English Manuscript Studies 1100–1700

English Manuscript Studies

1100–1700

VOLUME 12

Scribes and Transmission in English Manuscripts 1400–1700

Edited by

Peter Beal & A. S. G. Edwards

THE BRITISH LIBRARY

Manuscripts at Auction: January 2002 to December 2003
A.S.G. EDWARDS   254

Notes on Contributors   260

Index of Manuscripts   262

General Index   264

The Scribe Thomas Candour and the Making of Poggio Bracciolini's English Reputation

David Rundle

Twins—codicological twins—are at the heart of this tale. They were brought into this world by the same scribe and share a devotion to the same author. That author is Poggio Bracciolini (1380–1459), the most human of humanists: a moraliser and a womaniser, a papal secretary and a collector of ribald jokes, he was also the pre-eminent discoverer of forgotten classical texts, the reviver of the Ciceronian dialogue and the inventor of the humanist script, *littera antiqua*. It is, in particular, Poggio as writer of dialogues who is presented in these manuscript twins—though the optimism of the present tense I have just used needs to be tempered. For, these siblings, if not exactly separated at birth, have been divided in their fortune. One indeed suffered an early death, relatively speaking: only a century or so after its creation, it was torn apart, probably in Oxford, and now only a few relics of it survive, scattered fragments that have not previously been fully identified.[1] The city of its destruction is also the safe-haven of its twin, though the latter's arrival at the Bodleian may have been the result of a felicitous mistake. At its first flyleaf is a late-seventeenth-century donation note which reads:

> To the most illustrious Universitie of Oxford This manuscript of *Poggius* the Florentine, *writ by his Owne hand*, is humbly offered by Martin Lister.[2]

Despite the claim of the geologist and bibliophile, Dr Lister, the manuscript was not, in fact, written by Poggio himself; it, and its twin, are, instead, the work of one of the first Englishmen to practise the revived *littera antiqua*—Thomas Candour.

For scribes born into a culture of what are generically called gothic scripts, there were several methods through which they could engage with the humanist reform of handwriting.[3] At the most microscopic level, individual letter-forms could be imported into a script which remained mainly traditional.[4] In other cases, while the flow of the minuscules might reveal no Italianate influence, titles might be presented in humanist majuscules.[5] In contrast to these approaches that allowed only a smattering of humanist influence, other scribes attempted to become fluent in *littera antiqua*. For some it became one of a range of scripts they could practice; their manuscripts could oscillate between the new and the old handwriting with, in the case of the English scribe who worked for John Shirwood, the move from humanist book-hand to French secretary script being sometimes less a definite shift than a hardly perceptible slide.[6] Others might have considered such an approach half-hearted and instead set themselves the challenge of adopting *littera antiqua* to the exclusion of other scripts: this was particularly the case for those who learnt and practised the craft at its font in Italy—like the Scottish scribe, George of Kynnimond.[7] There was yet a further way of engaging with humanist scripts: every process of adoption necessarily involves adaptation, but, for some, adapting what they imitated was a self-conscious exercise. Something of this sort has been claimed for Nicolas de Clamanges' palaeographical experiments.[8] Something similar could be said for Thomas Candour.

Candour was not one of those ostentatious scribes who announced their presence in revelatory colophons: his identity was revealed only by A. C. de la Mare's deciphering of a half-erased note on the pastedown of one of his books.[9] In very large part because of the late Professor de la Mare's meticulous work, over a dozen extant manuscripts can now be identified for which Candour was partly or wholly responsible; a further group of manuscripts show him at work as an annotator, in particular collating copies of classical texts, like the first Decade of Livy [18]. He may well have earned money from his scribal activities, but it was not his primary profession: he held a series of clerical benefices in England, as well as having a role at the papal curia.[10] He was *cubicularius* to both Eugenius IV and Nicholas V and acted as proctor for various English figures like Richard, Duke of York. Not that his was a sedentary career in Florence or Rome: the sparse evidence available shows him shuttling between Italy and his homeland; the one occasion on which he appears in Poggio's epistolary is in a letter recommending him to Archbishop Stafford on such a journey back to England.[11] His activity as a scribe was similarly divided between the two countries: it appears that he was one of the many foreigners who learnt *littera antiqua* in Italy, but he also employed his skill in humanist script in manuscripts he wrote in England. This has sometimes made it difficult to attribute with confidence a particular manuscript to a particular place of production; there is rarely unambivalent textual proof or provenance information, leaving often only evidence garnered from the type of parchment used. In one case, it is suggestive that the manuscript is (unusually for a humanist codex) palimpsest, with the leaves having originally been used for fourteenth century shipping records, written in an Italian chancery hand [5].[12] More usually, the evidence comprises only the thickness and crispness of the parchment. Yet, for the manuscripts which concern us, his copies of Poggio's works, both the parchment and the text reveal these to be among the manuscripts he wrote in England. However, before we look at those manuscripts in detail, we should place them within their context by investigating how Poggio's works came to be known in this country.

Poggius Florentinus could not be accused of being parochial.[13] He was not averse to seeking employment far away from his homeland; he also proved solicitous in ensuring his literary writings achieved an international circulation. The foreign country with which he had most sustained direct contact was England, for he was here for over three years from 1419 as secretary to Henry Beaufort, bishop of Winchester.[14] When, by early 1423 at the latest, he returned to Italy and papal service, his English knowledge continued to prove professionally useful: he was responsible for much of the official correspondence sent to the Lancastrian kingdom.[15] We can also glimpse him in contact with former colleagues from Beaufort's household: one, Nicholas Bildeston, he recommended to his friend, Niccolò Niccoli, as *homo perhumanus et familiarissimus mihi*.[16] With another, Richard Petworth, Poggio exchanged letters after he returned to Italy—but not for long.[17] In 1425, Petworth seems to have taken offence at the tone of one of Poggio's letters, which was both indelicate about his weight and sententious about his clerical preferments.[18] Poggio, in turn, took offence at Petworth's petulant response and further lectured the Englishman with recondite classical references, of which he fully expected his correspondent to be ignorant.[19] Little wonder, then, that neither correspondent seems to have bothered to write again for the next ten years.[20]

When Poggio returned to Italy he was already in his early forties but his literary career remained ahead of him. He had, indeed, written some epistles intended for circulation, but his first dialogue, *De Avaritia*, was not published until 1428.[21] It was just under a decade later that Poggio began to promote his writings in England and, in the first instance, he did so through a fellow Italian. The Venetian lawyer and humanist, Pietro del Monte, was resident in London as papal collector between 1435 and 1440.[22] To him Poggio probably sent a manuscript of *De Avaritia*; he certainly furnished him with a copy of the 1435 epistolary dispute now known as the Scipio / Caesar controversy in which Poggio traded insults and classical references with Guarino da Verona.[23] Del Monte received that manuscript in 1439 and reacted by penning his own contribution to the controversy supporting Poggio in his republican diatribes against Caesar.[24] In 1440, before del Monte left England, he had a manuscript of the whole controversy produced and presented to Humfrey, Duke of Gloucester.[25] Del Monte's assistance in promoting Poggio's works may not have stopped there: after he returned to Italy, in late 1440 or early 1441, he sent to the Duke of Gloucester a *munusculum . . . hoc est libellum de nobilitate*—a lost manuscript most plausibly equated with Poggio's recently published dialogue of that title.[26]

Del Monte's use to Poggio as a conduit, trafficking Poggio's works to an English audience, may have lasted beyond his actual presence in this country, but it declined after he was once more dispatched across the Alps, this time to France (1442–45). Yet, in the same years, Poggio found he had another contact to whom he could send his works, and this time it was an Englishman, his former colleague Richard Petworth. Their correspondence had revived in 1438—but certainly not, in the first instance, for literary reasons. Instead, the purpose of Petworth's letters (for it seems to have been the Englishman who broke the silence) was two-fold: he wanted a political favour and he had a wedding-present for the recently married Poggio.[27] It is only two years later, with a letter from Poggio dated 24 May 1440, that humanist matters enter their discussions.[28] From this epistle, it would appear that Petworth had read some of Poggio's writings, including *De Avaritia*, and had written to their author complimenting him on his work.[29] It is not clear how Petworth had come by his copies—perhaps in part, it was through del Monte— but it would seem that they had not been sent to him directly by Poggio. If, however, the humanist had not initiated this interest in his works, he certainly was keen to capitalise on it. His letter of May 1440 described his most recent dialogue, *De Infelicitate Principum*, and promised to have it transcribed for his correspondent.

Poggio kept his word; two years later the 'English' copy of *De Infelicitate* was sent to Petworth, complete with authorial covering letter.[30] If humanists were skilled at creating around themselves the appearance of an exclusive circle of like-minded *amici*, this letter is the pre-eminent example of an humanist providing for himself an English group of friends. In this epistle (as elsewhere) Poggio combines images of intellectual and domestic companionship. *Humanissimus atque ornatissimus vir, dominus Adam prothonotarius* begins the letter; this is a reference to Adam Moleyns, whom Aeneas Sylvius Piccolomini complimented on his Latin, but whom Poggio considers endowed with *humanitas* because of his generosity.[31] He is not the only English character to inhabit this letter: there is also the nameless papal penitentiary who had acted as scribe to this volume, as well as another former colleague from Beaufort's household, William Toly.[32] Moreover, the epistle ends with a request that Petworth show the enclosed work to the Duke of Gloucester.

If Poggio here placed himself in this correspondence at the centre of an English circle, Petworth deftly employed it to create an image of himself as at the heart of a humanist coterie, promoting himself as particularly linked with Poggio.[33] It is not known whether Petworth heeded Poggio's bidding and had a copy of *De Infelicitate* made for Humfrey, Duke of Gloucester, but the work was certainly transcribed, complete with covering letter, by a visiting Paduan scribe, Milo da Carraria.[34] What is more, Petworth seems to have circulated Poggio's letters: for example, one late-fifteenth-century manuscript of letters by *Poggius philosophus,* though it does not include any directly referring to Petworth, appears to associate the collection with him.[35] In another instance, a letter-book was compiled at Christ Church, Canterbury, including Gasparino Barzizza's model letters, as well as some epistles of Guarino; between these two sections, there is a short set of letters by Englishmen.[36] This group is opened by a 1445 letter of Poggio's to Petworth; while we should perhaps not imagine that the following epistles were attempting to imitate a humanist style, they were clearly written mindful of the Italian example.[37] In one letter, Hugh Swynfeld complains to his correspondent, Petworth, about the vagaries of fortune, citing not just Aristotle and Solomon but also *tuo pogeo teste:* in effect, Poggio has become Petworth's writer.[38]

If Petworth promoted both himself and 'his' humanist, there was another person who was more self-effacing but equally instrumental in forging Poggio's English reputation, and that is the scribe Thomas Candour. It was Candour's contribution to compile what might be called a collected edition of Poggio's works, consisting of all the dialogues he had composed up to the early 1440s, as well as the Scipio / Caesar controversy. What is more, it is now clear that Candour produced at least two copies of his edition; the fragments of the second manuscript have previously been vaguely identified as from Poggio's letters, whereas, in fact, they provide sections from the same works as appear in the other codex that survives intact.[39] These two manuscripts, with their closely similar *mise-en-page* and same style of white-vine stem initials painted by Candour himself, can with justice be called twins.

While he was at the papal curia, Candour was certainly on friendly terms with Poggio, but his interest in the humanist's writings was hardly a function of their professional contact; on the contrary, that literary interest would appear to have developed at a physical distance from the author himself—and, indeed, without his prompting or assistance. One piece of evidence to suggest that Poggio was not directly supplying his English friend with copies for transcription involves the opening piece in Candour's edition. *De Avaritia* was, as we have seen, the first dialogue that Poggio composed, and it was one that, soon after its writing, he revised; thus it survives in two recensions—the first being the unedited version, the second the official one which Poggio himself circulated.[40] However, the version presented in Candour's manuscripts is (like all other extant English copies) the first, 'unofficial' recension.[41] Perhaps Candour had access to the same copy of the dialogue as Petworth had perused; certainly, in the case of *De Infelicitate Principum*, Candour would appear to be directly working from Petworth's manuscript, complete with Poggio's autograph letter which he, like Milo da Carraria, also transcribes.[42] Finally, in the case of the Scipio / Caesar controversy we can identify an extant manuscript from which Candour was working when compiling his edition. It is a workmanlike copy [16], written on paper by three English scribes, and including not just Poggio's and Guarino's texts but also Pietro del Monte's contribution; this copy may well derive directly from the presentation manuscript del Monte had made for Humfrey, Duke of Gloucester.[43] Candour would seem not to have had access to Humfrey's manuscript, but he did see this English copy: he not only adds at its first folio a rubricated title, but also corrects the text—suggesting, indeed, that he also had access to yet another copy of the controversy.[44]

The textual evidence about Candour's prototypes demonstrates that he was working from manuscripts available in England: his edition, in other words, is testimony to what was already circulating in this country. Its novelty lies not in the works it presents but in that it brings them together into one book devoted to the writings of Poggio Bracciolini. In other manuscripts made in England in the mid-fifteenth century, one or more of Poggio's dialogues is often twinned with specimens of the same genre by other writers, like, for example, Petrarch's *Secretum*.[45] In contrast, Candour's interest is not in type of text but in their particular author. In doing this, however far removed he was from Poggio himself, Candour was surely faithful to the humanist penchant for constructing an authorial persona. One technique used by humanists in the process of such construction was the provision of prefaces and of supplementary material, like the letter to Gregorio Correr and the poem of Carlo

Marsuppini that usually accompanied Poggio's *De Nobilitate*.[46] Candour not only includes those; he also inserts into his edition both the letter to Petworth and del Monte's Scipio / Caesar contribution, written in England and referring to the Duke of Gloucester—texts that allude to the local interest of this Florentine author. In other words, Poggio's persona as presented here has an English relevance. At the same time, the appearance of this as a particularly English humanist manuscript is assisted, I would suggest, by another element: by Candour's script.

While, across the range of books transcribed by Candour, his script could be characterised in general terms as a humanist bookhand, there is significant variation between the different manuscripts. This variation has been classified into 'three distinct styles', ranging from 'a current more or less gothic hand', through 'a variable humanistic script [which is] rather spiky', to 'a more formal rounded humanistic script', and these three styles have been designated (with more expediency than elegance) with the first three letters of the alphabet.[47] This description can not do full justice to the idiosnycracy of Candour's script, which even when it most closely emulates the new humanist canon has highly distinctive letter-forms, like the final *s* that is most often short but descends in a large arc below the line.[48] Such a tripartite classification is, unavoidably, a simplification but it does lucidly encapsulate the key differences. Yet, why should Candour have used this particular range of scripts? To answer this, let us concentrate on his Poggio collection.

In the complete extant manuscript of his Poggio collection [6], while some pages have a gothic aspect (hand 'a'), for the most part its script has been classified as in the second category (hand 'b')—as a *littera antiqua* but one which 'still has a very gothic look' [PLATE 1].[49] Such phrasing could permit an inference that the variation reflects Candour's development as a scribe, with the gothic elements declining as he became more proficient in the new script. Yet, such a notion of progress is flatly contradicted by what we know of the dating of his manuscripts. It appears that Candour was practising his fully-developed *littera antiqua* by 1437 at the latest [8], but Candour's complete Poggio codex was patently produced at some point after 30 July 1442, the date of the letter to Petworth.[50] In other words, though Candour had already proven his competence in *littera antiqua*, he chose not to parade his skill in this most humanist of manuscripts. That is not to say that he considered Poggio unworthy of humanist treatment: indeed, the fragments of the other copy of this Poggio collection—the textual twin to the complete codex—are all written in Candour's humanist bookhand. The two manuscripts may have been twins, but they were non-identical ones. Indeed, with these two codices he demonstrated that he could move

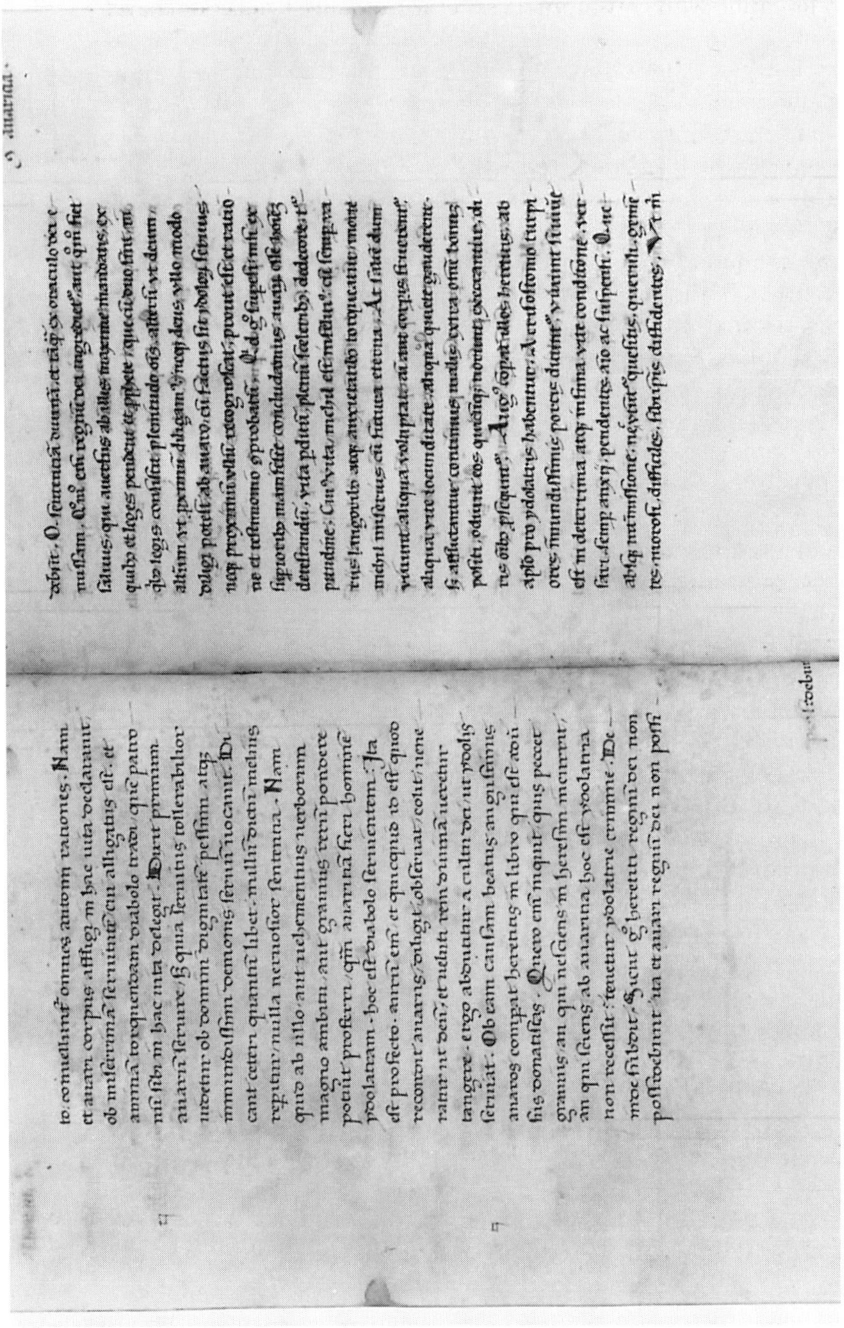

PLATE 1. *Two pages of Candour's edition of Poggio written in his hand 'b' and hand 'a': Oxford, Bodleian Library, MS Bodley 915, fols 32v–33r. (Each original page size 238 × 172mm.) Reproduced by permission of the Bodleian Library, University of Oxford.*

between imitating with consummate skill the humanists' new bookhand and electing not to use it.

I should hasten to add that Candour was like other English scribes who did not confine their use of the *littera antiqua* to what might seem appropriate humanist works.[51] In particular, there are two notable manuscripts in which Candour gives the poems of the twelfth-century Canterbury monk, Nigel Witeker, the full humanist treatment [2 & 3].[52] *Pari passu*, Candour's use of a more inventive script was not confined to one Poggio manuscript: he also employed it for the plays of Terence [7] and for a codex of the Church Father beloved of Florentine humanists, Lactantius [1]. In short, just as chronology cannot explain why Candour wrote in one or other script, so choice of text can provide no simple rationale. Nor can place of production: both the Witeker manuscripts and the Poggio fragments show that he employed his *littera antiqua* in his homeland. That said, and also accepting that not all of Candour's work can be firmly localised, there does seem to be something of a geographical division: his 'Italian' codices seem all to be in humanist script; all those manuscripts in which Thomas Candour is at his most eclectic or inventive appear to share an English provenance. Thus, while he was in his homeland, he could employ a fully-formed *littera antiqua*, but, at times, he also mingled this with more indigenous styles. Indeed, what he might be considered to be doing is experimenting with an English adaptation of the humanist agenda of 'classicising' handwriting.

The bookhand which the humanists christened *littera antiqua* is only the most famous example of an archaising script.[53] There were, in fifteenth-century England, indigenous attempts to emulate the bookhand of a previous generation, most notably in a remarkable manuscript from St Albans Abbey in the time of John Whethamstede: in that, the elegant script is derived from 'models of different dates in the twelfth and thirteenth centuries which could have been found at St Albans'.[54] It might be tempting to parallel this archaising codex with Candour's own activities, especially as it has been suggestively commented that his gothic might itself be 'an imitation of [an English] late twelfth-century hand'.[55] But Candour and the St Albans scribe were no kindred spirits: Candour does not limit his emulation to a narrow range of models all displaying a similar type of script. 'All archaising hands are hybrids' for, in them, the contemporary and the anachronistic collide; but Candour appears to relish such a collision.[56] What, on my submission, makes Candour notable is that in both those scripts which are definably not *littera antiqua* (hands 'a' and 'b'), he sets himself the task not of strict emulation but of inventively combining various different elements.

So, for example, in Candour's so-called gothic script there are features which are decidedly neither gothic nor protogothic: only contemporary humanist fashion can explain his willingness to use *lunulae*, or to construct the *–bus* suffix in the very unEnglish style of a *b* followed by an inverted *c*, or, indeed, to form his *g* with a single bowl and a snaking open descender.[57] Perhaps, in some cases, though, his letter-forms reflect knowledge of both the original as well as the revived *littera antiqua*—for example, his insistence on using an upright *r* to the exclusion of the gothic '*z*-shaped' form. In terms of aspect, for all its gothic spikiness, Candour is concerned with legibility, but some of his favoured techniques for achieving this could be called late-gothic strategems: in particular, he avoids a mass of minims by frequently differentiating between a *u* form and a *v* form. Perhaps a concern for legibility also explains a notable idionsycracy: Candour insists on writing *et*, avoiding the use of either the ampersand or the tironian abbreviation. This habit is repeated in Candour's 'variable humanistic' script (hand 'b')—as, indeed, are many of the characteristics just described.[58] The humanist influence in this version of his script is apparent in the decreased use of florid hairline-strokes and the generally larger letter-forms, yet in some features there is a notably narrow canon of gothic letter-forms employed: for instance, in this script, the *d* is insistently curve-backed, while in the 'gothic' script (hand 'a'), it was freer to oscillate between the two available forms, curved and straight-backed.

What these details emphasise is the conscious and eclectic construction of a canon of letter-forms: if this is archaising, it is as it would be practised by a magpie. The result is not an English parallel to the revived *littera antiqua*, but rather a domestication of the humanist reforms, mingling them or mediating them with English traditions. This, moreover, is an experiment that Candour considers appropriate for works of classical authors and, most strikingly, for a manuscript of the works of Poggio Bracciolini. Contrast this to his humanist treatment of Nigel Witeker: the twelfth-century English author, Candour's *littera antiqua* seems to announce, deserves a new international audience; with Poggio, Candour's hybrid scripts imply that this is an author relevant in an English context. The scribe appears knowingly to be casting both author's against type (or, rather, script), a strategy that affects even orthographical details. At least once at the first folio of one of Candour's Witeker manuscripts, the *ae* diphthong is marked with a light subscript abbreviation [PLATE 2].[59] In Candour's Poggio manuscripts, by contrast, no such markings occur. Indeed, to take the example of Poggio's letter to Petworth, which Candour apparently transcribed from the original—that is, the copy written by one of the leading proponents of

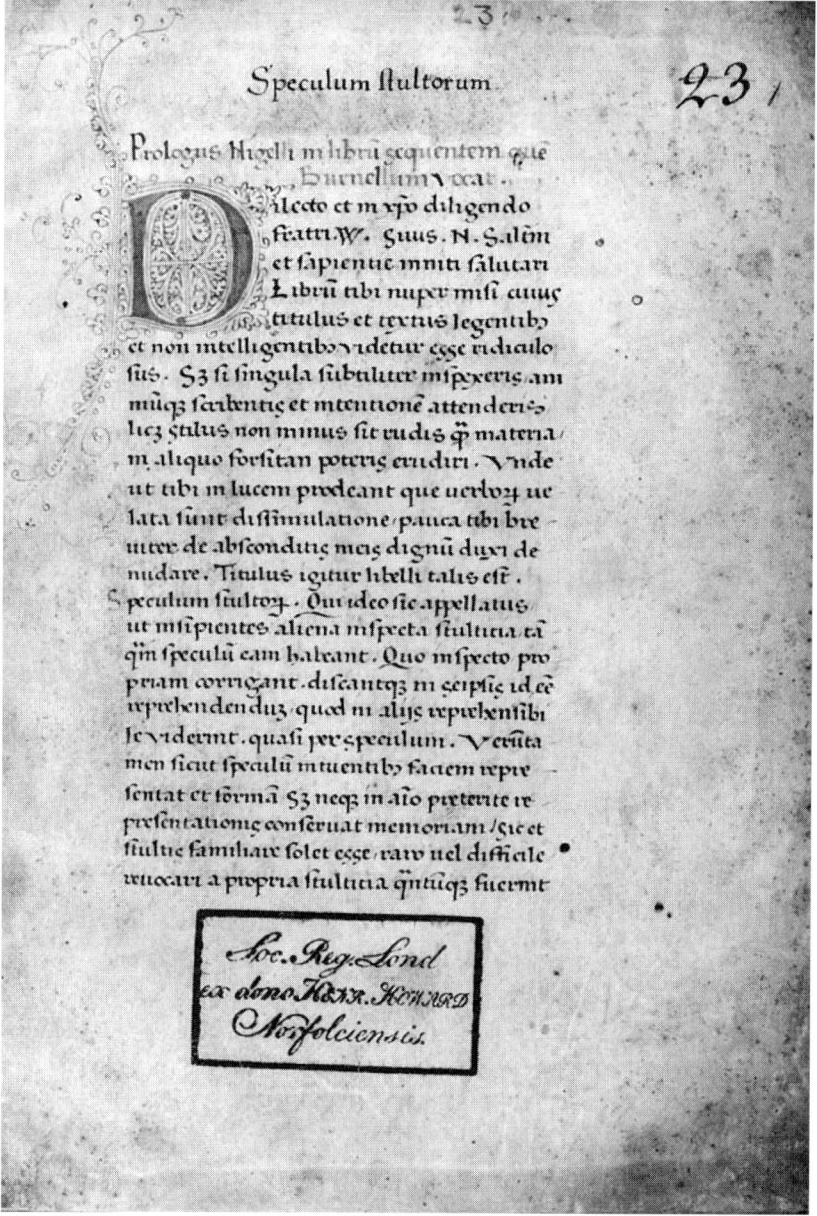

PLATE 2. *A page of Nigel Witeker, written by Candour in his hand 'c', with diphthong marked at l. 26: London, British Library, MS Arundel 23, fol. 1r. (Original page size 245 × 182mm.) Reproduced by permission of the Board of the British Library.*

humanist orthographical reforms—all diphthongs are unmarked, and to words like *mihi* the medieval *c* is added. Candour is not merely transcribing, he is translating the humanist into his new insular setting.[60] In fine, Candour has 'Englished' Poggio.

My purpose here has been to emphasise English engagement with the activities of the humanists. If the history of humanism has been conventionally described as virile 'dissemination' engendering timid 'reception', I have pitted against this terribly grand narrative a modest vignette. True, it has included a moment of humanist hauteur as Poggio dismissed his 'friend', Richard Petworth, as unlettered, but its keynote has been the autonomous intervention of Englishmen in the fortunes of the *studia humanitatis*. Such engagement can take various forms: Petworth is an example of the book-owner who understood his possession of a text could be used to promote both himself and its author. Thomas Candour, on the other hand—the scribe whose identity was for so long hidden—effected a more subtle intervention. Without recourse to their author, Candour compiled an edition of Poggio's works tailored to his local context, both in content and in aspect. Moreover, both Petworth's and Candour's activities were moments in the construction of a humanist's identity that the author could not fashion himself. For their works to reach foreign markets, as the authors often desired, a humanist like Poggio needed local contacts. But when the texts arrived unescorted in the far-off country, their fortunes depended on the goodwill of such ambassadors, and in the hands of our man *in Britannia* a work could easily go native. Indeed, in the hand of Thomas Candour—which 'Englished' humanist works just as it 'humanised' Anglo-Latin texts—this is precisely what transpired.

APPENDIX

A brief listing of manuscripts copied or annotated by Thomas Candour

The purpose of this checklist is to gather together the information we have of Candour's activities as scribe and annotator. The information provided is intentionally brief, including only a select bibliography. The information is, in very large part, testament to the work of Professor A. C. de la Mare, much of it presented in *DH&EH* and in *MSS at Oxford*. For access to some of the unpublished files of her researches, held in the

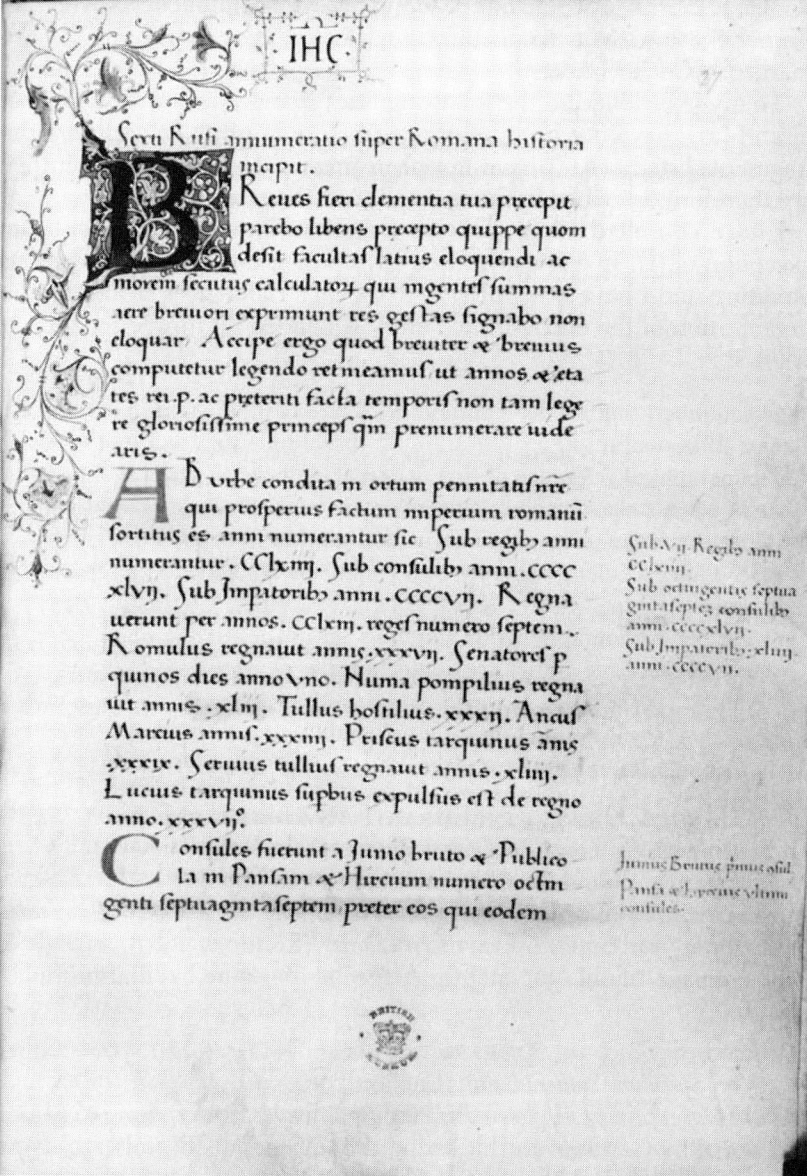

PLATE 3. *A page of Sextus Rufus, written by Candour in his hand 'c' and illuminated in his distinctive style of vine-stem initial: London, British Library, MS Harley 2471, fol. 27r. (Original page size 270 × 189mm.) Reproduced by permission of the Board of the British Library.*

deciphered at end pastedown. Written on thick suede-like parchment. *D&D Oxford,* No. 834; A&T, No. 575.

[11] OXFORD: NEW COLLEGE, MS 250—Cicero, *De Oratore, Brutus* & *De Partitione Oratoria* (Rome?).

DH&EH, No. 33: suggests there are two scribes, the first writing fols 1–41v, l. 32 in a 'fairly blobby' humanist script, and the second, identified as Candour, writing fols 41v, l. 32–98v. However, there are clearly three scripts here, with Candour's hand 'c' used for the last item (fols 87–98v) and the rubricated titles throughout. The script of the middle section (fol. 41v, l. 32—fol. 86) is a distinct *littera antiqua,* probably by another scribe; it is similar in letter-forms to Candour's script (and perhaps influenced him), but different in detail, and in aspect is smaller and less stiff. In the first two items, but not in the section he writes in his hand 'c', Candour regularly annotates the manuscript in a tiny humanist-influenced script, as well as correcting the text in his hand 'c'.

A&T, No. 966.

[12] OXFORD: NEW COLLEGE, MS 256—Guarino, *De Diphthongis* and works on vocabulary.

DH&EH, No. 56: written on Italian parchment. Written throughout by Candour but his script is remarkably changeable over the course of the manuscript: at times, it is definably hand 'c' (eg. fols 1r, 11r, 163r–v, 170r–v) and this script is also used for corrections and additions throughout the manucscript (eg. fols 22, 30, 41, 89, 155v [with Greek word]); however, more often, the script tends to be thicker, slightly slanted and less regular. *DH&EH* described this as hand 'b', but it has no parallels among the instances of that script; it is perhaps better to consider it a humanist cursive script with increasing Italian gothic influence.

A&T, No. 1001.

[13] OXFORD: NEW COLLEGE, MS 271, fols 157–167, l. 10—Maffeo Vegio, *Aeneid XIII.*

DH&EH, No. 59: hand 'c'; Candour's vine-stem initial (fol. 157). ACdelaM notes: unidentified coat-of-arms (fol. 3) also appears at CAMBRIDGE: UNIVERSITY LIBRARY, MS Ee. v. 5. The main part of this manuscript (Vergil, *Aeneid*) is written in an Italian late gothic script [A&T, No. 915], while, following Candour's intervention, there is a further addition (fol. 167, bottom half—172: Maffeo Vegio, *Astyanax*), written in a second English humanist script, perhaps influenced by Candour's hand. The last section also has an English imitation of a vine-stem initial, in the same style as, for example, those in LONDON: BL,

Add. MS 10344 (Doget, commentary on Plato's *Phaedo*) [*DH&EH*, No. 96; but cf. K. L. Scott, *Later Gothic Manuscripts, 1390–1490* (London, 1996), II, 333–4] and OXFORD: BODLEIAN, MS Auct. F. 2. 19, fol. 1 (Cicero, *Tusculan Disputations*; owned: John Tiptoft) [not previously noted; on the manuscript, see *DH&EH*, No. 74; {Bodleian exhibition catalogue}, *Duke Humfrey's Library and the Divinity School, 1488–1988* (Oxford, 1988), No. 59].
A&T, No. 609.

[14] OXFORD: NEW COLLEGE, MS 280—Eutropius; Victor Vitensis, *De Persecutione*; Pomponius Mela.
DH&EH, p. 32: suggests this manuscript was written by Candour 'in a very gothic version of style 'c'.' However, while Candour adds at the top of fols 1 and 151 his 'IHC' mark (also seen in [5], [8] and [11]), and while he writes some of the rubricated titles (fols 2v, 7v, 151, 153v–154, 168, 179v, 180, 186v, 190, 194, 195v) as well as annotating the volume, he is not responsible for the text itself. There are, in fact, two human-ist-influenced scripts here, though both are possibly by the same scribe. The first, thick-set but moderately sized, appears at fols 1–150; the second, which is very large and box-shaped, is used for fols 151–202. These scripts share distinctive letter-forms (e.g. the open-bowled but neckless *g*; the rather squat ampersand, and the *ct* ligature) which are quite different from those found in any of Candour's scripts.
A&T, No. 605.

[15] Fragments of a manuscript of Poggio's works, in Candour's hand 'c' (with curve-backed *d*). Written on crisp, smooth parchment (like quires vi–ix of [6]), with 28 long lines to a page (compared to 26 in [6]); variable written space: 180/185 × 120/121mm; fully ruled, with double borders, leaving reddish mark. The original order of these fragments would have been: [iv], [i], [v], [ii], [iii]. These fragments have no anno-tations, nor any other evidence for early provenance. The manuscript was in Oxford by the second half of the sixteenth century at the latest; it was probably there that it was dismantled and used in bindings, most likely during the period 1570–1585 (the binding of [ii] has centrepiece xviii, datable to that period [D. Pearson, *Oxford Bookbinding 1500–1640* (Oxford, 2000), p. 80]).
[i] LONDON: BRITISH LIBRARY, MS Harl. 5915, fol. 16—one leaf, with all lines present, but cropped to leave very little marginal space. Text is from *De Infelicitate Principum*: ed. D. Canfora (Rome, 1998), pp. 42 (l. 2)–43 (l. 27) [[16v] magistratus contissi nulla graviora consilia . . . Sed stultum atque imperitum vulgus / [16r] non hec eorum dampna

animadvertit . . . affligebar animo illorum stul| |]. This fragment is part of the collection of John Bagford (*d.*1716).

[ii] LONDON: PRIVATE COLLECTION—a fragment of a former flyleaf. Text is from Guarino's contribution to the Scipio / Caesar controversy: R. Sabbadini ed., *Epistolario di Guarino*, II (Venice, 1916), pp. 242, ll. 727–741 & 750–765 [| |endicarint . . . favorem om| | ; | |ori tempore . . . copiosissimam| |].

[iii] Oxford: Christ Church, printed book f. 3. 7—pastedowns [N. R. Ker, *Pastedowns in Oxford Bindings*, (Oxford, 1954), No. 1891]—two fragments from Poggio's *Defensiuncula*: Canfora ed., *La Controversia*, pp. 151–52, ll. 445–460 [{Sueton}ij verba quem . . . deposuerit debere] & pp. 148–9, ll. 320–340 [{n}equeat et tamen . . . in hac sua inep{ta}].

[iv] OXFORD: MERTON COLLEGE, MS E. 3. 35, Nos 3–5—two small former flyleaves, with one torn into two pieces—fragments from consecutive leaves of Poggio's *De Avaritia* (first recension): printed in *Opera omnia*, I, 22–24 [[3ʳ] quam pauca loqui . . . dedit tribunos| | . . . [3ᵛ] ante se iussit pelium . . . dabit. Et| | . . . [4r & 5r] est quam in alios . . . triumphantis currum. Quid| | . . . [4v & 5v] vero quod dixisti . . . mutua cum sit| |].

[v] Oxford: Merton College, printed book 76. a. 6—flyleaf [Ker, *Pastedowns*, no. 1663]—a near-complete sheet of which the first leaf is from Poggio's *De Infelicitate Principum*: Canfora ed., pp. 53 (l. 11)—54 (l. 33) [gravibus affligatur civis . . . Sed maxime tamen / principibus via virtutis ignota . . . temeritas in quo nullum consi{lium}]—and the second from his letter to Scipio Mainente: edited by G. Crevatin, 'La politica e la retorica' in *Poggio Bracciolini 1380–1980* (Florence, 1982), pp. 281–342, pp. 309 (l. 1)—311 (l. 2) [Poggius plurimam | | . . . civem pernitiossimum patr{ie quam ceteris gentibus imperan} / tem in servitutem redegit . . . milites post civilem| |] (the letter appears to lack a title, in contrast to [6], fol. 100v). Candour's vine-stem initial (rather rubbed), including an open-winged bird.

Manuscripts annotated by Candour

[16] CAMBRIDGE: TRINITY COLLEGE, MS O. 9. 8—Scipio / Caesar controversy; humanist formulary.
MSS at Oxford, p. 96. Candour's interventions confined to the first fascicule; he adds the title at fol. 1, and corrects the text at, for example, fols 9, 13, 24.
Rundle, 'Of Republics and Tyrants', pp. 334–41.

[17] OXFORD: NEW COLLEGE, MS 265—Boethius, *De Consolatione Philosophiae*.

A&T, No. 912. Annotations by Candour at fols 1, 2–5, 6v, ?10, 20r, 20v (with long-fingered *manicula*), 26v, 45v.

[18] OXFORD: NEW COLLEGE, MS 277—Livy, Decade I (Florence, s. xv$^{2/4}$)

DH&EH, No. 32. Candour's extensive interventions take two forms: (i) corrections on the line, erasing text and replacing in black ink in hand 'b'; (ii) marginal alternative readings written in a very thin, very small humanist-influenced script. His marginalia also include references to Marcus Varro: eg. fols 6v, 22v; as it has been plausibly argued that this manuscript probably derives from Boccaccio's lost copy [S. Oakley, *A Commentary on Livy, Books VI–X*, I (Oxford, 1997), pp. 258—60], and as Varro was an author rediscovered by Boccaccio, might these notes reflect Boccaccio's own annotations? Candour adds his elegant *manicula* just once, at fol. 2.

A&T, No. 920.

[19] OXFORD: NEW COLLEGE, MS 278—Livy, Decade III
A&T, No. 920. Annotated copiously by Candour (up to fol. 40), in the same combination as previous manuscript.

[20] OXFORD: NEW COLLEGE, MS 279—Livy, Decade IV
A&T, No. 920. Only one annotation by Candour, a note (now rubbed) at the final folio (fol. 111v), concerning the number of the books that should follow.

[21] OXFORD: ST. JOHN'S COLLEGE, MS 116—Seneca, *Epistolae* (Italy, 1385)
Candour annotates in a very small *littera antiqua* (fols 4v–6, 14v, 49–74, etc) and adds text in hand 'a' (verging on hand 'b'): fols 55v, 61, 66v–68, 74, 83, 84, 85, 86v, 88, 89r–v, 91, 92, 95v, 102, 106v, 108, 112, 114r–v, 116v, 121–23, 127v, 129v, 133v–134, 136v–137, 138, 139, 141v–142, 145, 148r–v, 149v, 150v–152, 153).
R. Hanna, *A Descriptive Catalogue of the Western Medieval Manuscripts of St John's College Oxford* (Oxford, 2002), pp. 163–64 & plate 2 (plate 2b showing Candour annotations). Note that there is a previously unnoticed erased inscription at top right of fol. 1, which reads: liber Petri Icheford[?].

Discounted manuscript

OXFORD: NEW COLLEGE, MS 274—Pliny, *Historia Naturalis* (St Albans, s. xiii^{in}). [R. W. Hunt], 'Richard de Bury's Books from the Abbey of St. Albans', *Bodleian Library Record*, 3 (1950–51), pp. 177–9 (p. 179), notes that this manuscript contains annotations 'in an elegant English humanist hand of the fifteenth century'. A. C. de la Mare later commented that the script 'has a very strong Italian flavour and suggests the influence of Guarino . . . [The notes] might conceivably be "Thomas S." but that is a very tentative suggestion' [letter to Richard Hunt, copy in the Bodleian, file 'Letters about Bodley MSS V']. The full list of these annotations is: fols 2, 23v, 25, 39, 61v, 63, 71, 98v, 113, 119, 121, 122, 123v–124, 183, 184v. They appear, however, to be larger and less skilfully written than the known examples of Candour's annotations.

NOTES

I would like to thank Drs X. van Binnebeke, C. de Hamel and M. Kauffmann for their assistance in preparing this article, and to record my immense debt to the late Professor A. C. de la Mare.

In this article, the following abbreviations are used:

A&T	J. J. G. Alexander & E. Temple, *Illuminated Manuscripts in Oxford College Libraries*, 2 vols (Oxford, 1985).
BRUO	A. B. Emden, *Biographical Register of the University of Oxford to A.D.1500*, 3 vols (Oxford, 1957–9).
Colophons	[Bénédictins da Bouvert] *Colophons des Manuscrits Occidentaux*, 6 vols (Fribourg, 1965–82).
D&D Oxford	A. G. Watson, *Catalogue of Dated and Datable Manuscripts c.435–1600 in Oxford Libraries* (Oxford, 1984).
DH&EH	[Bodleian exhibition catalogue] *Duke Humfrey and English Humanism* (Oxford, 1970).
Harth	Poggio Bracciolini, *Lettere*, ed. H. Harth, 3 vols (Florence, 1983–7).
MSS at Oxford	[Bodleian exhibition catalogue] *Manuscripts at Oxford: R. W. Hunt memorial exhibition* (Oxford, 1980).
Rundle, 'Of Republics and Tyrants'	D. Rundle, 'Of Republics and Tyrants: aspects of quattrocento humanist writings and their reception in England, *c.*1400–*c.*1460' (unpublished D.Phil. thesis, Oxford University, 1997).

1   All the known manuscripts by this scribe are listed in the Appendix; the fragments are listed as [15].

2   [6], fol. i. On Martin Lister (1635?–1712), see *Dictionary of National Biography*, 21 vols (Oxford, 1917) *sub nomine*; J. Stoye, *English Travellers Abroad* (London, 1987) pp. 296–301.

3   A brief survey of the arrival of humanist scripts outside Italy is provided by B. Bischoff, *Latin Palaeography* (Cambridge, 1989), pp. 148–49.

4   For a few examples from Winchester Cathedral Priory, see J. Greatrex, 'Humanistic script in a monastic register: an outward and visible sign?', *Studies in Church History*, 14 (1977), 189–91; for continental examples, see for instance M. Steinmann, 'Die lateinische Schrift zwischen Mittelalter und Humanismus' in G. Silagi, *Paläographie 1981: Colloquium des Comité International de Paléographie. München, 15–18 September 1981* [Münchener Beiträge zur Mediävistik und Renaissance-Forschung, 32] (München, 1982), pp. 193–99.

5 Two English examples of this phenomenon are (1) Dublin: Trinity College, ms 438 (John Manyngham's miscellany), on which see *DH&EH*, No. 21, and Rundle, 'Of Republics and Tyrants', pp. 348–54, esp. p. 348; (2) Oxford: Bodleian Library, MS lat. misc. d. 34, where the scribe, Robert Sherborne, imitates Antonio Beccaria's style of capitals—see the image of fol. 1 at N. Mann, 'Petrarch's Role in Humanism', *Apollo*, 94 (1971), 176–83 (ill. 8); this manuscript is discussed at *DH&EH*, No. 23.

6 Oxford: Corpus Christi College, MSS 60, 92 & 93, discussed at *DH&EH*, No. 102; the first and second of these appear as *D&D Oxford*, No. 768 & 771 (cf. plate 706).

7 Listed in A. Derolez, *Codicologie des Manuscrits en Écriture Humanistique sur Parchemin* (2 vols) (Turnhout, 1984), as scribe 136 [p. 137], with three manuscripts cited; to those, further signed manuscripts can be added: *Colophons*, No. 4641, 4989 and 5048, and Madrid: Biblioteca Nacional, MS 12708. A. C. de la Mare tentatively equated him with the Scotsman, Georgius de Clarmond, who copied Paris: BN, MS lat. 5805 in 1453 ['Lo scriptorium di Malatesta Novello' in F. Lollini & P. Lucchi (ed.), *Libraria Domini: i manoscritti della Biblioteca Malatestiana: testi e decorazioni* (Bologna, 1995), pp. 35–93 (n. 15)], though that manuscript is in a semi-humanist script. From the other manuscripts, it is known that Kynnimond was employed as a copyist in Rome in the 1450s by Cardinal Calandrini.

8 G. Ouy, 'Nicolas de Clamanges (ca.1360–1437). Philologue et calligraphe: imitation de l'Italie et réaction anti-italienne dans l'écriture d'un humaniste français au début du XVe siècle', in J. Autenrieth (ed.), *Renaissance- und Humanistenhandschriften* [Schriften des Historischen Kollegs Kolloquien, 13] (München, 1988), pp. 31–50. More generally, on the use by early-fifteenth-century French scholars of 'pré-humanistique' and 'italianisante' scripts, see F. Gasparri, *Introduction à l'Histoire de l'Écriture* ([Louvain], 1994), p. 125 & plates 54–65.

9 The note occurs at [10], end pastedown. The name was first read simply as 'Thomas S'; it is under that designation that Professor de la Mare introduced him in *DH&EH*, pp. 32–35. His identity was more fully revealed by her in *MSS at Oxford*, pp. 95–96.

10 On his clerical career, see *BRUO* and M. Harvey, *England, Rome and the Papacy, 1417–1464* (Manchester, 1993), pp. 34–35.

11 Harth, III, ep. I / 3.

12 On the rarity of humanist codices on palimpsest, see Derolez, *Codicologie*, p. 25, though, as a corrective, note, for example, that two of Sanvito's earliest manuscripts were on palimpsest: A. C. de la Mare, 'Bartolomeo Sanvito da Padova, copista e miniatore' in G. Baldissin Molli, G. Canova Mariani & F. Toniolo (ed.), *La Miniatura a Padova dal Medioevo al Settecento* (Modena, 1999), pp. 495–511 (p. 495).

13 The standard biography remains E. Walser, *Poggius Florentinus* (Leipzig, 1914); see also *Dizionario Biografico degli Italiani, sub nomine*.

14 The dates of Poggio's time in England sometimes cause confusion. He entered Beaufort's service in November 1418 at Mantua, travelled back with him via Rouen, where he met Henry V in March 1419, and probably reached England that summer [G.L.Harriss, *Cardinal Beaufort* (Oxford, 1988) pp. 97, 100; M.C.Davies, 'Friends and enemies of Poggio: studies in quattrocento humanist literature' (unpublished Oxford D.Phil. thesis, 1986), pp. 50 & 58 {ll. 235–6} (an earlier version in *Rinascimento*, 2nd Ser., 22 (1982), 152–82)]. So, Poggio's comment in June 1422 that he has been in England *quattuor annis* is an exaggeration [Harth, I, ep. 18 {l. 30}]. His last letter from England is dated 25 June 1422, where he suggests that it will be at least two months before he sets out; his first from Rome, addressed to Leonardo Bruni, is dated 16 March 1423 [Harth II, ep. 1/10; Harth I, ep. 20 is dated 12 February 1423 but, as

Davies, 'Friends and enemies', pp. 17–18, shows, this is Florentine style: i.e. by modern practice, it is dated 1424]. Poggio returned to Italy along the Rhine route and passed through Florence, albeit briefly [R.Sabbadini, *Le Scoperte dei codici latini e greci* [repr.] (Florence, 1967), I, 83–84; Harth II, ep. 1/10 {ll. 13–14, 39–40}]. This body of evidence would suggest that he left England between autumn 1422 and the first days of 1423.

15 S. Saygin, *Humphrey, Duke of Gloucester (1390–1447) and the Italian Humanists* (Leiden, 2002), esp. pp. 271–77.

16 Harth I, ep.48, ll.23–5. On Bildeston generally, see *BRUO;* on his literary interests, see D. Rundle, 'Two Unnoticed Manuscripts from the Collection of Humfrey, Duke of Gloucester, Part II', *Bodleian Library Record*, 16 (1998), 299–313.

17 On Petworth, see *BRUO.*

18 The offending letter is Harth II, ep. I/11 (correctly redated by the editor); Petworth's side of the correspondence is completely lost but his response to this letter can be inferred from Poggio's next epistle: Harth II, ep. I/13.

19 Harth II, ep. I/13, ll. 53–54.

20 Harth II, ep.VIII/2, dated 28 April 1438, is the next surviving letter; its opening section in which Poggio says Petworth's recent letters reminded him of *antiqua nostra consuetudo* strongly suggests that the letter had been preceded by a lengthy gap. Contrast the assumption of R. Weiss, *Humanism in England during the fifteenth century* [3rd edn] (Oxford, 1967), p. 20, that theirs was a lifelong contact.

21 An example of an epistle intended for publication is Poggio's description of the death of Jerome of Prague [Harth, II, ep. IV / 15]; an early copy of this which circulated in England survives at London: British Library, MS Harl. 2268, fols 15v–18, on which see Rundle, 'Of Republics and Tyrants', pp. 393–414. Poggio's *De Avaritia* survives in two recensions [see below, p. 6]; the first recension is printed in P. Bracciolini, *Opera Omnia*, ed. R. Fubini, I (Turin, 1964), 1–31, while the second is edited by G. Germano, *Dialogus Contra Avaritiam* (Livorno, 1994).

22 On del Monte generally, see A. Zanelli, 'Pietro del Monte', *Archivio storico lombardo*, 34 (1907), 317–78 & 46–115; D. Quaglioni, *Pietro del Monte a Roma* (Rome, 1984); *DBI.* On his time in England, see J. Haller, *Piero da Monte* (Rome, 1941); D. Rundle, 'On the Difference between Virtue and Weiss' in D. Dunn (ed.), *Courts, Counties and the Capital* (Stroud, 1996) pp. 181–203 (pp. 194–97); and ibid., 'Carneades' Legacy: the morality of eloquence in the humanist and papalist writings of Pietro del Monte', *English Historical Review*, 117 (2002), 284–305.

23 Del Monte certainly had access to *De Avaritia* as he follows it very closely in his *De Vitiorum inter se Differentia;* on this, see Rundle, 'Of Republics and Tryants', pp. 188–93. On the Scipio / Caesar controversy generally, see now D. Canfora, *La Controversia di Poggio Bracciolini e Guarino Veronese su Cesare e Scipione* (Florence, 2001).

24 Del Monte's contribution is printed in P. Bracciolini, *Opera omnia*, ed. R. Fubini, IV (Turin, 1969), 615–39; for discussion, see Rundle, 'Carneades' Legacy'.

25 The presentation copy to Humfrey survives as Cambridge: University Library, MS Gg. i. 34 (i), on which see D. Rundle, 'Two Unnoticed Manuscripts of Humfrey Duke of Gloucester: Part I', *Bodleian Library Record*, 16 (1998), 211–24.

26 A. Sammut, *Unfredo duca di Gloucester e gli umanisti italiani* (Padua 1980), p. 154; the editor assumed that the work alluded to was del Monte's own dialogue *De Vitiorum inter se Differentia*, but this is implausible as its theme is not nobility. An alternative identification could be Buonaccorso da Montemagno's dialogue on that theme, but the dating and del Monte's previous contacts with Poggio make that the more likely text. Poggio's *De Nobilitate* is printed in *Opera omnia*, I, 64–83.

27 Harth II, ep.VIII/2, ll. 34–36, 55–58; Poggio had written to Nicholas Bildeston with the news of his marriage in February 1436: Harth II, ep.V/6.

28 Harth II, ep.IX/18.

29 *Pace* Weiss, *Humanism*, p. 20n, it does not appear that Poggio sent Petworth a copy of his dialogue. For that to be the case, there would have to have been an extra letter which is now lost. However, there are a couple of reasons to think that the correspondence at this point is complete. The first involves Petworth's wedding-present of purses: two had reached Poggio by 1438 when he was expecting another one; the third does not seem to have arrived by February 1439 [Harth II, ep.IX/2] and in the 1440 letter he thanks Petworth for a *marsupium* [Harth II, ep.IX/18, l. 34]. The second reason is that there are references in the 1440 letter to the 1438 epistle: compare the opening of ep.IX/18 with ep.VIII/2, ll. 59–74 & ep.IX/18, ll. 34–35 with ep.VIII/2, ll. 49–53.

30 The letter is edited, from a derivative manuscript copy, by Walser, *Poggius*, p. 454. The dialogue is edited by D. Canfora (Rome, 1998); Petworth's copy does not survive.

31 On Adam Moleyns, and Piccolomini's praise of him, see D. Rundle, 'Humanism before the Tudors' in J. Woolfson (ed.), *Reassessing Tudor Humanism* (London, 2002), pp. 22–42 (pp. 22–23).

32 This scribe, referred to both here and in ep.IX/18, is frustratingly difficult to identify. One might imagine that Thomas Candour was the most likely candidate but there is no sign that he ever held a position in the penitentiary; it would seem, then, that there was another Englishman in Rome who could write *littera antiqua*. Poggio seems to mean the English minor penitentiary; in the mid-1430s, this was John Bloxwych and by 1443, it was James Blakedon [E. Göller, *Die Päpstliche Penitentiarie* I/2 (Rome, 1907), pp. 122–24; Harvey, *England, Rome*, p. 32] but there is no clear evidence for the intervening years. On Toly, see J. Stratford, *The Bedford Inventories* (London, 1993), p. 425.

33 In addition to the *De Infelicitate*, Poggio later offered to have book IV of *De Varietate Fortunae* transcribed for Petworth: Harth, III, ep.II/15, ll. 14–17 (perhaps implying that he already had the preceding books; no English copy survives).

34 The copy in Milo da Carraria's hand is Oxford: Bodleian, MS Rawl. C. 298 [Canfora (ed.), *De Infelicitate*, p. lxxxvi]. On this itinerant scribe, see *DH&EH*, pp. 13–14 and *Colophons*, Nos 13834–7. Judging from what we know of Milo's travels, this manuscript must date from the second half of the 1440s; he was certainly in London in 1447, when he copied Florence: Biblioteca Riccardiana, MS 952, on which see now T. de Robertis & R. Miriello (ed.), *I Manoscritti datati della Biblioteca Riccardiana di Firenze*, I (Florence, 1997), No. 93.

35 The manuscript concerned is Cambridge: Jesus College, MS Q. G. 15, written in England in the second half of the fifteenth century by an otherwise unknown character, Thomas Armin; at the top of fol. 7v, *Ricardo Secretario episcopi Wyntoniensis* is written, clearly alluding to Petworth. On this manuscript, see Rundle, 'Of Republics and Tyrants', pp. 324–30.

36 Tokyo: Imperial University Library, MS A.100.1300. This manuscript—the Streeter Codex (after the canon who thoughtfully arranged for its departure from England)—is discussed in detail by K. Nishimoto, *Codex Streeterianus* (Tokyo, 1987); it was a gift of James Goldwell to All Souls, and is discussed, with full bibliography, by A. G. Watson, *A Descriptive Catalogue of the Medieval Manuscripts of All Souls College Oxford* (Oxford, 1997), pp. 271–72. R. Weiss, 'Some unpublished correspondence of Guarino da Verona', *Italian Studies*, 2 (1939), 110–17, prints four letters; W. Schirmer,

Der Englische Frühhumanismus [2nd edn] (Tübingen, 1963) p. 16, prints a letter by Petworth to an unknown correspondent, and discusses the other letters by Englishmen on pp. 18–19. These other letters by Englishmen remain unprinted, as do the final two humanist letters.

37 Harth, III, ep.I/1, but starting at l.10. The whole letter survives in another English manuscript: Seville: Biblioteca Colombina, MS 5/5/28, fols 137v–9, on which see P.O. Kristeller, *Iter Italicum*, 7 vols (Leiden, 1963–97), IV, 619a.

38 Tokyo: Imperial University Library, MS A. 100. 1300, fol. 78.

39 It is as Poggio letters that they are described in *MSS at Oxford*, p. 96.

40 On the process of revision, see H. Harth, 'Niccolo Niccoli als literarischer Zensor', *Rinascimento*, 2nd Ser., 7 (1967), 29–53.

41 One copy of the second recension did reach England, as it was this version that del Monte used in his *De Vitiorum inter se Differentia*. On this, see above n. 23.

42 Canfora (ed.), *De Infelicitate*, pp. lxxxiv–v, refuses to exclude the possibility that Candour wrote his copy in Rome, but his own textual study [pp. cxxix–cxxx] and my own collation of the letter to Petworth demonstrate that Candour was working from the same prototype as used for Oxford: Bodleian, MS Rawl. C. 298.

43 On the presentation copy, see above, p. 4.

44 Brief textual collation of the three manuscripts is presented at Rundle, 'Of Republics and Tyrants', pp. 337–38.

45 Oxford: Balliol College, MS 127; Oxford: Corpus Christi College, MS 88. Cf. Cambridge: University Library, MS Ff. v. 12, where late fifteenth-century copies of *De Nobilitate* (signed by 'Freman') and *De Avaritia* (first recension) were bound at an early date with a twelfth-century copy of Cicero's *De Officiis*, suggesting that Poggio's dialogues may also have been considered works of moral advice; this codex was in its present location by 1556–7: see P. D. Clarke (ed.), *The University and College Libraries of Cambridge* [Corpus of British Medieval Library Catalogues, 10] (London, 2002), UC7. 15.

46 The letter to Correr is printed in *Opera omnia*, I, 325–8, and Marsuppini's poem in *Carmina illustrium poetarum italorum*, VI (Florence, 1720), 282–4.

47 *DH&EH*, p. 32.

48 The final *s* is only occasionally tall: it is at its most frequent in [11].

49 *DH&EH*, p. 32. This manuscript actually also includes at least one section in hand 'c': see [6], fol. 10v, l. 1–13.

50 On the dating of [8] see, in particular, *MSS at Oxford*, No. XXII.2.

51 For the suggestion that there may have been a canon of works considered appropriate for humanist treatment, see Rundle, 'Of Republics and Tyrants', pp. 253–54.

52 On Witeker (or Whiteacre or Wireker or Longchamps) generally, see A. G. Rigg, *A History of Anglo-Latin Literature 1066–1422* (Cambridge, 1992), pp. 102–5, and R. Sharpe, *A Handlist of the Latin Writers of Great Britain and Ireland before 1540* (Turnhout, 1997), *sub nomine*.

53 The classic discussion of the invention of *littera antiqua* remains B. L. Ullman, *The Origin and Development of Humanistic Script* (Rome, 1960); on the humanist terminology, see S. Rizzo, *Il lessico filologico degli umanisti* (Rome, 1973), esp. pp. 114–35. More generally on archaising scripts, crucial is M. B. Parkes, 'Archaizing Hands in English Manuscripts' in J. P. Carley & C. G. C. Tite (ed.), *Books and Collectors 1200–1700: Essays presented to Andrew Watson* (London, 1997), pp. 101–41.

54 Oxford: Bodleian Library, MS Auct. F. inf. 1. 1, on which see *MSS at Oxford*, XX.2, and Parkes, 'Archaising Hands', pp. 108–9 (with quotation at p. 109).

55 *MSS at Oxford*, p. 96 (on the basis of Dr A. I. Doyle's observation). The temptation proved irresistible to J. P. Gumbert, 'Italienische Schrift—humanistische Schrift—Humanistenschrift' in Autenrieth (ed.), *Renaissance- und Humanistenhandschriften*, pp. 63–70 (p. 69); he terms Candour's gothic script an example of what he calls '"neoromanischen" Schriften'.

56 Quotation from Parkes, 'Archaising Hands', p. 101.

57 *Lunulae*, or *virgulae convexae*, appear at, for example, [6], fol. 38v, ll. 6–7, 43, ll. 6–7; on their humanist invention, see M. B. Parkes, *Pause and Effect* (Aldershot, 1992), pp. 48–49; and for another example of early English use, see Daniel Wakelin's article in this volume.

58 A rare sighting of a humanist-style ampersand is at [6], fol. 17v, l. 24. The ampersand appears more often in his hand 'c': see, for example, [4], [5] or [11].

59 Candour does also employ diphthongs, albeit fitfully, in, for example, [5].

60 Milo da Carraria in Oxford: Bodleian, MS Rawl. C. 298 also does not indicate diphthongs but follows the humanist reform in writing *mihi*.

influence of *On Husbondrie* is also visible in the format of the three extant manuscripts of *Knyghthode and Bataile*: Cambridge, Pembroke College, MS 243; London, British Library, MS Cotton Titus A. xxiii; Oxford, Bodleian Library, MS Ashmole 45 (part ii).[8] In all three identically sized manuscripts, the main body of verse is regularly disposed in eight rime royal stanzas to a leaf, with marginal letters marking them *a* to *d* on the recto and *e* to *h* on the verso (visible in PLATE I from Cotton), just as in the translation of Palladius. Similarly, in both poems Latin side-notes signal topics of interest, while across the top of each double page spread appears the running title and in the top right-hand corner of each recto appears Vegetius's or Palladius's book number and foliation in Arabic numerals. The marginal markings of book, leaf and stanza facilitate an alphabetical index of each poem's contents. [9] All in all, these resemblances suggest that *Knyghthode and Bataile* imitates *On Husbondrie*.

The repetition of such an elaborately designed work also probably required that both poems be transmitted in fixed exemplars, a feat more readily achievable in stanzaic verse than prose. First, it emerges from the close integration of poem and index that the poet's original plans for the poem's visual appearance and textual apparatus required him to take the part of, or to employ, a scribe during composition, in order to develop a fully made-up exemplar of his work. In the only other previous work in English which regularly circulated with an index, Trevisa's translation of Higden's *Polychronicon*, the sequential order of topics under each letter-heading reveals that the index was most likely composed by Trevisa as he translated.[10] By contrast, the index to *Knyghthode and Bataile* is a subtle device which methodically gathers up cross-references to particular topics from scattered parts of the poem, and thus makes connections only visible if the indexer read through the whole text of an already complete poem. Furthermore, given the reference-system, the index must have been compiled after the scribal activity of disposing the text (the equivalent of the printer's 'casting off') and of elaborately enumerating leaves and lettering stanzas. Indeed, a few of the index's lemmata include words prompted not by the English verse, but by the Latin side-notes which accompany it.[11] Whether or not the author himself was that scribe, the scribal preparation of a fixed exemplar was an integral part of the author's original process of completing *Knyghthode and Bataile*, poem and index.

Nevertheless, despite his best laid plans, individual extant manuscripts do differ from the original format described here, and those divergences suggest something of the text's subsequent transmission. Two prologues which reveal the poet's original Lancastrian allegiances appear before the first and third of Vegetius's four books in the earliest of the three extant manuscripts of *Knyghthode and Bataile*: Pembroke. This manuscript is probably therefore datable after the presentation scene it describes on 1 March 1460 and before Henry VI's deposition in March 1461. Pembroke is copied by a single scribe in a small secretary hand of the mid-fifteenth century, though with a sigma-shaped *s* more common to anglicana hands. However, although the earliest manuscript, it carries the foliated leaves and stanza-lettering, but lacks the index. As now rebound, it is difficult to be certain, but it seems that after the final page of text, the scribe left the final leaf of quire VII (signed *g*) blank (fol. 54), on to which fifteenth- and sixteenth-century hands have jotted some names and a warrant. Symmetrical ink-spots and stains on the final page of verse and on the rough jottings suggest that they have long lain adjacent, without any intervening index. Therefore, if Pembroke did ever have an index, it was probably a codicological addition to the book. For comparison, in the two mainly holograph manuscripts of *On Husbondrie*, the index was clearly added in a separate quire at the front of the book,[12] whereas, by contrast, the index in the two later manuscripts of *Knyghthode and Bataile* begins within the same quire as the last leaf of verse.[13] Could Pembroke have been the author's copy, which he read before composing the index? It is a possible but not a likely or necessary hypothesis: Pembroke's scribe could simply have chosen to omit the utilitarian index.

Omissions occur within the later manuscripts which allow the literary work to endure beyond the political events which prompted its composition. Cotton and Ashmole replace Henry VI's name with that of Edward IV (lines 121, 2880) and omit the two lengthy Lancastrian prologues. (Ashmole is now fragmentary but, given its references to Edward, it probably always lacked the prologues.) Given these changes, Cotton and Ashmole probably date from the reign of Edward IV: Cotton is on paper with watermarks most like a series of very similar specimens datable from 1464 onwards,[14] and both are copied in versions of the secretary bookhand used for English literary texts in the third quarter of the fifteenth-century.[15] It is in Cotton that we must seek the earliest evidence concerning the omission of the two Lancastrian prologues. (I will argue below that Ashmole is copied from Cotton.) Progress on the copying of Cotton was initially halting: changes of ink reveal four short scribal stints in the first quire (fols 1r–1v, 89–129; fol. 1v, 129–144; fols 2r–6v, 145–410; fols 6v–8v, 411–536), and that first quire may originally have contained only six leaves. Rebinding again makes this assertion uncertain; but if so, Cotton's prologue-less first quire initially ended where the first quire of eight would end in an exemplar once constructed like Pembroke (in eights, neatly signed), but from which those first two leaves of Lancastrian prologue had been excised. Only then did the scribe of Cotton add a second bifolium, and thereafter proceed in regular quires of eight (signed '2 quair' and so on). The other partisan prologue, to book III, was also clearly missing in the exemplar of Cotton: where it, on folio 17, would have been cut, Cotton reached the end of a quire but used as its catchwords on folio 16v the first words of folio 18r of Pembroke or its twin ('lo thus thelectioun'). We might wonder, however, whether the scribe knew that something had been expunged, for some awareness made him carefully allow his foliation to jump past folio 17, in order for the index to work; he did not always copy his exemplar's foliation correctly, as on folios 40–41 and 44–46. The early hesitancy and the later assurance suggest that Cotton's scribe was aware that some editorial modifications had been made to the exemplar he was copying.

Yet was that exemplar, otherwise identical to Pembroke with the index in an additional separate quire, close to the author's own text? This possibility emerges further from the presence in Cotton of seventy glosses. As noted, unlike *On Husbondrie*, sixty-two of the glosses to *Knyghthode and Bataile* are not in Latin but English, and usually offer alternative wording or phrasing, often rectifying *minutiae* of metre or grammar. There is no evidence that they were in the exemplar of Pembroke, which lacks them; however, like the expurgation of Lancastrian sentiment, they were already part of the exemplar of Cotton. In the line 'Omnipote*n*s, this is his champioun' (2011), the scribe firstly in eye-skip copied the second word of the interlinear alternative '*vel* almghty lord' as part of the poetic line and then deleted it ('Omnipotens [lord] / this is his Champioun').[16] These interlinear alternatives probably represent signs of a later revision in an authorial exemplar otherwise similar to Pembroke.

However, these are mere speculations about transmission from authorial drafts; what is more visible is scribal endeavour in transmitting the poem's linguistic and literary niceties with care. In fact, the interlinear alternative wording could equally betray literary activity at a later stage of textual transmission, for the glosses' perfectionism matches the scribes' own concern with the poem's language. Besides the carefully reproduced *mise-en-page*, the text itself is also duplicated with a rigour quite unlike the 'mouvance' or 'variance' for which vernacular writing is known. The scribes take care to preserve even its orthography and punctuation, that is the so-called 'accidentals' of the text as well as its substantive readings.[17] This care emerges, paradoxically, in their errors and rectification of them. Dyboski and Arend's printed edition only notes a few scribal corrections; in fact, there are at least twenty-

eight corrections in Pembroke; forty-one in Cotton; and thirty-seven in
the fewer leaves of the mutilated Ashmole. Each manuscript contains
corrections by the respective main scribe as he went along: three of
twenty-eight in Pembroke (fols 8v, 517; 9r, 559; 39r, 2215);[18] twenty-five
of forty in Cotton; and up to seventeen of thirty-seven in Ashmole.
Self-corrections are not unknown in fifteenth-century English manuscripts.[19] However, in each manuscript a second hand then works
through the text correcting it, often in the tiniest details. These corrections attest to a concern for the accurate reproduction of *Knyghthode and
Bataile* as a metrical and verbally distinctive literary work, rather than
as a utilitarian text whose significance lies only in its lessons. Each
manuscript betrays something different about the scribal attitudes and
activity.

In Pembroke, some twenty-one corrections were added in a slightly
darker ink, not always easily discernible, usually between the lines, and
so probably at a later stage in the production of the manuscript. The
corrector employed a much more elaborate letter *w* formed of three
loops, and a more cursive, almost inverted *e*; nevertheless, given the
pressures of space in so few interlineations, it is impossible to confirm
that the corrector was someone other than the main copyist. What is
evident is his close attention: he modifies all manner of smaller words
and sometimes simply a letter: *the* becomes *these*; *ege*, a battle-line or
Latin *acies*, becomes *egge* (fol. 34r, 1938, 1947). At seven points the darker-
ink corrector adds nothing more than an inflectional *e*: for example,
'Heer faught[e] thei . that hadde as yet no sheelde' (fol. 32v, 1853). This
orthographical nitpicking, for a language as open to variation as
fifteenth-century English, can only serve to maintain the poem's
rigorously formed iambic pentameter: the scribes seem concerned with
the poem's 'cadence', as the epilogue requested. Similarly, the later
correctors of the other two manuscripts also, if less commonly, rectify
metrical errors.[20] The scribe of Pembroke sounds the inflectional *e*,
except where it would be elided even by metrical purists such as
Hoccleve (as clarified recently by J. A. Burrow).[21] That the final *e*, if
written, is still sounded emerges from a couple of places in which the
scribes, in all three manuscripts, alter a rhyme-word to ensure that it
does or does not have a final *e* like its pair (for example, Pembroke 8r,
505; Ashmole 4v, 292; Cotton 4v, 294). Yet whereas, it has been argued,
Hoccleve's works, *On Husbondrie* and a few other pieces of metrically
skilful fifteenth-century verse employ the inflectional *e* consistently as a
formal, artificial poetic convention, as in French alexandrine verse,
rather than because it was customarily pronounced,[22] *Knyghthode and
Bataile* less artfully uses it only when it is necessary to give otherwise

unmetrical lines an iambic rhythm (or when it would, anyway, be elided). The strenuous reproductive effort required by other scribes like Hoccleve to preserve that consistently archaic *e* is surpassed, then, by the scribe of Pembroke who would have had to imagine the sound of the poem's metre in order to preserve the inflectional *e* so intermittently. Pembroke's scribe seems aware that fifteenth-century 'Ortographie' shapes a highly artificial 'cadence' and that, as a scribe, he has an important role in preserving it.

The original scribe of Cotton is less successful in preserving the poem's iambic pentameter: he often includes or omits inflectional *e* to the detriment of the poem's rhythm.[23] Yet the slow and diligent nature of the scribal process emerges in Cotton's other corrections. Someone added fifteen of the book's forty corrections in a noticeably greyer ink at so late a stage that the quires were already assembled into a complete book, and at some speed: on folio 7r, the start of the bifolium added to the first quire, he added the word *oone* and it left offset on folio 6v. Despite his speed and his late involvement, though, the grey-ink corrector also attended to metrical detail and other *minutiae*, such as adding a mere minim to the *e* in an explicable eyeskip *well* to render it *wall* ('Thus dike *and* wall is well x. foote in hight', fol. 8v, 536). Moreover, this nitpicker's efforts were always anticipated as part of the production process: the original scribe encountered seven words in his exemplar that he did not understand and therefore left spaces which, on all but one occasion, were filled with the requisite term by the grey-ink corrector, such as the unusual *wastom*, the *size* of a ship, or *wawerd*, the *vanguard* of an army (see fol. 47r, 2655, reproduced in PLATE 1, and also fols 3r, 223, 227; 7r, 440; 8v, 535; 12v, 736; 41r, 2322).[24] Ironically, the line about the *wawerd* continues with the translator's warning not to worry about the linguistic difficulties of a Roman military treatise: 'of termys is noo foors, | So the conceyt be had' (736–7); but this scribe did worry about the poem's unusual terms, just as the scribe of Pembroke worried about metre.

Does this planned, collaborative fine-tuning of the poem's linguistic details betray a formal scribal milieu or professional book production? Any speculation about the milieu of the Cotton scribe must account for certain similarities between his hand and the hand of the Ashmole manuscript of *Knyghthode and Bataile*. (The decorated initials on folio 18r of Cotton and Ashmole are also almost identical.) The hands are not the same. Overall, Ashmole has a slightly spikier aspect in the joins between some strokes, and it also uses a different display script for the first few words of each stanza later in the manuscript. The scribe's choice of spelling in unstressed vowels also differs from Cotton (between *e, i* and *y*).

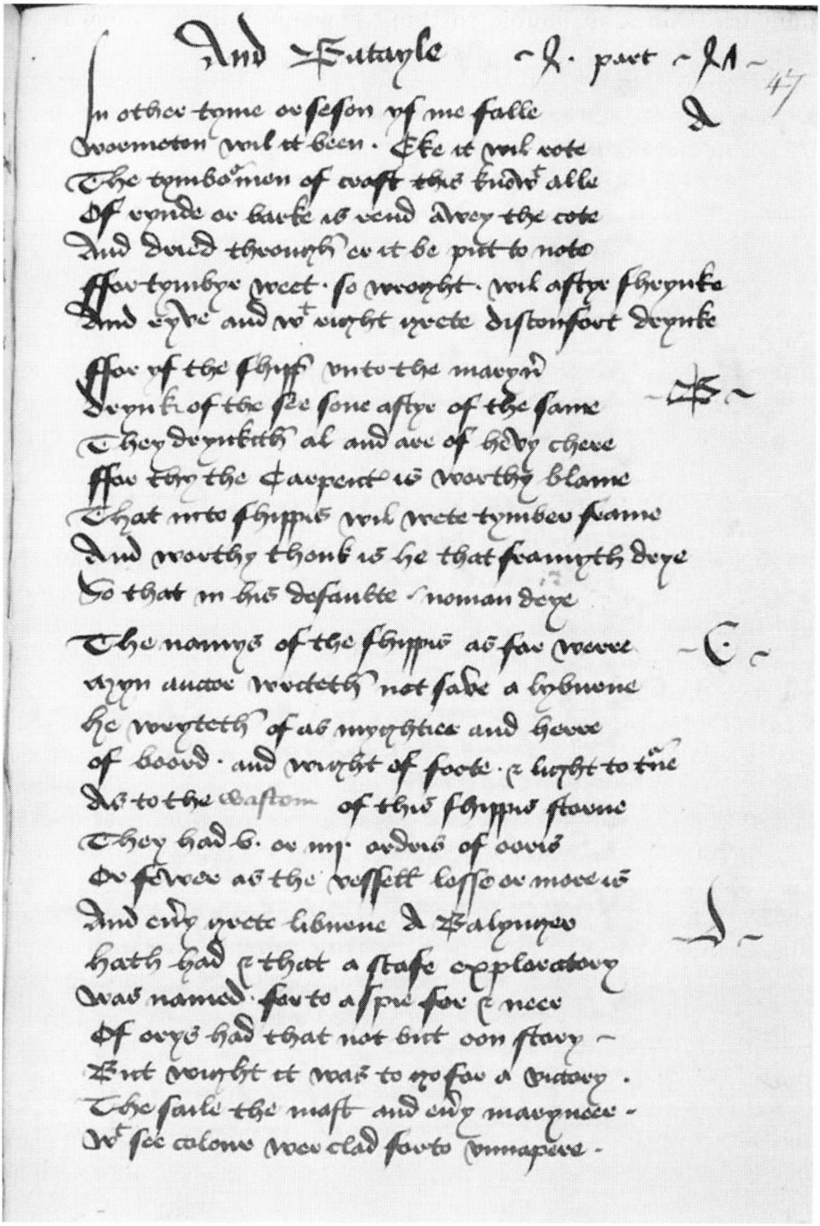

PLATE I. *A page in the Cotton manuscript of* Knyghthode and Bataile: *London, British Library, Cotton* MS *Titus A. xxiii, fol. 47r. (Original page size 216 × 146mm.) Reproduced by permission of the Board of the British Library.*

However, they form many graphs in identical ways (*a*, *s*, *w*, *y*) and, more intriguingly, ligatures and movements within such graphs: for example, an angular curve at the bottom of the ascender on *h* and a *v*-shaped *r* with only a hairline join between the down-stroke and a cursory crossbar (as seen in PLATE 2 and PLATE 3, line 16, *grymly* and *his*). Nevertheless, in other cases the manuscripts show different preferred graphs from an available variation. Cotton usually uses the elaborately looped ascenders on letter *d* more customary earlier in the fifteenth century and only a few loopless ascenders (for example fols 47r, line 24; 47v, line 9, seen in PLATE 2); Ashmole uses loopless ascenders still in a minority of cases, but more frequently.[25] Cotton usually puts a vertical stroke through majuscule *G* and *E* but only rarely through majuscule *C* (for example 42r, line 27 note): Ashmole has the opposite preferences, but still the same range of variants. Like a language in flux, these hands reveal permitted variations shared by two people but with shifting preferences among them. However, each manuscript does on rare occasions employ a couple of graphs never used by its peer: in Cotton a *p* formed with one swift loop leaving a tail; in Ashmole, a two-shaped *r*. It was of course possible for scribes to alter their range of graphs slightly over time, but the more limited range of similarities here suggests two different scribes, yet perhaps two scribes trained in the same hand and the same milieu.

The closeness of scribal milieux could be confirmed, for present purposes, by the textual connections between these two witnesses of the poem. In *mise-en-page*, glosses and in the finer points of textual detail, Ashmole is clearly close to Cotton, as the poem's editors first remarked.[26] For example, Cotton's corrector rewrites one line and it appears in its rewritten form in Ashmole ('lo this Citee wil all these assaile', fol. 42r, 2376). Moreover, the errors in Ashmole confirm the initial close relationship. Ashmole contains twenty corrections in an orange ink, and containing some graphs not found in the main hand: a highly cursive backwards *e*; *g* with a long shoulder-bar to the right; a sigma-shaped *s* with a long splay ahead of it. These orange-ink corrections reveal two points. Firstly, the main scribe originally copied Ashmole directly from Cotton. Richard Beadle has noted that the number of English-language manuscripts for which the exact exemplars have so far been identified is remarkably small:[27] these two manuscripts of *Knyghthode and Bataile* probably constitute a further rare example of direct copying. Secondly, and more intriguingly, the orange-ink corrector then checked the text copied from Cotton against a manuscript apparently identical, in at least these eighteen places, to the earliest manuscript, Pembroke (perhaps the manuscript from which Cotton had

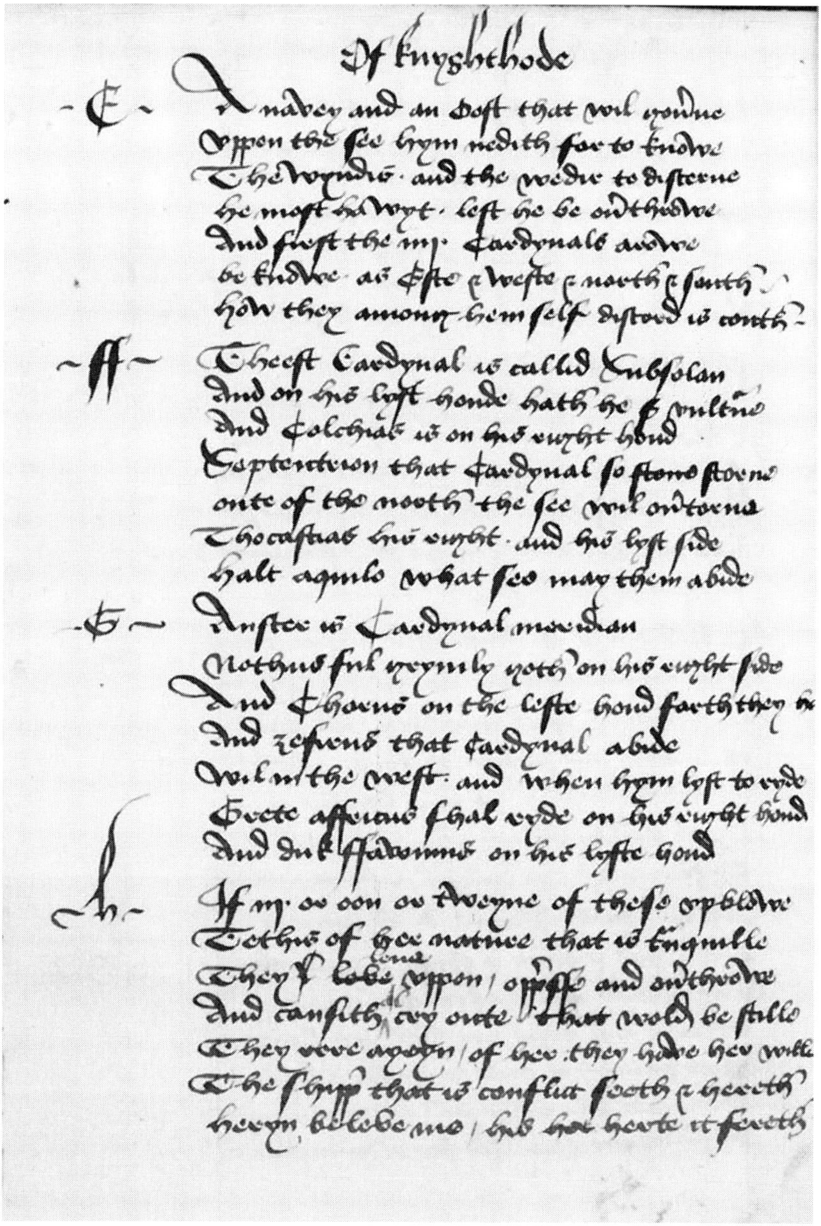

PLATE 2. *Another page in the Cotton manuscript of* Knyghthode and Bataile*: London, British Library, Cotton MS Titus A. xxiii, fol. 47v. (Original page size 216 × 146mm.) Reproduced by permission of the Board of the British Library.*

been copied). Cotton and Ashmole also, then, usefully illuminate not only close copying from one exemplar to another, but also the care exercised by some copyists to preserve the original text despite the errors in their exemplar.

Unfortunately, many leaves have been lost from Ashmole, but in the twenty-four extant leaves, some eighteen corrections identify passages in which Ashmole duplicates a clear error in Cotton but which has been corrected back again to resemble Pembroke.[28] Two examples must suffice:

43r	2422
Pembroke	Awey with euery hous . And mak a wal
Cotton	Awey with heuy hous and make a wal
Ashmole	Awey with [h]ev[er]y hous . and make a wal
48r	2715
Pembroke	Appereth / What is that the sterrys .vij.
Cotton	Appereth what is that ~ Thesteis vij.
Ashmole	Apperith . what is þat . Thest*is vij. *sterris *(added in the margin)*

The first example uses straightforward and typical amendments. In the second example, the copyist of Ashmole seems to have been misled by the particular graphic reproduction of *Thesteis* by the scribe of Cotton. Cotton's scribe here may have confused *the sterrys* with the nymph *Thetis* who appeared on the preceding page (47v, 2687), perhaps because his exemplar abbreviated *er*. Yet the first *e* and *s* of Cotton's *Thesteis* are not in fact joined cursively, although there is no space between them, and there may be a tiny feint loop over the second *e* to mark the abbreviation of *er*: Cotton's text may read *The stereis*. However, as my uncertainty shows, these features are not readily visible without more squinting than Ashmole's busy copyist presumably had time for. He appears to have copied quickly the graphs which look like *Thesteis* in Cotton; then, later noticing the flaws in this text, a second scribe collated Ashmole with another text of the poem.

This sort of scribal correction, in quest of a better text, is not unique. Ralph Hanna identified a prolific literary scribe correcting his copy of *Troilus and Criseyde* against a better exemplar. In 1476 the Norwich town clerk Geoffrey Spirleng corrected the errors of his young son in copying their private manuscript of *The Canterbury Tales*, and also made good the omissions in one exemplar (still extant, by chance) with a second. The main, probably authorial scribe of two manuscripts of *On Husbondrie* also corrected his assistant's handiwork.[29] As Hanna commented, some scribes did seem to seek to transmit their exemplars scrupulously or fastidiously, or to seek the best text; they were often simply hampered by the available exemplars.[30] So in Ashmole, someone sought to remove errors carried over from the exemplar, Cotton, because they recognized and had access to a better text of the poem. This textual collation may reflect the close-knit readership which the similar hands suggest. Yet also, contrary to theories which dismiss their literary interests, these corrections reveal fifteenth-century scribes fussily concerned with preserving the specific verbal form of the literary work. There is little 'mouvance' or 'variance' here.

One of the corrections in Ashmole may reveal the inspiration for such carefulness. On one page of Ashmole, as PLATE 3 shows, the orange-ink corrector adds to the text two *lunulae*, that is, the marks commonly called parentheses or round brackets, which were not found in the exemplar, Cotton:

47v	2692	
Pembroke	(Heryn beleve ⌈me⌉) his hert it fereth .	
Cotton	Heryn beleve me / his [het] herte it fereth	
Ashmole	[(⌈Herin beleve me [/][)] his hert it ferith ~	

The orange-ink corrector's addition of *lunulae* to Ashmole again restores the text found in Pembroke (as PLATE 4 shows); however, this correction concerns itself with punctuation alone. (He adds another punctuation mark, a *virgula*, on fol. 21v, line 1230.) Punctuation, like 'cadence' and 'Ortographie', is essential to the scribe's preservation of the text and its unambiguous meaning. As it happens, Pembroke contains 8 pairs of *lunulae*, in both brown ink and red:

iʳ	9	And she thi modir . (Blessed mot she be) .	red
iiʳ	48	Welcom (Here is tassay . entre to get .)	red
iiʳ	58	Heer wil I rede (he seith) as o psaultier	red
5v	358	And noo man (as thei seyn)~ is seyn prevaile	brown and red
11r	642	Virgile seith (an high poete is he)	brown
31r	1782	May brynge (as god defende) us to myschaunce .	re
36r	2045	But first (as seide is erste) is hem tassaile	brown and red
47v	2692	(Heryn beleve ⌈me⌉) his hert it fereth	brown and red

Unfortunately, only two pairs appear on leaves which still survive in Ashmole, and Ashmole does not copy the other pair (fol. 5v). *Knyghthode and Bataile*'s *lunulae* largely attribute speech or carry directly addressed

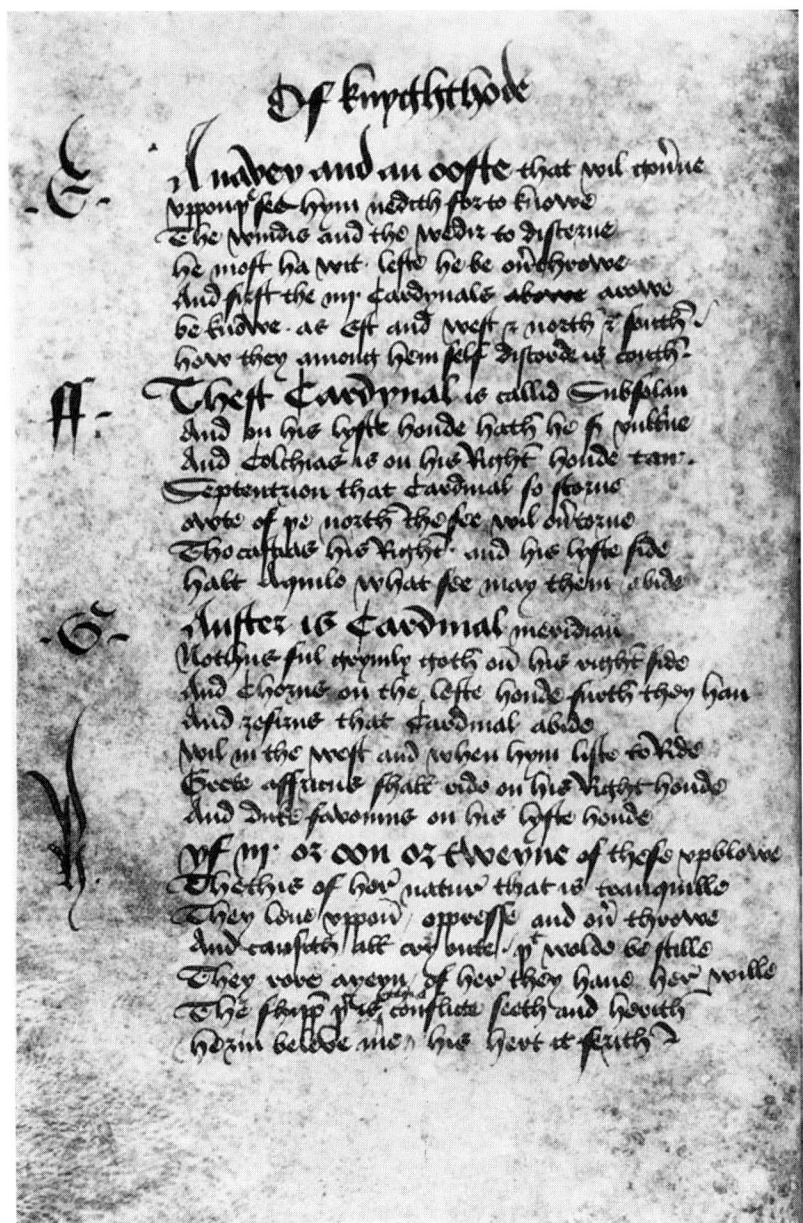

PLATE 3. *A page in the Ashmole manuscript of* Knyghthode and Bataile: *Oxford, Bodleian Library,* MS *Ashmole 45 (part ii), fol. 18v. (Original page size 206 × 137mm.) Reproduced by permission of the Bodleian Library, University of Oxford.*

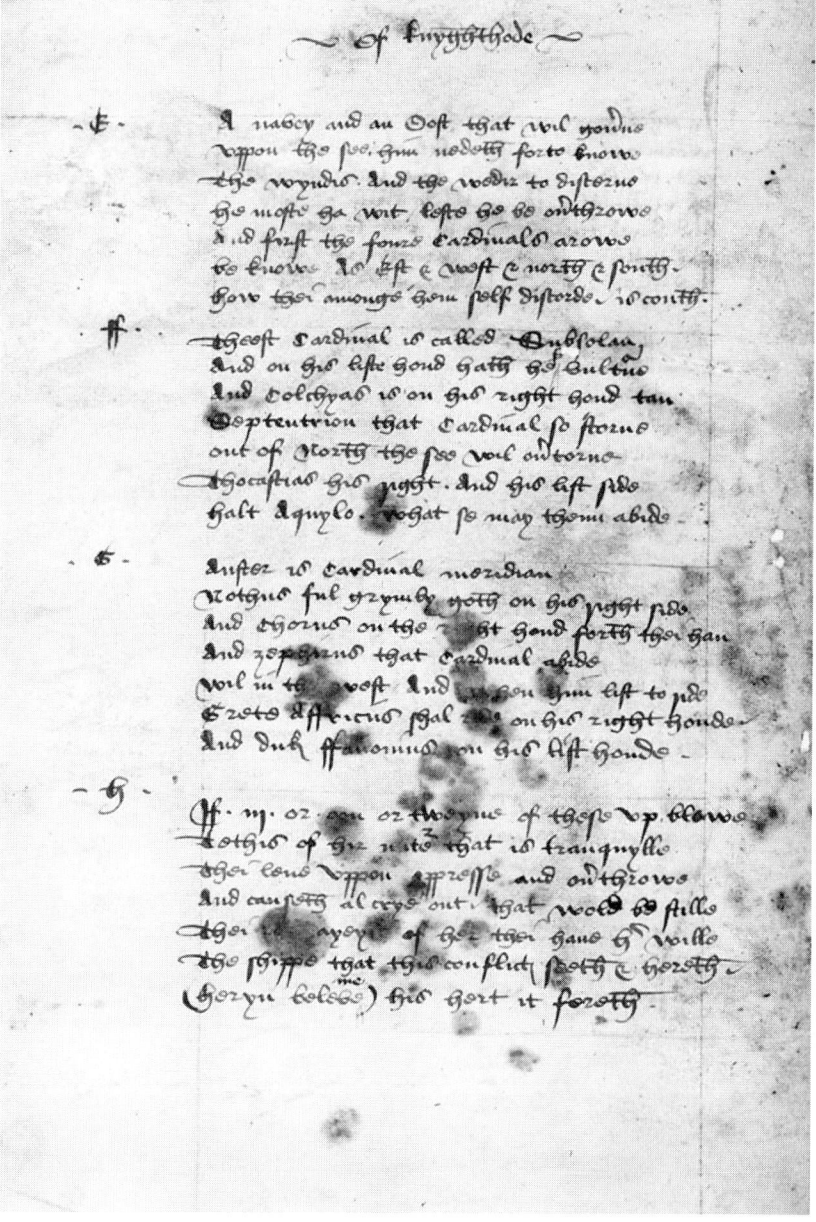

PLATE 4. *A page in the Pembroke manuscript of* Knyghthode and Bataile*:
Cambridge, Pembroke College, MS 243, fol. 49v. (Original page size 240 × 170mm.)
Reproduced by permission of the Master and Fellows of Pembroke College, Cambridge.*

theatrical 'asides', both of which remained familiar usages of *lunulae* in sixteenth-century England, according to John Lennard.[31] They clarify the complex text's varying voices and modes of address, and ensure an accurate reading.

Nonetheless, *lunulae* are extremely unusual marks to find in a fifteenth-century English vernacular manuscript. The standard histories of punctuation identify the first example from England in Pynson's 1494 print of Giovanni Sulpizio's neo-Latin grammar, although the mark does appear in an edition of Cicero's *Pro Milone* probably printed at Oxford in 1483 by Theodoric Rood of Cologne.[32] The mark was invented by Coluccio Salutati as early as 1398, but it was virtually unknown outside of manuscripts of grammatical treatises by Gasparino Barzizza, Jacopo Alpoleio and Guillaume Fichet. Historians have assumed that it spread only in the uniform typefaces based upon humanist script which increasingly homogenized European printing and punctuation in the late fifteenth century.[33] This chronology renders the *lunulae* in Pembroke and Ashmole chronological curiosities for the record book. Given that Pembroke is probably datable between 1 March 1460 and 4 March 1461, and at the latest before the death of Henry VI in 1471, it constitutes the first known use of the *lunula* in a text in the English language and is one of the earliest datable uses in any language in England or by an Englishman. David Rundle's article in this volume records that Thomas Candour, a scribe who cultivated a humanist hand, used them too. Their use so early suggests that the scribe of Pembroke, if not his imitator in Ashmole, also had some humanist connections. There are in fact many other *lunulae* in manuscripts from England in the second half of the fifteenth-century, but they appear in manuscripts produced by Italians living there or by English scholars who had pursued the *studia humanitatis* in Italy.[34] The *lunulae* suggest an unsurprising humanist influence upon *Knyghthode and Bataile*: this translation of a late classical work employs one of the signs of humanist neo-classicism.

Moreover, the use of *lunulae* by other English humanists illuminates the motives for, and connotations of, the use of *lunulae* in *Knyghthode and Bataile*. John Gunthorpe, scholar, diplomat and dean of Bath and Wells, was an early user of *lunulae*: for example, in some diplomatic speeches dated to 1468.[35] Then when he copied Horace's *Satires* in his humanist hand, he included five pairs in his first draft and, while reading, added eight more pairs in red ink and rubricated two earlier pairs. Gunthorpe's *lunulae* tend to enclose longer phrases than the brief asides 'bracketed off' in *Knyghthode and Bataile*; however, the increasing number of *lunulae* during his second, rubricating stint recalls the English poem.[36]

Gunthorpe's acquaintance John Russell, later Bishop of Lincoln, also added further *lunulae* to Fust and Schoeffer's edition of Cicero's *De Officiis*, a book which already contained some printed *lunulae*, and which Paul Saenger credits with disseminating the mark in northern Europe.[37] Russell and Gunthorpe also glossed their books, sometimes in English, in the same stints during which they punctuated them. For Salutati and his followers, the *lunula*, like other humanist innovations in punctuation, was crucially an aid to disambiguation and to comprehension of the elaborate rhetoric of the classical or classicizing text, as a gloss was. The scribes of the Pembroke and Ashmole manuscripts of *Knyghthode and Bataile* were equally concerned to clarify their text's ersatz classical style. Moreover, in Pembroke, the fact that seven of the *lunulae* and many other punctuation marks were originally or later rubricated suggests that these marks were proudly used elements of the book's distinctive *mise-en-page*. For Gunthorpe and for this vernacular scribe, punctuation, typified by the unusual *lunula*, is both integral to the text and a distinctive feature in its own right: the very verbal clarity of the text, achieved in a manner redolent of humanist writing and reading, is itself on display.

So two points emerge. First, the manuscripts of *Knyghthode and Bataile* suggest that all elements of the book, from punctuation to *mise-en-page* could have some importance for the author's and scribes' conception of the literary text, as argued by some recent bibliographers such as D. F. McKenzie.[38] The scribe rubricating these *lunulae* is not tinkering with 'accidentals' but clarifying both the meaning of individual lines and the broader 'meaning', the connotations, of *Knyghthode and Bataile* as a whole work. Secondly, the evidence of scribal attempts to preserve minute details of the text's verbal form in all three manuscripts suggests a care for the fixity of texts not attributed to vernacular scribes by Zumthor, Cerquiglini or Machan. A work of such learning could not be transmitted by author alone. It required the author himself to engage in, or to supervise closely, scribal activity in preparing an exemplar before he composed the index and transmitted the poem to other scribes in the desired visual format. More importantly, though, the further transmission of *Knyghthode and Bataile* required the considerable efforts of those other scribes in copying, correcting and punctuating its 'cadence' and 'Ortographie'. The poet pretends that 'Of termys is noo foors', but he was being disingenuous. These manuscripts suggest that both this poem and fifteenth-century vernacular scribes could be more literary in their taste and skill than is sometimes alleged.

Or are such scribal practices in *Knyghthode and Bataile* really characteristic of English vernacular scribes? Coincidentally, John Gunthorpe and John Russell were associates of the royal secretary William Hatteclyff and the chamberlain William Hastings, whose families were the probable earliest owners of the Pembroke and Cotton manuscripts. These links, and the poet's emulation of Duke Humfrey's *On Husbondrie*, all suggest that the poem was created and transmitted among a milieu with distinctly humanist tastes, albeit here manifested in the vernacular.[39] The scribes' evident concern for textual fixity and clarity, manifested in their careful corrections, displays attitudes towards the text analogous to those of humanist scholars. The use of *lunulae* also suggests some Italian or English humanist influence upon these scribes. Like the poet's own revision of Chaucer's gloomy 'Go, litil book' conclusion, the manuscripts of *Knyghthode and Bataile* reveal some new expectations and new habits for English vernacular scribes in the later fifteenth century.

NOTES

1 Quotations and parenthetical line references come from R. Dyboski and Z. M. Arend, eds, *Knyghthode and Bataile*, EETS, OS 201 (London, 1935).

2 See most recently Christopher Allmand, 'The Fifteenth-Century English Versions of Vegetius' *De Re Militari*', in *Armies, Chivalry and Warfare in Medieval Britain and France: proceedings of the 1995 Harlaxton Symposium*, ed. Matthew Strickland, Harlaxton Medieval Studies, VII (Stamford, 1998), pp. 30–45 (pp. 32, 35–36). Until Professor Allmand's longer study is published, the fullest accounts of Vegetius's transmission are Michael D. Reeve, 'The Transmission of Vegetius's *Epitoma rei militaris*', *Aevum*, 74 (2000), 243–354, especially p. 343, for *Knyghthode and Bataile*, and Foster Hallberg Sherwood, 'Studies in Medieval Uses of Vegetius' "Epitoma Rei Militaris"', unpub. doctoral diss. (University of California, Los Angeles, 1980).

3 See John Watts, *Henry VI and the Politics of Kingship* (Cambridge, 1996), p. 354; Julia Boffey, 'Books and Readers in Calais: Some Notes', *The Ricardian*, 13 [special issue: *Tant D'Emprises—So Many Undertakings: Essays in Honour of Anne Sutton*, ed. Livia Visser-Fuchs] (2003), 67–74; and Daniel Wakelin, 'Vernacular humanism in England *c*.1440–1485', unpub. Ph.D. thesis (University of Cambridge, 2002), pp. 121–29.

4 Geoffrey Chaucer, *Troilus and Criseyde*, book 5, lines 1786–99 in *The Riverside Chaucer*, ed. Larry D. Benson, 3rd edn (1987; Oxford, 1988), p. 584.

5 *MED*, *writer(e* (n.), sense (a).

6 Paul Zumthor, *Essai de poétique médiévale* (Paris, 1972), pp. 71–72, 507; Bernard Cerquiglini, *Éloge de la variante: Histoire critique de la philologie* (Paris, 1989), pp. 41–42, 58, 111; Tim William Machan, *Textual Criticism and Middle English Texts* (Charlottesville, VA, 1994), pp. 141–3, 165–76.

7 Mark Liddell, ed., *The Middle English Translation of Palladius De Re Rustica* (Berlin, 1896), prologue 65–112, I. 1182–1204.

8 As all three manuscripts were once foliated identically, for ease of comparison I cite the scribal foliation of each. The modern pencil foliations differ because: the prologue to book I was not originally foliated in Pembroke (and so I count those leaves as fols i–ii); a flyleaf in Cotton has been foliated by a later cataloguer (and so the pen-

cil foliation differs from the original foliation until the scribe omits fol. 17); and Ashmole has lost several leaves.

9 Compare Oxford, Bodleian Library, MS Duke Humfrey d. 2 and Glasgow, University Library, MS Hunter 104 (T. 5. 6), described variously by A.C. de la Mare, 'Duke Humfrey's English Palladius (MS. Duke Humfrey d. 2)', *Bodleian Library Record*, 12 (1985), 39–51, and Daniel Wakelin, 'An Imaginary Readership: Vernacular Humanism in Fifteenth-Century England', in *Borderlines: Insular and Continental Perspectives on Medieval Culture—the Proceedings of the First Five Borderlines Conferences*, ed. Stephen Kelly and Jason O'Rourke (Dublin: Four Courts, 2004 forthcoming).

10 Ronald Waldron, 'Dialect aspects of Trevisa's translation of the *Polychronicon*', in *Regionalism in Late Medieval Manuscripts and Texts: Essays celebrating the publication of* A Linguistic Atlas of Late Mediaeval English, ed. Felicity Riddy (Cambridge, 1991), pp. 67–87 (pp. 76–77). One bilingual manuscript of Chaucer's *Boece* contains a Latin alphabetical index (Cambridge University Library, MS Ii. 3. 21, fols 1r–8v), and an index was added to a bilingual copy of Walton's translation of Boethius (Cambridge, St John's College, MS G. 29, fols 81r–85v).

11 Compare for example 'Electioun of place' (Ashmole fol. 54v) and 'Electio loci' (fol. 31r, by line 1756 which does not use any cognate phrase).

12 Bodleian Library, MS Duke Humfrey d. 2, fols x–xviii and Glasgow, University Library, MS Hunter 104 (T. 5. 6), fols 1–6.

13 Cotton collates thus: i + I⁶, II², III–VIII⁸ + i (with an index on fols 54r–56v). Ashmole cannot be collated due to its considerable damage, but the last four leaves of verse and the three leaves of index seem to form one intact quire, with the final blank leaf cancelled.

14 C. M. Briquet, *Les Filigranes: Dictionnaire historique des marques du papier dès leur apparition vers 1282 jusqu'en 1600*, ed. Allan Stevenson, 4 vols (Amsterdam, 1986), specimens 9181–3 dating from 1464, 1467 and 1472.

15 For similar graphs, compare PLATE 3 to the hand of William Ebesham before 1469, in C. E. Wright, *English Vernacular Hands from the Twelfth to the Fifteenth Centuries* (Oxford, 1960), plate 24; or that of Roger Thorney in the reign of Edward IV, in P.R. Robinson, *Dated and Datable Manuscripts c.737–1600 in Cambridge Libraries*, 2 vols (Cambridge, 1988), plate 304.

16 More confusingly, at four other points, the scribe first copied and then deleted an interlinear phrase (fols 4r, 258; 5r, 323 twice; 32r, 1825). Dyboski and Arend, eds, *Knyghthode and Bataile*, only record the first example and do not mention its deletion.

17 See D. F. McKenzie, *Making Meaning: 'Printers of the Mind' and Other Essays*, ed. Peter D. McDonald and Michael F. Suarez, S. J. (Amherst, Mass., 2002), pp. 200–01.

18 Pembroke also has five corrections by the rubricator, who added much punctuation too.

19 See for example Mary Hamel, 'Scribal Self-Corrections in the Thornton *Morte Arthure*', *Studies in Bibliography*, 36 (1983), 119–37 (pp. 124–9).

20 Orthographic corrections which affect only metre appear in Pembroke at fols 8r, 505; 15r, 887; 26r, 1501; 28v, 1626; 30r, 1724; 32v, 1853; 43v, 2456; in Cotton at fols 4v, 294; 32v, 1853; in Ashmole at fols 2v, 178; 4v, 292; 49r, 2764; 52r, 2921.

21 Thomas Hoccleve, *Complaint and Dialogue*, ed. J. A. Burrow, EETS, OS 313 (Oxford, 1999), pp. xxx–xxxi.

22 On fifteenth-century metre, see Hoccleve, *Complaint*, ed. Burrow, p. xxix; B. A. Windeatt, '"Most conservatyf the soun": Chaucer's *Troilus* metre', *Poetica*, 8 (1977),

44–60 (pp. 47–49); Eleanor Prescott Hammond, ed., *English Verse between Chaucer and Surrey* (Durham, NC, 1927), pp. ix, 17–24; Eleanor Prescott Hammond, 'The Nine Syllabled Pentameter Line in Some Post-Chaucerian Manuscripts', *Modern Philology*, 23 (1925), 129–52 (pp. 131–32).

23 For example compare in Pembroke and Cotton fol. 47v, lines 2674 (*tan* omitted in Cotton), 2687 (*natur* and *nature*), 2689 (*out* and *oute*). Cotton frequently harms lines by spelling *out* as *oute* (see also fol. 42r, 2381).

24 See *MED*, *wastme* (n.), sense 2.(c), meaning 'size'; *MED*, *vaunt-ward(e* (n.).

25 M. B. Parkes, *English Cursive Book Hands 1250–1500* (London, 1969), pp. xx–xxi, 12, describes the loss of looped ascenders in later fifteenth-century secretary hands.

26 *Knyghthode and Bataile*, ed. Dyboski and Arend, p. xv.

27 Richard Beadle, 'Geoffrey Spirleng (*c.*1426–*c.*1494): a Scribe of the *Canterbury Tales* in his Time', in *Of the making of books: Medieval manuscripts, their scribes and readers. Essays presented to M.B. Parkes*, ed. P. Robinson and R. Zim (Aldershot, 1997), pp. 116–46 (pp. 118–19, n.7).

28 See Ashmole fols 2v, 178; 5v, 361; 7r, 440; 20v, 1194; 21v, 1223; 22v, 1285; 41r, 2325; 41v, 2351; 43r, 2422; 47v, 2691, 2692; 48r, 2715; 48v, 2741; 51r, 2884; 52r, 2921, 2922, 2925; 53r, 2988.

29 See respectively Ralph Hanna, 'The Scribe of Huntington HM 114', *Studies in Bibliography*, 42 (1989), 120–33 (p. 127); Beadle, 'Geoffrey Spirleng', pp. 117, 133; and see the corrections marked in the *apparatus criticus* throughout Liddell, ed., *On Husbondrie*.

30 Hanna, 'The Scribe of Huntington HM 114', pp. 125, 128–29.

31 John Lennard, *But I Digress: The Exploitation of Parentheses in English Printed Verse* (Oxford, 1991), pp. 20–22. I follow Erasmus and Lennard in using *lunula* to distinguish the graphic mark from the whole parenthesis (which denotes the marks and the words between them all together).

32 M. B. Parkes, *Pause and Effect: An Introduction to the History of Punctuation in the West* (Aldershot, 1992), pp. 48–52. See also Marcus Tullius Cicero, *Pro Milone* (Oxford: Rood, *c.*1483), in fragments now in the Bodleian Library, Arch. G. d. 33, sig. b3ʳ, and Oxford, Merton College, P. 3. 2 and P. 3. 3a, sigs c6ʳ, d2ᵛ (*STC* 5312).

33 Paul Saenger, 'The Implications of Incunable Description for the History of Reading Revisited', *Papers of the Bibliographical Society of America*, 91 (1997), 495–504 (p. 497); Evencio Beltran, 'Un Traité inconnu de Guillaume Fichet sur la ponctuation', *Scriptorium*, 39 (1985), 284–91 (p. 290).

34 See their use by Italians in England throughout: for example, Cambridge, Trinity College, MS B. 14. 47 (Surigone, *De Institutionibus boni viri libellus*, dedicated to the prior of Great Malvern), and London, Lambeth Palace Library, MS 450 (Traversagni, *Triumphus amoris domini nostri Jhesu Christi*, dated in London, 1485, fol. 6r). One odd vernacular example appears in a late fifteenth-century anthology of lyrics to introduce the title of a secular song upon which a godly *contrafactum* has been based: 'A song in þe tune of (And I were a mayd *etc*' (Bodleian Library, MS Eng. poet. e. 1, fol. 47v). Lennard, *But I Digress*, pp. 17–21, notes the use of a single *lunula* to mark lemmata from the original text in commentaries; the *contrafactum*'s title may reflect an analogous separation of original text and response.

35 Bodleian Library, MS Bodley 587, fols 79r, 84r–84v, printed in Pierre Chaplais, *English Diplomatic Practice*, 2 vols (London, 1982), I, pp. 242, 247–48.

36 Lambeth Palace Library, MS 425 fols 74v–75r, 78r, 80v, 84r, 87r, 88r, 105r, 109r. [Richard Hunt and A.C. de la Mare], *Duke Humfrey and English Humanism in the Fifteenth Century* (Oxford, 1970), pp. 55–56 (No. 93).

37 Marcus Tullius Cicero, *De Officiis, Paradoxa* (Mainz: Fust and Schoeffer, 1465), in a copy now catalogued as Lambeth Palace Library, MS 765: for example, fol. 2r. See Saenger, 'Implications', p. 497, and A.B. Emden, *A Biographical Register of the University of Oxford to A.D. 1500*, 3 vols (Oxford, 1957–59), III, 1609–11, s.v. Russell.

38 See for example McKenzie, *Making Meaning*, p. 215.

39 On which, see Daniel Wakelin, 'The Occasion, Author and Readers of *Knyghthode and Bataile*', forthcoming in *Medium Ævum*.

Scottish Manuscript Miscellanies from the Fifteenth to the Seventeenth Century

Priscilla Bawcutt

'Mo sterres, God wot, than a payre'

(Chaucer, *The Parliament of Fowls*, 595)

My starting-point is a very bright star in the Scottish firmament, the Bannatyne Manuscript. Recently termed, with some hyperbole, 'the most important literary document of early Scottish literature',[1] it has been closely scrutinised by many scholars, especially in the last quarter of a century. Yet despite all the undoubted advances in our knowledge, this manuscript poses many unsolved problems, and I am increasingly uneasy at the way conjecture, unverified assumptions and hypotheses, and even downright errors are rapidly acquiring the status of fact. Michael Lynch thus erroneously claimed, in *Scotland: A New History*, that the collection contains 'more love poetry than anything else', and that it was 'compiled' in 1565–66.[2] The wide dissemination of such beliefs is ensured by the well-deserved popularity of his important book. Enshrined in the very title of *Poetry of the Stewart Court*, an anthology based solely on the Bannatyne Manuscript, is another tenacious yet dubious notion, that it is a 'court anthology'. In the tart words of Denton Fox, 'to describe the whole contents of the manuscript as court poetry is to stretch the term out of all reason'.[3] Several modern preconceptions can be traced ultimately to one great man: Sir Walter Scott, who viewed George Bannatyne in the light of his own Romantic beliefs and assumptions and imputed to him the patriotic and antiquarian plan of 'saving the literature of a whole nation'.[4] Another current idea—that 'the collection was destined for the printer'—can likewise be traced ultimately to Scott's speculation that Bannatyne 'designed' the work 'to be sent to the press'.[5]

The Bannatyne Manuscript, above all, is perceived as unique: many distinguished scholars have studied it, but few have questioned this unique status, or made much attempt to view it in the context of other manuscript miscellanies, whether English or Scottish. The one exception is a curious long-standing rivalry with the Maitland Folio (Appendix, No. 6); when John Pinkerton, in the eighteenth century, called the Folio 'the chief treasure of ancient Scottish poetry', he was vigorously attacked by the defenders of Bannatyne.[6] In this paper I shall look at a number of Scottish literary miscellanies—a subject inherently interesting in itself, I believe—and then return to the Bannatyne Manuscript, and re-examine it in the light of these other manuscripts. Such a comparison, as I hope to show, is profitable.[7]

Quite a large number of Scottish anthologies survive, and in the past there must have existed many more. Only one Catholic devotional collection is now extant (London, British Library, MS Arundel 285; Appendix, No. 4), and it is inherently unlikely that no others were produced. Yet these manuscripts are, in general, not well known, and have been curiously neglected by scholars. In the first half of the twentieth century excellent transcripts of some were published by the Scottish Text Society (Appendix, Nos. 2, 3, 4, 5, 6 and 7); yet their apparatuses were sketchy, and until recently few have been followed up by further study. There now exist good facsimiles of the Bannatyne Manuscript and Oxford, Bodleian Library, MS Arch. Selden. B. 24 (Appendix, No. 1).[8] Useful descriptive studies of the Asloan Manuscript (Appendix, No. 3) and MS Arundel 285 have also been published;[9] but nothing comparable exists for any other miscellany. A few manuscripts have been printed in part, often modernised, bowdlerised, or with the order of their contents rearranged. In 1899, for instance, William Walker published *Extracts from the Commonplace Book of Andrew Melville 1621–1640* (Aberdeen University Library, MS 28; Appendix, No. 16); he omitted much, including a bawdy sonnet, and the very first item, a substantial prose piece, at the beginning of which is inscribed in a nineteenth-century hand (probably Walker's): 'An Essay on Women—not complimentary'. Another small verse miscellany (Edinburgh University Library, MS Laing III. 447; Appendix, No. 18) has been printed, but the order of items is totally rearranged, for no obvious reason; what is even more misleading, it is published in the Scottish Text Society's Montgomerie Supplementary volume, although it contains only three poems certainly by that poet (*The Cherrie and the Slae*; No. vi; and No. xxx).[10] None of the later manuscripts has been described carefully and systematically; information about them is difficult to find, muddled and sometimes quite misleading. When I first came across a reference by Mrs Helena Shire to the Melvill Buik of Roundels (Appendix, No. 13) I was intrigued by the title, but wondered why she mentioned only two poems and gave no further description of the manuscript's contents. It is symptomatic that W. H. Auden, who also showed some awareness of this work in *An Elizabethan Song Book*, said that 'the only known manuscript' was in Australia. In fact, it has been owned by the Library of Congress in Washington since 1945.[11]

There are many different and legitimate ways of approaching a manuscript. We all, editors and critics alike, seek out what we can understand, interpret, or find interesting: ballads perhaps, or works in a specific genre, or new poems by a particular poet—Dunbar, Montgomerie, Ayton. Above all, Scottish scholars have looked for works authentically Scottish. The history of Bodleian Arch. Selden. B. 24 is typical: one item from it, *The Kingis Quair*, has been reprinted again and again, and it has sometimes been called 'the *Kingis Quair* manuscript'; its other, largely Chaucerian, contents have been virtually ignored in Scotland. Today, in somewhat the same patriotic spirit, the seventeenth-century song manuscripts are searched for 'the music of Scotland'; the presence in them of works by English composers is rarely mentioned. I do not wish to be misunderstood. To assemble the lost, scattered, or forgotten compositions of Scottish poets and musicians is a worthy enterprise.[12] Nonetheless, silent selectivity, whether inspired by nationalism or some other motive—extracting merely the plums, like little Jack Horner—may lead to distortion and falsification, not only of a manuscript's character but of a society's literary and musical culture.

In recent decades there has been a remarkable resurgence of interest in late medieval and early modern manuscripts. One feature of modern codicology that I find particularly significant is the concern with the manuscript as a whole, not just as a quarry from which choice items may be selected. An analogy might be drawn with the motives of modern archaeologists: no longer mere treasure-seekers, they analyse the structure and social significance of a site. As Derek Pearsall comments: 'the methods of compilers and manuscript editors of all kinds, whether professional or amateur, need to be studied, if we are to understand the reception and readership assumed for the literary works contained in their collections'. Yet nothing is ever wholly new. Long ago M. R. James urged scholars not to neglect 'anything that a manuscript can tell us as to its place of origin, its scribe, or its owners. Names and scribblings . . . which to one student suggest nothing, may combine in the memory of another into a coherent piece of history'.[13] A second point (to which I shall return) concerns the relationship of manuscripts and printed books. Today it is widely recognised that scribal activity, both professional and amateur, continued to be important for centuries after the invention of printing: the late date of the Robert Tait Manuscript

(Appendix, No. 20) should be noted. Poems were not only preserved, but also transmitted, and, in a sense, published in manuscript.[14] In the field of Scottish studies, however, there still remains a tendency to privilege the printed book.

In the Appendix below are listed twenty Scottish miscellanies mentioned in this article (bracketed numbers refer to this list). They are arranged in approximately chronological order, from the late fifteenth century to the last quarter of the seventeenth century. In fact I shall say little of numbers 1–4 and 20, despite their considerable interest. I shall be chiefly concerned with a shorter and more homogeneous period: the 1560s to the 1640s. Even so, it is clearly impossible to discuss every aspect of every miscellany. I shall give more prominence to some manuscripts than others, and focus on such questions as who compiled them, what they contain, where their material came from, and how they are arranged.

I must stress at the outset the diversity of these manuscripts, in size as in other respects. At one extreme is the Asloan Manuscript (No. 3), which even in its present imperfect condition contains over 300 leaves (230 × 170mm); at the other is the much smaller Maxwell Manuscript (No. 9), which has only thirty-six leaves (approximately 125 × 100mm). Time has treated these works very differently. Some, such as the Maitland Quarto (No. 7), are still in a state of remarkably good preservation; others, such as the Maitland Folio (No. 6) are worn and damp-stained. Perhaps in the worst state of all is the fragmentary manuscript in the National Archives of Scotland in Edinburgh (RH 13/35; No. 8), which has been 'sadly ravaged by time, damp, and mice'.[15] Later owners of some manuscripts cut out leaves—the stubs of many such can be seen in the Robert Edward Manuscript (No. 19); the owners of others attempted to preserve and embellish them by rebinding, but this too led to damage and the loss of important features vital for explaining a manuscript's make-up.

What can be discovered about the copyists, compilers or owners of these collections? (Sometimes one person was all three.) Predominantly they were young men; educated, but not highly learned; members of the middle classes rather than great noble families; notaries, ministers, schoolteachers, and lairds. One exception to this generalisation is the owner of Arch. Selden. B. 24 (No. 1), who is thought to have been the nobleman Henry, Lord Sinclair (d.1513); he was the patron of Gavin Douglas, who eulogised him as 'fader of bukis'. This manuscript is exceptional also for its elaborate decoration to which there is no parallel in other Scottish miscellanies.[16] In some cases (EUL MS Laing. III. 467; No. 18) we know nothing of the owner. All that we can say of those who compiled Cambridge University Library, MS Kk. 1. 5, No. 6 (No. 2), and BL MS Arundel 285 (No. 4: PLATE 1) is that, judging by the contents, they were good Catholics; by contrast, the contents of Edinburgh, National Library of Scotland, Adv. MS 19. 3. 6 (No. 10), suggest that the compiler was no less devout, but a Protestant. Other copyists, however, have placed their names not only at the beginning or end, but throughout the manuscript: 'per manum Iohannis Asloan'; 'be me Maxwell of Southbar 30ungar'; 'the penner Robertus Edwardus'; and 'by me R Taitt' or 'per me R Tatium'. From these and other data scholars have plausibly identified John Asloan as a notary, active in Edinburgh in the first thirty years of the sixteenth century. The scribe of NAS RH 13/35 also seems likely to have been a notary, called Thomas White, who lived in the Haddington area of East Lothian, and apparently compiled this miscellany for the Cockburns of Ormiston, a family largely sympathetic to the Reformers. John Maxwell, however, was probably a Catholic, and came from a different area of Scotland; he was heir to the estate of Southbar in Renfrewshire, and lived until 1606. A young amateur versifier and translator from Latin, he copied some poems and composed others, largely, as he says, 'for spoirt / me to conforte' (fol. 5r).[17] Robert Edward and Robert Tait were conservative in their tastes, and, although they lived in the seventeenth century, preserved much verse and music from the preceding century. Robert Edward (c.1616–96) was a graduate of St Andrews and minister of Murroes in Angus; his patron was the Earl of Panmure, in whose family his manuscript was preserved.[18] A little more is known about the career of Robert Tait, a 'doctour', or assistant teacher, in Lauder parish, and a supporter of Episcopalianism and James VII. He was appointed session clerk in Lauder on 7 January 1677, but seems to have been removed from office after the Revolution in 1688, because of his anti-Presbyterian views. His manuscript, compiled between 1676 and 1689, contains verse in Scots and Latin, as well as an important repertory of songs.[19]

Several manuscripts are associated with the name of Melvill, and the north-east of Scotland. The Andrew Mevill of Aberdeen University Library MS 28 (No. 16) was not the famous Reformer, but a teacher at the Aberdeen song school between 1621 and 1640. When Melvill was appointed master in 1637, he was said to be of 'gude lyff and conversatioun', and qualified in the 'airt of musick'. Unfortunately, his manuscript contains no song-settings, although there are copies of printed works on musical theory. Among its contents are rhyming proverbs, moral and religious verse, and, at the end (fols 79v–80r) an interesting list of 'the buiks in my pressis', which includes the romance 'Gray Steill' and the 'feables Easope'.[20] David Melvill was apparently his brother,

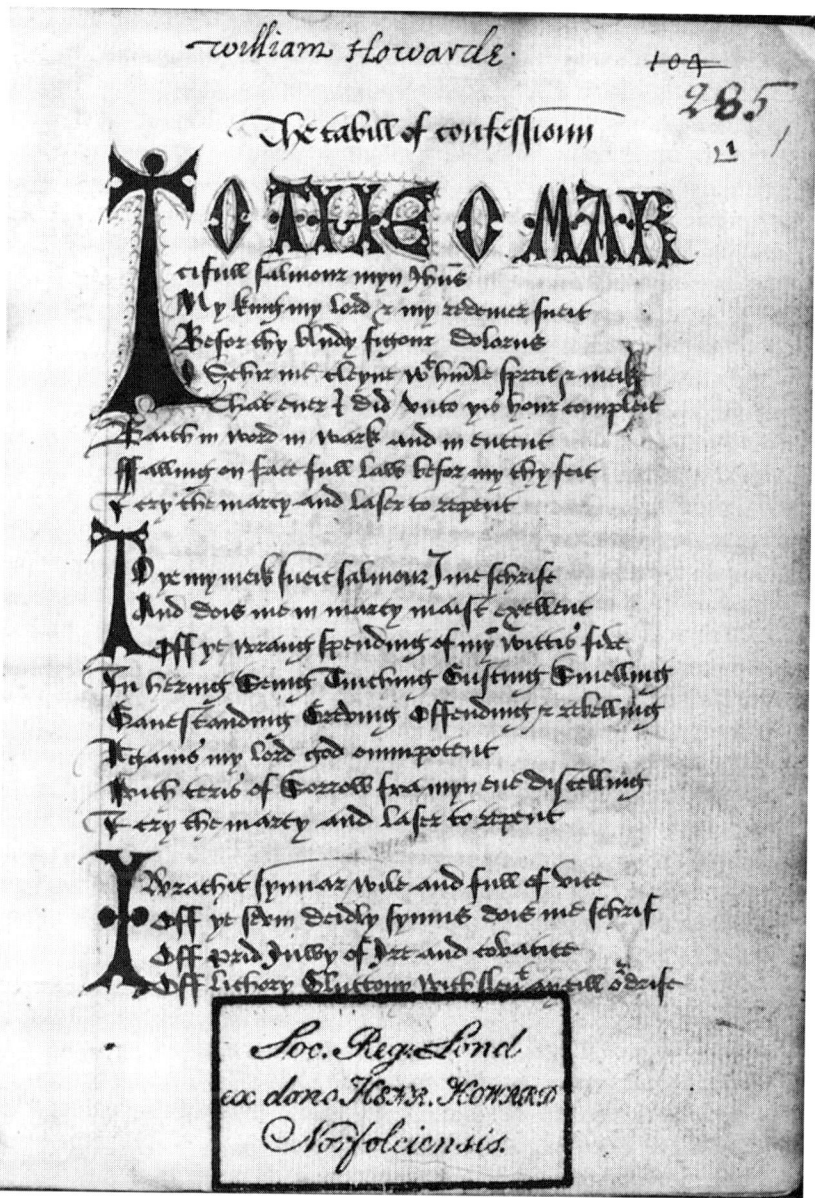

PLATE I. *Opening stanzas of William Dunbar's devotional poem 'The Tabill of Confessioun', bearing the signature of the later owner Lord William Howard, in the Arundel miscellany: London, British Library, Arundel* MS *285, fol. 1r. (Original page size 190 × 133mm.) Reproduced by permission of the Board of the British Library.*

contains extracts from the 1599 print of the *Poems* of Alexander Hume. David Melvill says that he 'collected' his roundels in 1612, but gives no hint of their source. The Roxburghe Club editors of this manuscript suggested that they derived from 'the floating material of the day'. William Ringler, however, has shown that all but ten—both texts and tunes—were taken from two works of Thomas Ravenscroft, *Pammelia* and *Deuteromelia*, printed in London three years earlier, in 1609. (Only four items in the Buik of Roundels are definitely Scottish.) *Deuteromelia* also supplied a song for the compiler of EUL Laing III. 447 (No. 18): 'Glade am I, glade am I'.[47] Earlier it was mentioned that the editor of selections from the Andrew Melvill Manuscript (No. 16) omitted the first item. This too derives from a print, whose title, copied word for word by Melvill, gives some idea of its tone and contents:

> The Arraignment of Lewd, Idle, Froward, and Vnconstant
> Women . . . Pleasant for Married men, Profitable for
> Young men, and hurtful to none.

This work was first printed in London in 1615, but Melvill probably used a reprint published in 1629 by John Wreittoun.[48]

One particular type of print, the broadside ballad, interested several compilers. Andrew Melvill included a pair of religious poems that circulated on the same broadsheet: one on the Nativity, the other on the Passion, beginning respectively, 'Jewry came to Jerusalem' and 'Turn your eyes that are affixed'.[49] NLS Adv. 19.3.6 contains a pious poem with a title more intriguing than its text: 'Certaine wise sentences of Salomon to the tune of Wigmores galliard'. Here too the source is a broadside, dated in the first quarter of the seventeenth century: 'An excellent ditty, shewing the sage sayings and wise sentences of Solomon. To the tune of Wigmore's Galliard'.[50] The origins of another poem, in EUL Laing III. 447 (No. 18), are particularly interesting. 'Some men for suddane joy do weip' is a religious poem, consisting of 112 lines arranged in quatrains. Although printed in the Montgomerie Supplement, the editor wisely denied it to Montgomerie, noting anti-Catholic gibes at 'the hour [whore] of rome', and attributed it instead to Alexander Hume. In fact the poem was written very much earlier; it is a ballad associated with the name of John Carewell, a Protestant martyr executed in the reign of Mary Tudor. First printed in 1564, it became immensely popular—a snatch is quoted by the Fool in *King Lear*—and may indeed have been known to Hume.[51]

Who were the likely readers of these manuscripts? A printed book's readership was potentially large, geographically dispersed, and mostly unknown to author or publisher.[52] A manuscript's readership was likely to be smaller, close at hand, and more intimate. One might roughly analyse its components as the compiler; his (or her) family and friends; and later generations of the family. There is clearly an element of the informal commonplace book in some of these miscellanies. Along with poems, they record practical information and memorable dates (of battles or children's birthdays). Some also have a self-recreational function, well expressed by John Maxwell: 'to exercise my awin ingyne' (fol. 23v). Others were manifestly intended for the extended family— those related by blood or marriage, those who had been to the same university, or who held the same religious beliefs, or had similar tastes, whether for bawdy jokes, or music. Obvious illustrations of this are seen in the dependence of the Reidpeth Manuscript upon the Maitland Folio, or in the song manuscripts, which were clearly designed for communal use. The layout of the Robert Tait Manuscript shows that it was used 'for actual part-singing, or playing across the table', since Tait copied both secular and sacred music in such a way that two voices appear rightside up, whereas the other two are upside down.[53]

Later generations of a family evidently continued to take interest in some of these manuscripts. Indeed they often contributed to them, using scripts and spellings that may be distinguished from those of the first compiler, even if they are not always precisely datable. Additions of this kind may have important implications. Literary historians have sometimes been unaware that the colophon to a poem was not, in every case, written by its original copyist. There is a poem in the Maitland Folio (No. lxxxviii), which begins: 'Gif bissie branit bodeis ȝow bakbyte'. A conventional attack on slanderers, it belongs to the same genre as two pieces by Dunbar ('Musing allone this hinder nicht', and 'How sould I rewill me or in quhat wys'). Like another copy of the same poem in the Maitland Quarto (No. xliii), the text in the Folio was originally anonymous. Later, presumably in or after 1595, someone added to the Folio text the following: 'Quod Iohne Maitland . . . Chancellor of Scotland and died 3 October 1595'.[54] This attribution may perhaps be correct, yet there is surely a question mark over John Maitland's authorship of this poem, as there is over the few other vernacular pieces attributed to him. There is much better evidence for his having been a Latin poet.[55]

The Maitland Folio also contains a marginal entry, unmentioned by its editor, placed on page 318, to the right of Dunbar's 'In to thir dirk and drublie dayis' (No. cxliii). It is short but metrical: 'The Lord is onlye my support / and he that doth me feed'. This sounds like the opening of the 23rd Psalm, and the wording is indeed identical with a version of that psalm in *The Forme of Prayers*.[56] Such an origin suggests a reader belonging to the Reformers; elsewhere in the Folio there are added verses from *The Gude and Godlie Ballatis*.[57] What is more, the location next to Dunbar's melancholy poem may be no accident, but an interesting example of reader response—a kind of 'contrapoyson', or antidote.

To return to the Bannatyne Manuscript: does it differ from the other Scottish miscellanies as strikingly as is sometimes assumed? George Bannatyne was twenty-three when he completed the manuscript 'in tyme of pest' in 1568. He came of a Forfarshire family, but spent most of his life as a merchant in Edinburgh. He thus resembled many of the other compilers in youth and social status. The manuscript is undoubtedly impressive in its sheer size: the main section contains 375 leaves, and there is, in addition, a draft manuscript, which contains 58 pages. It should be noted, however, that the Asloan Manuscript, although incomplete, contains over 300 leaves. The Bannatyne Manuscript is also remarkable for the rich variety of its contents. The notion that it contains more love poetry than anything else can be refuted simply by looking at it, by noting the number of leaves devoted to different sections, and by observing the satirical nature of many of the 'ballatis of luve'. Critics are inclined to disregard the high proportion of space that Bannatyne devotes to moral and religious verse; this is an area, however, where he is closely akin to other compilers, especially John Maxwell and Andrew Melvill. It is striking also how many items supposedly 'unique' to Bannatyne occur in other manuscripts. A good illustration is the advice poem that begins 'Grund the in patience' (No. 91; fol. 74r); this is described as 'a unique copy', although I have encountered at least six other copies.[58] Explicit didacticism does not please us today, but it clearly appealed to Bannatyne and his contemporaries. Although the Bannatyne Manuscript contains no music, it is now recognised that the 'ballatis of luve' look forward, interestingly, to the seventeenth-century song collections. The Robert Edward Manuscript contains settings (not necessarily texts) of at least seven of these poems.[59] It is curious that one small clue to Bannatyne's inclusion of songs was long disregarded. The manuscript contains the popular poem 'O lusty May with Flora quene' (No. 279; fol. 229v), which appears in other miscellanies, including the Melvill Bassus (PLATE 3); yet, although it has been printed in several modern anthologies, the tell-tale use of *bis* after a phrase in line eight is rarely reproduced.[60]

The Bannatyne Manuscript also resembles other Scottish miscellanies in containing a large yet rarely acknowledged English element: there are poems by Chaucer, Lydgate, Hoccleve, Walton, Heywood, and Wyatt, together with various anonymous pieces. Many of these are noted in the Introduction to the Scolar Facsimile, but by no means all;

PLATE 3. *Song 9, 'O lustie may with flora quene', in David Melvill's Bassus part-book: London, British Library, Additional MS 36484, fol. 5r. (Original page size 200 × 272mm.) Reproduced by permission of the Board of the British Library.*

a small instance is No. 107 (fol. 75v), 'Now quhen ane wreche is sett to he estait', which is a moralising extract from Lydgate's *Fall of Princes* (IV. 3151–70).[61] Among Bannatyne's 'ballatis mirrie' there is a curious work called 'The nyne ordour of knavis' (No. 223), which—so far as I know—has been totally ignored by all critics, except Denton Fox. In an unpublished note he shows that it is closely related to a work published in London some time during the 1560s by John Awdelay, known as 'The xxv Orders of Knaves'. A work in the rogue tradition, it may have had an appeal similar to *Colkelbie Sow*.[62]

Bannatyne famously described his sources as 'copeis awld mankit and mvtillait' (p. 59),[63] but this phrase should not be interpreted as referring solely to other manuscripts. Much of his material came from prints. Seven of the poems with erroneous attributions to Chaucer derive from Thynne's Chaucer, probably from the edition published *c*.1545–50.[64] Two poems by John Bellenden (Nos 4 and 403) seem to derive from Davidson's edition of Bellenden's translation of Hector Boece.[65] Other printed sources include Douglas's translation of the *Aeneid* (1553), Heywood's *Epigrams* (apparently from either the 1562 or the 1566 edition), and *The Forme of Prayers* (either 1564 or 1565).[66] Careful comparison with these prints would shed light on Bannatyne's practices as a copyist. Perhaps the most significant of his printed sources is William Baldwin's *Treatise of Morall Philosophye*. This sententious work seems unreadable today, but was immensely popular in its own time—especially among Protestants—and Ringler has demonstrated that Bannatyne used an edition pirated by Palfreyman which was printed in July 1567. This, it should be noted, supports Bannatyne's own dating of his manuscript in 1568.[67]

Bannatyne's printed sources also included broadside ballads.[68] A particularly interesting instance is No. 246 (fol. 215v), one of the 'ballatis of luve', which begins:

> Was nocht gud king Salamon
> reuisit [ravished] in sindry wyis
> With every lufely paragon
> Glistering befoir his eis.

It is termed a 'unique copy' by Fox and Ringler, although the colophon provides a disregarded clue to its origin: 'Quod ane inglisman'. This poem is, in fact, a lightly Scotticised version of a broadside, written by William Elderton, called 'The Pangs of Love and Lovers' Fitts'. Only a single copy of the print now survives, dated 22 March, 1560,[69] but the ballad's great popularity is well attested.[70] There is a parodic version in *The Gude and Godlie Ballatis*, which begins:

> Was not Salomon, the king
> To miserie be wemen brocht?[71]

The tune to which it was sung (which may well have been known to Bannatyne) is found both in the Dublin Virginal Manuscript and the Mulliner Book.[72] Bannatyne's version is very close to the print, but contains a final extra stanza, which ends:

> Quhy suld nocht I, pur sempill man,
> La[d]y, la[d]y,
> Lawbour and serwe ȝow the best that I can,
> My deir lady.

It is tempting, but rash, to attribute this addition to the punning pen of Robert Sempill.

Probably the most original feature of Bannatyne's miscellany is its fivefold division into 'ballatis of theoligie', 'ballatis of moralitie', 'ballettis mirrie', 'ballatis of luve', and 'fabillis'. There exists no close analogue, so far as I am aware, to his interesting attempt at an arrangement that is both thematic and generic. Nonetheless, the care that was lavished on the manuscript and several features of its layout are paralleled in other Scottish miscellanies. Like the Asloan Manuscript, the Maitland Quarto, the Buik of Roundels and others, the Bannatyne Manuscript is a handsome 'buik' in its own right, and I am unconvinced by suggestions that it was designed for printing. The table of contents, as I have shown, has parallels in several miscellanies; it does not necessarily constitute proof 'of an editor anticipating a printed form for his collection'.[73] Bannatyne ends with a verse valediction, from 'The wryttar to the redar', beginning: 'Heir endis this buik writtin in tyme of pest' (fol. 375r). A. A. MacDonald said of this: 'it is scarcely credible that [Bannatyne] wrote such stanzas for his own benefit'.[74] Indeed not: but why must we assume, anachronistically, that the only 'buiks' read by sixteenth-century readers were printed? Why, incidentally, must we also accept the linked proposition that Bannatyne's Protestantism resulted from censorship or 'an eye for the market', not from deep inner conviction? Bannatyne's closing words belong to the double tradition of the scribal colophon and the poet's *envoi*. His manuscript was certainly read by later generations of his family, who during the sixteenth and seventeenth centuries made their own contributions to it, ranging from moral epigrams to bawdy love poems.

Bannatyne says that his poems came from 'diuers new and ancient poettis' (fol. 211r). Neither these words nor his choice of texts suggests to me the self-conscious antiquarian, who regarded older Scottish poetry as an endangered species. To think this is surely critical hindsightism, born of Romantic nostalgia. What the collection magnificently displays is Bannatyne's eclecticism and lack of literary nationalism. It also demonstrates the remarkable variety of vernacular poetry that was available to him in the 1560s from many sources, 'new and ancient', Scottish and English, manuscript and print. (It is relevant surely, that in the next decade Scottish printers were still prepared to publish not only comparatively recent writers, such as Sir David Lindsay and John Rolland, but also more 'ancient' ones, such as Barbour, Blind Hary, Henryson, and Douglas.) Other Scottish miscellanies likewise illuminate the taste of their compilers, and the wider culture to which they belonged. Sometimes their contents merely confirm social or literary trends that are well known; at other times, however, they correct long-established yet over-simplistic views, most strikingly perhaps the notion that seventeenth-century Scotland was 'more prone to religious strife than indulgence in the arts'.[75]

This article has a double purpose: to describe some salient features of Scottish literary miscellanies, and in so doing to provide a context for the Bannatyne Manuscript. It is, inevitably, a brief introduction to a very large subject. Far more material exists than has been mentioned here, especially from the neglected seventeenth century. What seems a desirable goal for future scholarship is to provide a detailed register of these miscellanies, and good analytic descriptions of their contents. To accomplish this well, however, is a task in which literary scholars must co-operate with historians and musicologists.

APPENDIX

Summary List of Scottish Manuscript Miscellanies

The manuscripts are listed in chronological order, in so far as this can be ascertained.

Brief information is supplied on the following: name of the manuscript, where one is in common use today; present location and shelfmark; scribe or compiler (where known), followed by early owner (where known); geographical location; and printed editions and facsimiles (with the abbreviation STS given for the Scottish Text Society). Further scholarly information concerning the manuscripts is found in the notes. The last column indicates the number of folios in a manuscript, or pages (where it is paginated). The nature of the contents is indicated thus: V (Verse); P (Prose); and M (Music).

1. Oxford, Bodleian, MS Arch. Selden. B. 24   *c*.1488–1513   230 fols (V)
Henry, Lord Sinclair (owner),
Roslin, Midlothian.
The Works of Geoffrey Chaucer and the Kingis
Quair: A Facsimile of Bodleian Library, Oxford,
Manuscript Arch. Selden. B. 24, introd. J. Boffey
and A. S. G. Edwards (Cambridge, 1997).

2. CUL, MS   2nd half   55 fols (V, P)
Kk. 1. 5. No. 6   15th cent.
V de F.
Ratis Raving, and Other Early Scots
Poems on Morals, ed. R. Girvan (STS, 1939).

3. Asloan Manuscript   *c*.1513–32   304 fols (V, P)
Edinburgh, NLS, MS 16500.
John Asloan, Edinburgh.
The Asloan Manuscript, ed. W. A. Craigie,
2 vols (STS, 1923–5).

4. London, BL, MS Arundel 285   *c*.1540?   224 fols (V, P)
Lord William Howard of Naworth
(late 16th cent. owner)
Devotional Pieces in Verse and Prose from
MS Arundel 285 and MS Harleian 6919, ed.
J. A. W. Bennett (STS, 1955).

5. Bannatyne Manuscript   completed   375 fols
Edinburgh, NLS, MS Adv.1. 1. 6.   1568   +58 pp (V)
George Bannatyne, Edinburgh.
The Bannatyne Manuscript, ed. W. Tod
Ritchie, 4 vols (STS, 1928–34).
The Bannatyne Manuscript: a Facsimile, introd.
D. Fox and W. A. Ringler (London, 1980).

6. Maitland Folio   *c*.1570–86   366 pp (V)
Cambridge, Magdalene College, Pepys
Library, MS 2553.
Family of Sir Richard Maitland of Lethington.
The Maitland Folio Manuscript, ed. W. A.
Craigie, 2 vols (STS, 1919–27).

7. Maitland Quarto   1586   140 fols (V)
Cambridge, Magdalene College,
Pepys Library, MS 1408.
Marie Maitland, Lethington (owner).

The Maitland Quarto Manuscript, ed.
W. A. Craigie (STS, 1920).

8. Edinburgh, NAS, RH 12/35	*c.*1582–6	Fragmentary
?Thomas White, Haddington. Family	(V, P)	
of Cockburn of Ormiston (?owners).		
Unpublished.		
9. Maxwell Manuscript	1584–9	36 fols (V, P)
Edinburgh, EUL, MS Laing III. 467.		
John Maxwell of Southbar, Renfrew.		
Unpublished.		
10. Edinburgh, NLS, MS Adv. 19.3.6	1st half	76 fols (V, P)
Unpublished.	17th cent.	
11. Melvill Bassus	*c.*1604	71 fols (V, M)
BL, Add. MS 36484.		
David Melvill, Aberdeen.		
Unpublished.		
12. Tolquhon Cantus	1611	20 fols (V, M)
Cambridge, Fitzwilliam		
Museum, MS Mu 689.		
David Melvill; A. F. (owner).		
Unpublished.		
13. Melvill Buik of Roundels	1612	151 pp + 27
Washington, Library of Congress,		unnumbered
MS M1490. M535. A5.		pp
David Melvill.		(V, M)
The Melvill Book of Roundels, ed.		
G. Bantock and H. O. Anderton		
(Roxburghe Club, 1916). Modernised.		
14. Reidpeth Manuscript	1622–3	69 fols (V)
Cambridge, CUL, MS Ll.5.10.		
John Reidpeth; Christopher Cockburn		
(owner), Berwickshire.		
Unpublished.		
15. Robertson Manuscript	*c.*1630?	(V)
a) NLS, MS 15937 (19th-cent. transcript)		215 fols
b) BL, Add.MS 29409 (19th-cent.		
partial transcript)		21 fols
Margaret Robertson, Bonskeid,		
Perthshire. Unpublished.		

16. Aberdeen, AUL, MS 28 Andrew Melvill, Aberdeen. Published only in part. *Extracts from the Commonplace Book of* *Andrew Melville 1621–1640*, ed. W. Walker (Aberdeen, 1899).	*c.*1637	81 fols (V, P)
17. Edinburgh, NLS, MS Dep. 314, No. 23 Lady Margaret Wemyss, Fife. Unpublished.	*c.*1643–4	177 fols (V, M)
18. Edinburgh, EUL, MS Laing III. 447 In *Poems of Alexander Montgomerie:* *Supplementary Volume*, ed. G. Stevenson (STS, 1910).	1st half 17th cent.	84 fols (V)
19. Robert Edward's Manuscript Edinburgh, NLS, MS 9450. Robert Edward, Murroes parish, Angus. Unpublished.	? 1635–70	79 fols (V, M)
20. Tait Manuscript Los Angeles, William Andrews Clark Memorial Library, MS T135Z B7 24. Robert Tait, Lauder. Unpublished.	1676–89	193 fols (V, M)

NOTES

1 T. van Heijnsbergen, 'The Interaction between Literature and History in Queen Mary's Edinburgh: the Bannatyne Manuscript and its Prosopographical Context', in *The Renaissance in Scotland: Studies in Literature, Religion, History and Culture Offered to John Durkan*, ed. A. A. MacDonald, M. Lynch and I. B. Cowan (Leiden, 1994), pp. 183–225 (p.183).

2 *Scotland: a New History* (London, 1991; rev. edn, 1992), p. 213.

3 See *Poetry of the Stewart Court*, ed. J. Hughes and W. S. Ramson (Canberra, 1982); and Fox's review in *TLS*, 30 September 1983.

4 W. Scott, 'Memoir of George Bannatyne', cit. in *The Bannatyne Manuscript*, ed. W. Tod Ritchie, 4 vols (STS, 1928–34), I, pp. cxxix–cxxx.

5 Ibid, pp. cxxix, cxxxii; for later expressions of this view, see ibid, p. xxxviii; and two articles by A. A. MacDonald: 'The Bannatyne Manuscript: a Marian Anthology', *Innes Review*, 37 (1986), 36–47 (pp. 41–42); and 'The Printed Book that Never Was: George Bannatyne's Poetic Anthology (1568)', in *Boeken in de late Middeleeuwen*, ed. J. M. M. Hermans and K. van der Hoek (Groningen, 1994), pp. 101–10 (p. 105). For further discussion of Bannatyne's motives and methods, see D. Fox, 'Manuscripts

Surrey's Martial Epigram: Scribes and Transmission

A. S. G. Edwards

Manuscripts of the poems of Henry Howard, Earl of Surrey, are not large in number, especially when compared with those of his contemporary, Sir Thomas Wyatt. Indeed, only a small number of his poems survive in more than one manuscript version. One poem, however, does seem to have enjoyed a relatively extensive circulation. The various forms in which it was transmitted afford some insight into the scribal environments in which Surrey's lyrics were copied.[1]

Surrey's translation of Martial's *Epigram*, X. 47[2] comprises sixteen lines in cross rhyming couplets. Six manuscript versions of this poem are recorded. These are as follows:[3]

1) London, British Library, Additional MS 36529, fol. 54v.[4] The manuscript is the largest surviving manuscript collection of Surrey's poems, assembled by Sir John Harington the elder (1520?–82) and his son, also Sir John Harington (1560–1612), comprising twenty-seven poems, between fols 50 and 65. One copyist seems to have been responsible for all the poems between fols 50–59 except for the first poem on fol. 59; he writes in a fluent semi-cursive hand. Another, writing in a more formal text hand with some italic features, was responsible for the first poem on fol. 59 and for all the poems between fols 58v and 65v.

2) London, British Library, Cotton MS Titus A. xxiv, fol. 80, where this is the only Surrey poem in the manuscript. It is written in a semi-cursive hand of the second half of the sixteenth century. There is a note in the upper outer margin, 'Martialis lib. 9'. The poem is subscribed 'finis Surre'.

3) Cambridge, Trinity College, Capell W. 1, an edition of Tottel's *Songes and Sonettes* (1557); the poem is copied on the verso of the final leaf, fol. [120], in a mid-sixteenth-century hand.

4) A copy written on a blank leaf in a copy of the Aldine edition of Martial's *Epigrams* (Venice, 1501).[5] This volume was sold at Sotheby's, 13 March, 1979, lot 443, as the property of J. M. Burwell-Nugent, for

£400 to Alan Thomas and exported in December of that year to a private buyer.[6] This poem (PLATE I) is the only content of the page on which it appears, apart from a cropped title (the first words of which appear to be 'vita qua'), and a cropped page or leaf number. The page measures approximately 145 × 235mm., and the text is written in a mid-sixteenth-century semi-cursive hand with some italic features.[7] A photograph of this page is now also in the British Library, Department of Manuscripts (RP 1845).

5) London, British Library, Additional MS 12049, p. 150. This manuscript is in the hand of Sir John Harington the younger, and dates from *c*.1603. The poem appears in the fourth book of his *Epigrams* and is titled 'A translation of the Earl of Surreys | out of Martiall directed by him | to one Maister Warner'. It was printed, with minor errors of transcription, in the *Gentleman's Magazine*, 97, ii (1827), 392.[8]

6) Washington, DC, Folger Shakespeare Library, MS V. a. 249, pp. 200–1. This is another manuscript in the hand of Sir John Harington and contains substantially the same texts as BL Add. 12049.[9] It is titled 'A translation of the Ear of Surreys | out of Martiall directed by him to | one Maister Warner'. It also seems to have been compiled early in the first decade of the seventeenth century.[10]

Also relevant to the present enquiry are two printed forms of the poem:

7) The first printing by William Baldwin in his *A Treatise of Morall Phylosophie* (1547/8: STC 1253), sig. Qi[v].[11] This is the earliest datable version of the poem and was printed during Surrey's lifetime, albeit without attribution.[12]

8) The version printed in Tottel's *Songes and Sonnettes* (1557: STC 13860), sig. Di[v] where it is titled 'The means to attain / happy life'.[13]

In addition, forms of the opening words appear to introduce pieces of music in two sixteenth-century manuscript music books: BL Add. MS 30513, fol. 65v, and London, National Archives, SP 1/246, fol. 22v.[14]

In spite of the numerous versions in both manuscript and print, no scholarly edition has taken into account all relevant witnesses. My present concern is briefly to assess the relationship between these witnesses and to consider the implications of the scribal transmission of this poem.

In what follows I use the following sigla to identify the various versions:

A: BL Add. MS 36529
B: William Baldwin, *Treatise of Morall Phylosophie*

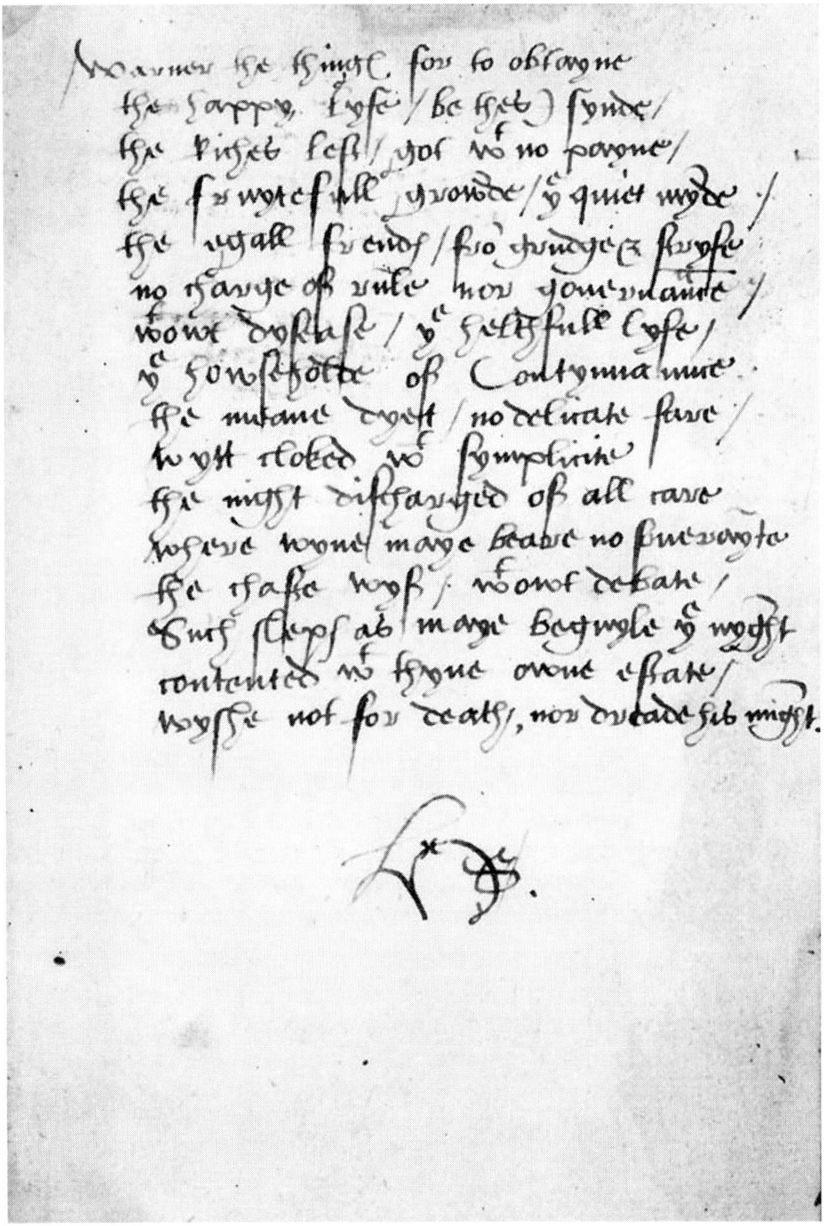

PLATE I. *Manuscript text of Surrey's translation of Martial's* Epigram X. 47 *written on the terminal blank leaf of an exemplum of Martial's* Epigrammata *(published by Aldus Manutius, Venice, 1501). Reproduced by courtesy of Sotheby's, London.*

C: Trinity College, Cambridge, Capell W. 1
F: Folger MS V. a. 249
G: BL Add. MS 12049
L: BL Cotton MS Titus A. xxiv
O: The version sold at Sotheby's, 13 March 1979, lot 443
T: Tottel (1557), sig. Di^v

I begin by printing below the version that appears in *O*, a version that has not previously been printed. The reasons for doing so here will emerge in subsequent analysis. In the following transcription some contractions have been expanded and italicized, but not self-evident ones such as 'w^t', 'y^e' and the ampersand. The manuscript punctuation has been preserved. This is chiefly the virgule; only in the final line is there a comma and a period.

<pre>
 1   Warner the thinges for to obtayne
          the happy lyfe / be thes I fynde /
          the Riches left / got w^t no payne /
          the fruytefull grownde / ye quiet mynde /
 5   the egall frendes / from grudge & stryfe
          no charge of rule nor gouernaunce /
          w^{t}owt dysease / ye helthfull lyfe /
          ye howseholde of Contynuaunce
          the meane dyet / no delicate fare /
10   wytt cloked w^t symplicite
          the night discharged of all care
          where wyne maye beare no soueraynte
          the chaste wyf / w^{t}owt debate /
          Such slepes as maye beguyle ye nyght
15   contented w^t thyne owne estate /
          wyshe not for death, nor dreade his might.
                                        H S.
</pre>

I set out below the full list of substantive variants from *O* for all the relevant witnesses:

1. Warner] *A* Marshall, *T* Martiall, *C* My frendes, *B L* My frende; for to] *B C L T* that do; obtayne] *A B C L T* attayne
2. be] *G* ar
3. left] *C* leste; got w^t no] *A B C F G L T* not got with
4. grownde] *G* field
5. frendes] *A B C L T* frind; from] *A B C F G L T* no; &] *A G* nor, *B C T* no, *L* ne
6. rule] *L* life; nor] *F G* or, *L* no

7. helthfull] *B C L* healthie;

9. delicate] *B C L* dayntye; *F* delicate, *G* delicate (*with* daintie *written above the line.*)

10. wytt cloked] *A B C F G* wysdom ioyned , *L* riches yoyned, *T* Trew wisdom ioyned; symplicite] *B C L T* simpelnes

12. maye beare no soueraynte] *B C T* the wyt may not opresse, *L* the will dothe not oppresse

13. chaste] *B C L T* faythfull, *F G* chast plain; wyf] *A* wise wyfe;

15. contented w^t thyne owne estate] *B C L* Content thy selfe with thine estate

16. wyshe not for] *A B F G* Neyther wisshe death, *C* ne the wyshe, *L* not wishinge, *T* Ne wish for; nor] *C T* ne; dreade] *A B C* T fear

Before discussing these variants it should be noted that there are also a number of differences between the contexts in which the poem appears, between its form of presentation and between the texts themselves.

The version in *O* is important in part because it provides an unusually precise context for its circulation. In it the poem is directed to an individual within Surrey's circle, Sir Edward Warner, who had married the widow of Sir Thomas Wyatt, and who was called on to testify against Surrey at his trial.[15]

F and *G* are the only other manuscripts to address the poem to Warner. They are also the only witnesses to suggest a specific occasion for the poem: 'A translation of the Earle of Surreys out of Martialle, directed by him to one Maister Warner'. All the other witnesses are less specific in the form of reference. In *A* the opening word is 'Marshall', presumably an orthographic variant of 'Martiall', the form in *T*. In the other versions, the opening words are 'My frende(s)', a reading which obviously indicates adaptation to a wider, more generalized audience.[16]

The forms of presentation also differ. *C* and *L*, for example, present the poem as quatrains, the former separating the first, second and third stanzas with spacing and paraphs. In addition, *L* copies the text in a variant order: lines 1–4, 9–12, 5–8, 13–16, which also suggests derivation from an exemplar that had set the poem out as stanzas. And in *C* and *O* it is copied as a flyleaf poem, a fact that suggests informal circulation, possibly even associated with memorial transmission.[17] Such different forms suggest a fluidity in the poem's transmission.

The variation between witnesses, both in manuscript and in those printed forms which seem to reflect independently derived manuscript witnesses, also suggests a curiously divergent process of transmission. *O* contains a number of unique readings:

3. got w^t no] *A B C F G L T* not got with
5. from] *A B CF G L T* no; &] *A F G* nor, *B C T* no, *L* ne
10. wytt cloked] *A B C F G* wysdom ioyned , *L* riches yoyned, *T* Trew
wisdom ioyne
16. wyshe not for] *A B F G* Neyther wisshe death, *C* ne the wyshe, *L* not
wishinge, *T* Ne wish for

Several of these readings are demonstrably harder in *O* and hence
potentially have more claim to originality than those elsewhere; for
example, the syntactic inversion in lines 3 and 16 and the difficult, but
still defensible syntax of line 5: 'the egall frend*es* / from grudge & stryfe'
with the suppressed verb, all seem more likely to be authorial than
scribal. The variant in line 10 is particularly striking since it suggests a
line of independent transmission for *O*, as the readings of the other
witnesses could not have been derived from it.

In addition, the few other points where *O* and *F* and *G* agree, against
all other witnesses (apart from the opening word), provide some additional support for *O*'s superiority:

1. obtayne] *A B C L T* attayne
5. frendes] *A B C L T* frind

In line 1 the Latin reads *Vitam quae faciant beatiorem* (Latin text line 1) and
is susceptible to either form in translation. In line 5, however, the Latin
plural *pares amici* (7) supports *O F G* against the other witnesses.

But *F* and *G* do contain a small number of unique variants:

2. be] *F G* ar
4. grownde] *F G* field
6. nor] *F G* or

None of these is demonstrably inferior to *O*'s readings at these points: in
line 2 both readings are renderings of Martial's plural *sunt* (2); in 4, both
forms are acceptable translations of Martial's *ager* (4); and in 6 there is
no equivalent in the Latin. The possibility has to be considered that the
different *O F G* readings at these points could both reflect Surrey's inten-
tions: that is, that he himself circulated more than one version of this
poem.

Variants in the other witnesses suggest processes of transmission that
seem to have involved arbitrary substitutions; for example:

6. rule] *L* life
9. delicate] *B C L* dayntye; *G* ^{daintie}delicate
12. where wyne maye beare no soueraynte] *B C T* the wyt may not
opresse, *L* the will dothe not oppresse

13. chaste] *B C L T* faythfull, *G* chast plain; wyfe] *A* wise wyfe[18]
16. dreade] *A B C T* fear

What is suggestive about these variants is that they all occur at points either where both versions are acceptable renderings of the Latin or where they are both least close to the Latin. Thus in 6, 'no charge of rule [*or* 'life'] nor gouernaunce' is a free rendering of *toga rara* (5). In 9, both 'no delicate fare' and 'no dayntye fare' represent *sine arte mensa* (8). Both versions of line 12 render *nox non ebria* (9). The multiple variants for 'the chaste wyf' in line 13 reflect different senses of the potentialities of Martial's *non tristis torus et tamen pudicus* (10). And 'dreade, and 'fear' are both acceptable translations of the Latin *metuas* (13). A similar point can also be made about line 15 where the witnesses diverge, albeit in slightly different groupings:

15. contented w^t thyne owne estate] *B C L* Content thy selfe with thine estate

Both reflect different possibilities of translating Martial's *quod sis esse velis nihilque malis* (12).

Certain conclusions emerge from the variation between the surviving witnesses. It is clear that there was more than one line of transmission for this lyric: that represented by *O*, *F* and *G*, and at least one represented by the other versions of the text. As I have already suggested, *O* seems to offer a form of the text that is, in a number of instances, demonstrably superior. *F* and *G* seem independently derived from either the same source as *O* or one close to it. But *G* clearly derives either from some conflation of different versions or from a version that contained alternative readings, possibly therefore a draft close to an authorial version. The evidence for this point comes from its inclusion in line of both variant readings, 'daintie' and 'delicate', either of which is defensible.

All the other witnesses, to a greater or lesser degree, seem the product of either a different tradition or of some form of scribal conflation. *A* in particular seems to embody readings from different branches of the tradition. And other versions may include readings that were the result of independent substitutions by scribes which produced easier readings, most obviously, of course, with the poem's opening word.

The fact that one version, in *B*, achieved print status while Surrey was alive, provides an indication of its circulation in environments over which he may have little control. But the possibility remains that some of the indifferent variations may derive from Surrey's own circulation of more than one version of his poem, and that a lyric originally conceived for an individual was adapted by the poet himself for a wider circulation.

Surrey's Martial translation offers some insight into the variegated circumstances of the transmission of courtly verse in the mid-sixteenth century. This evidence suggests a fluid process of transmission in a variety of textual environments, involving the possibility of multiple authorial versions as well as scribal transmission through which the poem was adapted from coterie circulation to a wider audience or audiences.[19]

Without the survival of more detailed documentation, neither the creative nor the socially determined factors that bear on the processes of transmission lend themselves to clear-cut analysis.[20] But they do suggest that the manuscript circulation of Surrey's verse may merit more extensive examination.

NOTES

1 I am greatly indebted to Dr Peter Beal and Professor Julia Boffey for advice and assistance in the preparation of this article.

2 I quote throughout from *Martial Epigrams*, ed. D. R. Shackleton Bailey, 2 vols (Cambridge, Mass., 1993), II, 366–9.

3 All these are noted in Peter Beal, *Index of English Literary Manuscripts, Volume 1, 1450–1625, Part 2, Drayton-Wyatt* (London, 1980), Nos SuH 38–42 and 42.5; see also Hyder Rollins, in his edition of *Tottel's Miscellany*, revised edition (Cambridge, Mass., 1965), II, 150.

4 This version formed the basis for the most recent scholarly edition by Emrys Jones, *Henry Howard Earl of Surrey: Poems* (Oxford, 1964), pp. 34–35.

5 Its earliest recorded owner as noted in the Sotheby's catalogue was 'Robertus Pemberus', presumably to be identified with Robert Pember (*d*.1560), Fellow of St John's College, Cambridge, a prominent humanist; on whom see *DNB*.

6 I am indebted to Professor Ralph Hanna and Richard Linenthal for help in attempting to trace this item.

7 It may be helpful to observe that this hand is wholly unlike Surrey's own, as reproduced most accessibly in Anthony G. Petti, *English literary hands from Chaucer to Dryden* (Cambridge, Mass., 1997), p. 68, plate 20.

8 In line 2 in this transcription 'these' should be 'theise'; in line 3 'nor' should be 'not'; and in line 8 'healthful' should be 'healthfull'.

9 Apart from orthographical variants, the Folger manuscript omits the superscript 'daintie' in line 9.

10 For a brief description, see *Catalogue of Manuscripts in the Folger Shakespeare Library*, Volume 2 (Boston, 1971), pp. 172–3.

11 This was seemingly first noted by H.H. Hudson, 'Surrey and Martial', *Modern Language Notes*, 38 (1923), 481–3, and is recapitulated by Rollins, II, 150. The information is repeated, without reference to Hudson or Rollins, in J. M. Evans, 'The Text of Surrey's "The Means to Attain Happy Life"', *Notes & Queries*, NS 30 (1983), 409–11. For a dissenting view of Evans's editorial conclusions, see W. D. McGaw,

'The Text of Surrey's "The Means to Attain Happy Life"—A Reply', *Notes &
Queries*, NS 32 (1985), 456–68.

12 Rollins observes: 'Evidently Baldwin, in one way or another, had access to a manuscript copy, not improbably, to one given him by the poet' (II, 150).

13 I have not considered the numerous subsequent early printings of Tottel, for which
see *STC*, 1386 etc. Variants are recorded in Rollins, II, 270.

14 For details of these, see I. L. Mumford, 'Musical Settings to the Poems of Henry
Howard, Earl of Surrey', *English Miscellany*, 8 (1957), 9–20, and William Ringler,
Bibliography and Index of English Verse in Manuscript, 1501–1558 (London, 1992), TM
1036.

15 On Warner (1511–65), see *DNB* and W.A. Sessions, *Henry Howard The Poet Earl of
Surrey: A Life* (Oxford, 1999), pp. 381–2, 397–8.

16 In the musical settings for this poem in BL Add. MSS 30513 and NA SP 1/246, the
only words that occur are 'My freinds'.

17 On flyleaf poems, see R.H. Robbins, ed., *Secular Lyrics of the XIVth and XVth Centuries*
(Oxford, 1952), pp. xxx–xxxi, and Julia Boffey, *The Manuscripts of English Courtly Love
Lyrics* (Cambridge, 1985), pp. 27–29.

18 This reading is printed in the latest modern edition, by Jones, from *A*. It seems in
obvious respects inferior since it is clearly identifiable as the result of a combination
of homoeographic and dittographic scribal error. It also destroys the octosyllabic
line.

19 Of crucial importance is the role of the Harington family, responsbile for the preservation of three manuscript versions of this poem as well as another important collection containing verse by Surrey, the Arundel-Harington manuscript. I discuss
their role as well as other aspects of Surrey's manuscript circulation in 'The
Manuscripts of Surrey's Verse', *Huntington Library Quarterly*, 67 (2004), 283–93.

20 For valuable discussion of such tendencies in this period see Arthur F. Marotti,
Manuscript, Print, and the English Renaissance Lyric (Ithaca, NY, 1995), especially
pp. 135–47 and the further references cited there.

Obliterature

Reading a Censored Text of Donne's
'To his mistress going to bed'

Randall McLeod

One of the verse miscellanies in the Rosenbach Museum & Library in Philadelphia, 'Commonplace book MS 239/22',[1] shows heavy deletion in opening 52v–53r. The spectacular image of these two pages shown in the next opening (PLATE I) seems to justify a recent report, that the poem is 'totally obliterated by ink smears'.[2] This censored text will be the focus of my essay, for I aim to read it anyway: line for line, word for word, letter for letter—darkness legible.

But first, in plain daylight, let us get our bearings by scrutinizing the dozen lines of seventeenth-century handwriting at the top of the verso page, to see in detail just what the manuscript looks like unravaged. The horizontal pen-stroke below the last of these twelve lines strongly suggests that they lie at the *end* of a poem. (The smearing that begins right after, and extends through just the page and a half you see here, must cover at least the *start* of the next poem.)[3]

PLATE I (next opening). *Two pages of the Rosenbach Manuscript containing Donne's poem, heavily deleted: Philadelphia, The Rosenbach Museum & Library, MS 239/22, fols 52v–53r. (Original size of each page 171 × 99mm.) Reproduced by permission of The Rosenbach Museum & Library.*

By yt the greatest shame to mans estate
Fallos on vt to be cal'd effeminate
Though you be much lou'd in the shrin'd hall
These things that seeme exceed substantiall
Gods when you fum'd on altars were pleas'd w
Because you were burnt not yt they lou'd the sm
You ar loathsome being taken smelly alone
shall we loue ill things ioynd and hate eath o
If you were good, yo good would soone decay
And you ar rare that takes yo good away
All my perfumes I owe most willingly
T'embalme thy fathers coarse. what will he d

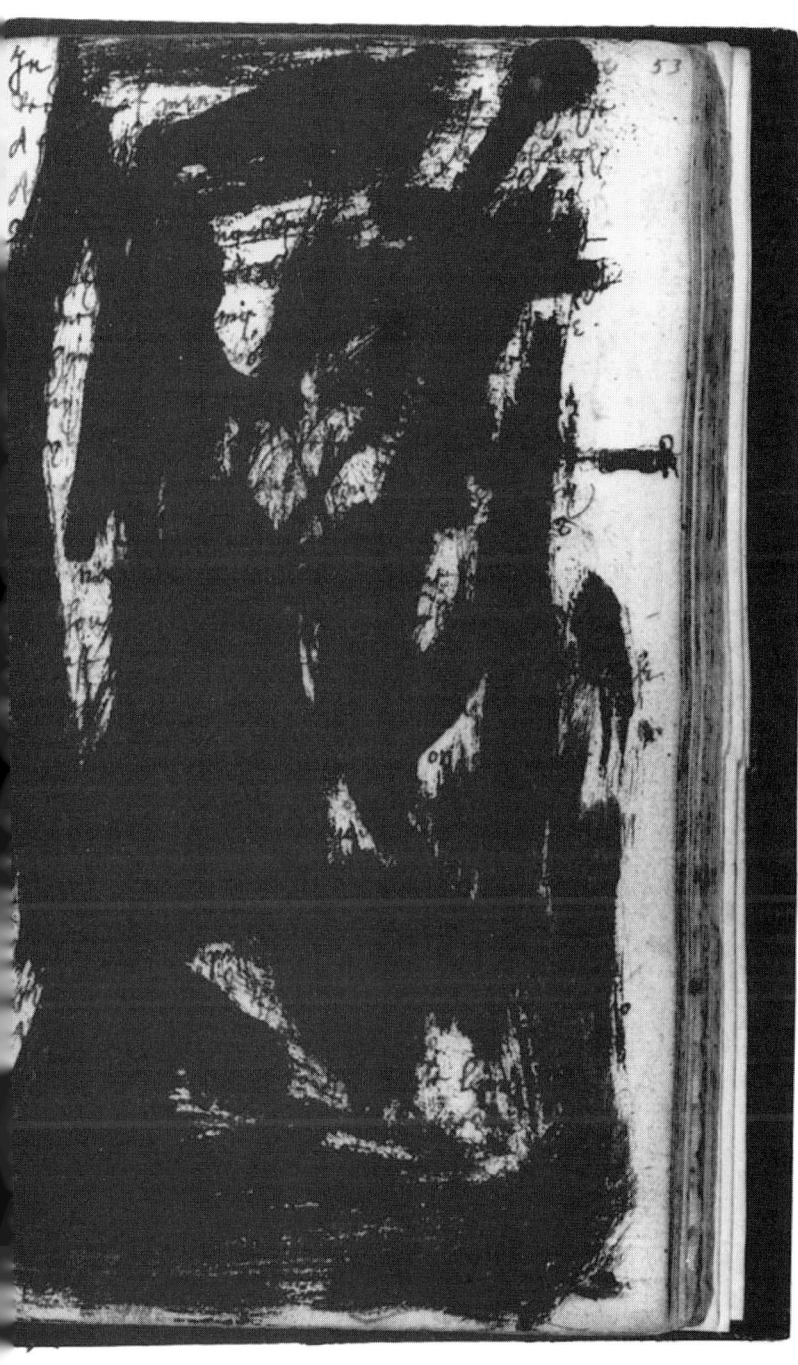

1   By thee the greatest staine to mans Estate
2   ffalles on vs to be calld effeminate
3   Though you be much loued in the Princes hall
4   These things that seeme exceed substantiall
5   Gods when you fumd on altars were pleasd well
6   Because you were burnt not y^t they loue the smell
7   You are loathsome being taken simply alone
8   Shall we loue ill things ioynd and hate each one?
9   If you were good, yor good would soone decay
10 And you are rare that takes yor good away
11 All my perfumes I giue most willingly
12 T' embalme thy fathers coarse. what will he dye?

On the previous recto of the manuscript, 'J. D.' stands at the head of this poem. These letters are a sign of authorship, not a title. Despite a few unfamiliar readings in the portion quoted above, it is recognizably John Donne's 'ELEGY IV. *The Perfume.*', so titled in the second edition of his *Poems*, 1635 (*STC* 7046), or simply '*Elegie IV.*', as it is called in the first edition, 1633 (*STC* 7045 and 7045.2).[4] For comparison, I will here reproduce the corresponding lines atop H2r from this first edition (PLATE 2). Beside it, I will supply verse numbers to match those for my transcription from the Rosenbach Manuscript. And, in the list of substantive variants below, I will also provide (in parentheses) the numbers for these verses in modern editions of the poem (though they do not quite match those of the 1633 edition, which, like eleven of the fifty early manuscripts, does not have an early couplet in the poem, vv. 7–8, which is found in the other thirty-four manuscripts that also have the verses immediately before and after, vv. 6 and 9).[5]

		MS	*1633*
4	(64)	These	There
5	(65)	you	yee
6	(66)	loue the	lik'd your
7	(67)	loathsome	loathsome all
9	(69)	would	doth
10	(70)	yor	the

Among the editors of Donne, Grierson (1912) did not know of the existence of this Rosenbach Manuscript. He held that the 1633 edition offered a good text of 'The Perfume' (with vv. 7–8 supplied from else-

Poëms.   *51*

0   By drawing in a leprous harlots breath,
1   By thee, the greatest staine to mans estate
2   Falls on us, to be call'd effeminate;
3   Though you be much lov'd in the Princes hall,
4   There, things that seeme, exceed substantiall.
5   Gods, when yee fum'd on altars, were pleas'd well,
6   Because you' were burnt, not that they lik'd your smell,
7   You' are loathsome all, being taken simply alone,
8   Shall wee love ill things joyn'd, and hate each one?
9   If you were good, your good doth soone decay;
10   And you are rare, that takes the good away.
11   All my perfumes, I give most willingly
12   To'embalme thy fathers corse; What? will hee die?

PLATE 2. *Page 51 (sig. H2r) of John Donne,* Poems *(London, 1633: STC 7045), actual size.*

where—from *1635*, it seems); and so *1633* served as his copy. He essentially perpetuated the traditional view of the text, which had been based on the poem as printed. Gardner (1965), by contrast, did know of this Rosenbach Manuscript, but she also used *1633* as her copy-text.[6] The recent Variorum edition (2000) departs from these editors' printed copy-text, in favour of a manuscript known to both of them, the Westmoreland Manuscript in the Berg Collection of the New York Public Library (3171/NY3). Holding it to be very close to the lost sources, the Variorum uses this manuscript as copy-text for all twelve of the elegies it contains and also for their sequence. Despite this radical and provocative shift in copy-text, all these editors read substantively as *1633* in these lines from 'The Perfume'. Like many a miscellany, then, Rosenbach MS 239/22 is not deemed to be very high on the tree of textual transmission. (One will have to find other reasons to love it.)

    Not unusually for the period of this manuscript (1638–45)[7], the punctuation of this passage in Rosenbach MS 239/22 is much lighter than

Regina

regionum

Italia.

Parentes

sunt quorum

nos semen

de semine

sanguis

de sangui[-]

ne, caro

de carne

sumus.

Come Madam come

all rest my powers

defye Vntill I

labour, I in labour

lye The foe oftimes

hauinge ye foe in sight

is tyrd w^{th}

standinge

though

yey neeuer

fight.

Il ne fault pas bransler le Pique

it causeth Frenzyes, cramps & other

boddily indispositions.

poem. In the three decades after Keynes' revelation, editors have continued to speak of the 1669 edition as the first.[13] (Who listens to bibliographers?) But at last, in the twenty-first century, a scholarly edition, the Variorum has stated clearly what Keynes revealed in 1973; and it has collated the earliest printed edition in detail.

Although refused a license to be printed, the poem circulated in manuscript, as did those that had been printed in *1633*. An astonishing number of handwritten copies of this poem that survive from the seventeenth century, more than for any other of Donne's elegies, except 'The Anagram' (a text that had *not*, been refused a license).[14] Peter Beal's *Index of English Literary Manuscripts* listed sixty-four manuscripts of our poem in the body of the book, with a sixty-fifth (the hitherto unidentified Rosenbach text we are dealing with here) mentioned in the Addenda. Since publication of the *Index* in 1980, Beal has learned of two more copies, one a manuscript in University College of North Wales (3190.5), and the other owned by the Duke of Bedford (3195.5), both of which have now also been taken into account in the Variorum edition (as WB1 and P1 respectively).

But the discovery of manuscripts is not over yet—may never be. Mark Bland has found a sixty-eighth item, a marginal quotation, *c.*1640, of the first two couplets of the poem, in the hand of Charles, Lord Stanhope (1593–1675), in his copy of John Selden's *Mare clausum seu de dominio maris*, 1635, now Bodleian MS Add C. 262 (PLATE 3). Stanhope, Bland reports, 'generally . . . used his [printed] books to write down whatever came into his rather disordered mind', there usually being 'no link between the marginalia and the text' of the books he wrote in.[15]

Interſerenda

Regʋnd
regʋonum
manis, Britannicæ, de quo capite ſuperiore. Suas au-
rem ——

Pag. 155. l. 17.

Italia.
——Vopiſco. Ita ſerè Proconſul Aſiæ totum ſub ſua diſpoſitione habebat Helleſpontiacum fretum uſque in Europæ
litora, ut capite oſtenditur decimo quarto. Non alio

Parentes
ſunt quorum
certè——

Pag. eadem l. 21.

nos men
De ſemine
Sanguis
De ſangui
——Comes habendus eſt. Id quod maximè etiam
firmatur ex alio ipſius Dignitatum Notitiæ loco, ubi de
Comitum præfecturis quæ ſub diſpoſitione Viri illuſtris
Magiſtri Peditum præſentalis, agitur. In libris Notitiæ
editis ita legitur,

ne, caro
De carne
ſumus
*Sub diſpoſitione Viri Illuſtris Magiſtri pedi-
ditum Præſentalis, Comites Militum infraſcriptorum.*

Come Madam come
Italiæ.
att reſt my power
Africæ.
defye Vertue of
Tingitaniæ.
Labour, J in Labour
Tractus Argentoratenſis.
Britanniarum.
Eye of the foe oftimes
Litoris Saxonici per Britannias.
hauynge ye foe in ſight

is tyrow
tam in Alciati quàm Pancirolli editione legitur, ut heic,
ſtanding
Militum infraſcriptorum. Dubitari nequit, quin pro Militum, Limitum fuerit ſubſtituendum. Neque enim ratio
though
officiorum Imperialium patitur ut Militum ibi locum
habeat. Et certiſſimum eſt ex eis quæ ſequuntur, Ita-
liam, Africam, Tractum Argentoratenſem, Britannias
they neeuer
& litus Saxonicum ſuos habuiſſe Comites, ut Comites
fight
limitum, non aliter ac Territoria quæ ibi proximè ſub-
junguntur; velut Mauritania Cæſarienſis, Tripolitani,
aliæ

... ne fault nos, transler le pique
... causeth Frenzyes, crampſ & other
boodily indigeſtions.

This new version of the opening lines of the Donne poem (the third of these four entries) does not yield any substantive readings not already known from other manuscripts. But even so, the particularities of Stanhope's hand do offer valuable insights. It is interesting to see how effectively capitalization communicates the verse structure in the absence of either end-of-verse punctuation or conventional verse lineation. Also, note that the density of ink is strong at the start of the first and third verses, but progressively lessens toward the ends of the second and fourth. (It seems also to be generally faded by subsequent wear and tear at the outer edge.) The replenishing of ink on the nib thus appears to follow a literary, not a graphic logic: the pen returned to the inkwell only after writing out a full couplet, the structural unit of the elegy.

And most startling is the novel context of the other marginalia: they provide insight into the fit of Donne's verse in the somewhat reconstructable mental life and erotic musings of a near contemporary. Stanhope's excerpt of lines about sexual frustration and about Donne's curious man 'in labour'[16] is positioned after his pronouncement on the commonality of seed, flesh and blood between parent and offspring, and before one on the perils of male masturbation.[17] (Do we read Donne any differently today, I wonder?)[18]

In this regard, Stanhope's quotation from this elegy compares with another of the newly reported copies, that by another identified reader, Francis, fourth Earl of Bedford (1593–1641). Close to the last entry in his vast unfinished—unfinishable—encyclopedic commonplace book, he quoted twenty-two verses or part verses from Donne's poem, and annotated them with reference numbers in preparation for their eventual export for arrangement severally under various heads. In the case of one of the surviving slips associated with such numerical annotations for another extract, the numbers assigned to various phrases within it were matched on the slip with the headings 'loue', 'Lerning', 'youth', 'flatery', 'desier', 'will', 'disposition' and 'wemen'—which name but a few of Bedford's many organizational topics. Unfortunately for us, the Earl's work on Donne's poem seems to have been left unfinished. Though the quotations from it were certainly numbered for export, the key to the thematic sorting seems now to be lost or was never prepared, and the quotations have not found their intended homes. Nevertheless, Bedford's selections from almost half of the verses of the poem give a

PLATE 3 (previous page). *A page of John Selden's* Mare clausum seu de dominio maris *(1635: STC 22175) with manuscript annotations by Charles, Lord Stanhope: Oxford, Bodleian Library, MS Add. C. 262, p. 314 (sig. Ss1v). (Original page size 182 × 151mm.) Reproduced by permission of the Bodleian Library.*

clear idea of just what parts of it stood out for this very close and systematic reader, another near contemporary of Donne's.[19]

****

Back to the Rosenbach Museum, and to the manuscript in hand, and to a close reading of its obliterated text. I *did* say that I aimed to read it—and read it 'letter by letter'. But how?

Since the early 1980s, a new technology, called infrared reflectography, has made its name at police headquarters (in forensic work), and at the art gallery (by revealing the under-drawing of paintings). It turns out that, though the smearing ink certainly blocks light in the range visible to the human eye, it may be relatively transparent to light off the lower end of the visible spectrum. Thus, to infrared light, opaque smears like those in the Rosenbach Manuscript can dissipate merely into a fog. The question, of course, is whether at such a frequency the scribe's ink will also leave not a wrack behind. In this case, luck is with us; the two inks are chemically different. Infrared light can indeed *penetrate* the censor's smears; but the scribe's pen strokes below it are able to *absorb* incident radiation, whereas the white paper around them *reflects* it back through the smears. Our eyes cannot detect this reflection, but an infrared-sensitive camera can, and hence can read the difference between the paper and the scribe's ink for us, and so 'dis-cover' the lost text, as Donne's age would have said.

The relatively straightforward technology for infrared reflectography of the manuscript does not exist at the Rosenbach Museum itself, and so the Curator, Elizabeth Fuller, kindly deposited the manuscript in the Conservation Department of the Philadelphia Museum of Art, where the analysis was carried out by its photographer, Joe Mikuliak, in the spring of 2000. His equipment consisted of a Hamamatsu infrared video camera, a Scion Frame Grabber, and a personal computer. The output of the camera was examined on a video monitor, and the contrast and density of the digital file was enhanced before it was saved. In this case, the camera took in a height of about nine lines at a time, one frame capturing the beginnings of lines in this range, and another frame the ends. Each of the eighteen images needed to cover the text overlapped its neighbours, so that the printed outputs from the saved files could be coordinated with one other (and, if one so desired, edited into a composite image).

In the next opening, for contrast, are a visible-light photograph of the upper right corner of the recto page, 53r (PLATE 4), and the corresponding infrared image (PLATE 5). (This is one of the clearer infrared images.) Throughout the infrared image, you can detect the smear as a

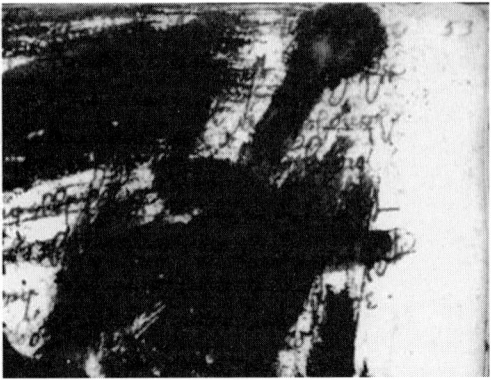

PLATE 4. *A portion of fol. 53r of the Rosenbach Manuscript in visible-light photography, actual size. Reproduced by permission of the Rosenbach Museum & Library.*

thin haze, and even make out its changing densities. The text is not fully naked; but the smear no longer censors. Curiously, the letters we can now see and read are of more varied density than we should have expected from what we saw in the twelve unobliterated lines atop the verso page. Whether the censoring ink selectively altered the scribe's work (dissolved some of it, say) or is merely still partially and unevenly covering it, is not sure. And so, with this particular infrared equipment, we may not yet have the optimal picture of what remains of the original text under the smear. Illuminating the manuscript with an infrared source of tuneable frequency might be able to improve the quality of the image either generally or in specific areas, and thus lead to the recovery of more text. Accordingly, the following transcription of the manuscript from the infrared reading of it is provisional, and should not be deemed the last word. But let it stand until someone performs the analysis again, with superior equipment or a sharper eye.

Here, then, is the whole 'infra-read' text as I make it out from this photograph. Or perhaps I should call it the 'hole' text, because of the numerous gaps where it is indecipherable. Of course, my 'th[ ]m' in v. 25 must originally have been 'them', even though not all the letters can now be observed. But I do not offer 'them', because my transcription is a record just of what can be made out today—the so-called 'existential text'. As you can see, the handwriting appears to be uniform with that of the uncensored lines atop 52v, and this fact tells us what to expect as we peer into the mist.

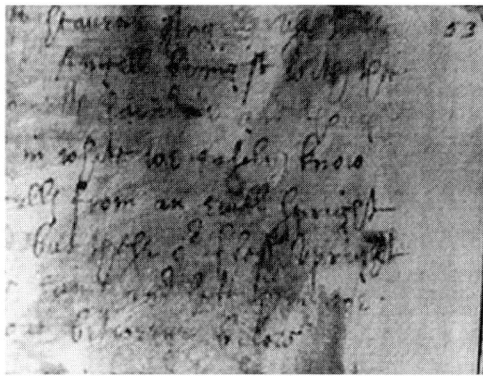

PLATE 5. *A portion of fol. 53r of the Rosenbach Manuscript in infrared photography, actual size. Reproduced by permission of the Rosenbach Museum & Library.*

19	bes heauens A̲ngells v̲s̲e̲ to bee̲	53
20	Angell bring̲s̲t̲ wi̲t̲h̲ t̲h̲e̲e̲	
21	o[ ]etts Pa[ ]dise a̲[ ] t̲h̲o̲u̲g̲h̲	
22	in w̲h̲ite we easily k̲n̲o̲w̲	
23	e̲l̲l̲s̲ f̲r̲o̲m̲ an euill spright̲	
24	but these oʳ flesh vprig̲h̲t̲	
25	g han[ ] and lett th[ ]m g̲o̲e̲.	
26	o̲ue betweene belo̲w̲	

Two *ad hoc* conventions of my transcription need explanation. (1) In square brackets, I enclose the space where no text is legible in either infrared light or visible light. (2) And I underline letters and spaces between words that can be read in daylight. Curiously, letters that are apparent in daylight are not always clear or even detectable in the infrared images. (Contrast the final letter of 'though' at the end of v. 21: it is legible in the original and so in the visible-light photograph; but it is absent in the infrared photograph.) Establishing the obliterated text thus requires recourse to different modalities: one cannot look either to visible or infrared light alone to provide a full view.

****

I will turn now to preparing two versions of the entire censored poem in Rosenbach MS 239/22. The first continues the kind of Swiss-cheese representation just offered. The second will attempt to fill in the gaps with 'restrained conjecture'. One of my ugly texts will offer too little information, the other too much. I have sought out these uncompromising representations carefully as critiques of editorial unity and pulchritude, for the focus of the conclusion to this essay is divided between the practice of reconstruction and a critical distrust of conjecture.

Now, an accurate reading of the digitalized images is often very difficult to establish. Without a detailed knowledge of the extensive variation in the more than three-score surviving manuscripts of this poem, I confess, I would not have been able to recover as much text as I have or to recover it with any degree of confidence. I did not so much *read* the text I offer below, as *deduce* it. If the poem had been one hitherto unknown, I doubt I could have satisfactorily grasped it. But, having read all the many manuscripts of this text of Donne's in preparing a photographic facsimile edition of them (under the working title *License My Roving Hands*), I have come to realize that the uncertainty of reading this specific Rosenbach Manuscript is really only an extreme version of the general condition of grasping seventeenth-century handwriting, in which one often has to read, read and re-read a passage to get it right—if it *can* be got right. Even if all the handwritten letters of a text are clear and uniform (as we are accustomed to think of letter-shapes in printing), the non-use of punctuation in manuscripts of this period still would make for a highly ambiguous text.

I have sought hard to avoid guess-work in the following transcription, and have used square brackets enclosing different lengths of space to indicate unreadable stretches. With regards to punctuation, my transcript indicates periods in vv. 18, 25 (though this one may merely be stray ink), and 46, and question marks in vv. 30 and 40. As the scribe's inking of punctuation, especially of commas and periods, could have been subtle, and as the smearing ink of the censor could either have dissolved such evidence or could continue to block it to infrared radiation, readers should regard my representation as apt to be more accurate in letters and spaces between words than in pointing. However, as the commentary on the uncensored twelve lines in the opening has already established, punctuation by this scribe is light, and there may well not have been any more points than are here recorded.

As you will see, the text is forty-eight verses long and is, therefore, an *untitled* version of this poem. (Stabbing in the dark, however, the Variorum edition had ventured the existence of a 'damaged' title.) The numbering assigned to each verse is traditional, and is as found in all scholarly editions. (It is nevertheless prejudicial, of course, for it sees vv. 31–32 as 'repositioned'.)

1   Come Madam [ ]o[ ]e all rest my powers defye
2   V[ ]till I la[ ] I in labou[ ] lye
3   The foe oft times hauing the foe in sight

4   [ ] ti[ ]ed with standing thou[   ] fight.

5   Of with that gir[ ] lik[ ] heau[   ] zone glistering

6   [   ] farre <u>faire</u>[ ] wor[ ] encompassing

7   [   ] y^t <u>spangled</u> brestplate y^t you <u>weare</u>

8   That I may see [   ]hrine that shines so faire

9   Vnlace yor selfe for that harmonious chime

10   [ ]ls me [   ] y^t now tis yor bedd time

11   <u>Of</u> with that happy buske that I enuy

12   T[ ]at still will be and still can stand so nigh

13   Y[ ] gowne[ ] going of such b[   ] state re[ ]<u>al</u>[ ]

14   A[] when from flowery meads hills shadowes ste<u>al</u>[ ]

15   [   ]<u>oure</u> [   ]nett an[ ] show

16   [   ]at on you doth grow

17   [   ] and <u>then</u> <u>softly</u> tre<u>ad</u>

18   <u>In this</u> [   ] <u>hallowe</u>[ ] <u>temple</u> th[ ] <u>soft</u> bed.   *[end of 52v]*

19   <u>In such white robes</u> heauens <u>Angells</u> <u>vse</u> to bee 53   *[start of 53r]*

20   <u>Recea</u>[ ] <u>of men</u> t[ ] Angell bring<u>st</u> wi<u>th thee</u>

21   <u>A</u> heauenly Maho[ ]etts Pa[ ]dise <u>a</u>[ ] <u>though</u>

22   <u>A</u>ll Spirits walke in w<u>h</u>ite we easily <u>know</u>

23   <u>By</u> this t[   ] <u>Angells from</u> an euill spright

24   They set o^r hair[   ] but these o^r flesh vpri<u>ght</u>

25   Lice<u>nce</u> my roui<u>ng</u> han[ ] and lett th[ ]m go<u>e</u> .

26   Be<u>hind</u> before [ ]<u>boue</u> betweene <u>below</u>

27   O m<u>y</u> Ameri[ ] my new found [ ]and

28   Th<u>y</u> kingdome [ ]s <u>safest</u> w<u>hen</u> with one man m[   ]d

29   My Mi[   ] of preci<u>ous</u> sto<u>nes</u> [ ] my Emper<u>y</u>

30   [ ]ow blest am I in this dis[   ]<u>?</u>

33   full <u>n</u>akednesse all eyes are d<u>ue to</u> thee

34   As s<u>ou</u>les vnbodyed bodyes vncloathd must bee

35   To t<u>ast</u> whole ioyes gemmes that you weam[   ]<u>se</u>

36   Are as Atlanta[ ]s bals cast in men[ ] views

37   That when a f[   ] ey[ ] lighteth <u>on a</u> gemme

38   his greedy eye must cou[ ]tt th[   ] them

39   Like vnto bookes with gaudy couerings made

40   ffor lay men [   ]ll weomen thus arraid?

41   Themselues are musick bookes [   ] only wee

42   (<u>W</u>hom th[   ] imp<u>u</u>[   ] will dig[ ]fye

43   <u>M</u>ust bee reuea[ ]d <u>then</u> S[   ] <u>know</u>

44   <u>A</u>s liberally a[ ] to a <u>midwife</u> [   ]

45   Thy []el[ ] cast all <u>yea thi</u>[   ]<u>ite linnen</u> [   ]e

46   Ther is no pennance [   ] to [ ]<u>nnocence</u>.

31   [ ] enter in [   ] to be free

32   There wher my [   ] is sett my [ ]ale [ ]all bee
47   To teach the[   ] nak[   ] f[   ] than
48   What needs [   ]u [   ] more c[ ]uering then a man

****

Now to prepare for the more sophisticated (too sophisticated) version of this text, which will appear on pp. 123–33. But two important clarifications first. I am not offering to *restore* the text, but rather to fill in some of blank areas in square brackets in the first transcription with my *conjectures*—sometimes even *optional* conjectures. I do not want to base these conjectures on personal aesthetics, but rather on something objective, readings found in other manuscripts. But it is not that *any* reading in *any* manuscript qualifies as a candidate. As in organ transplants, shouldn't one try to match donors and recipients? I will limit the range of options by drawing conjectural readings only from those texts that bear a 'family resemblance' to that of Rosenbach MS 239/22.

But what is this family I am speaking of? The Variorum edition has organized the manuscripts into a more complex tree than ever before: variants within a specific *line of transmission* might be organized into *divisions, branches, families, subfamilies,* and *sub-subfamilies*. One thinks of a tree as recording progressive deterioration of the text, as one moves through time and away from the roots. In order to sense what family resemblances the Rosenbach Manuscript bears, we need to grasp this impressive new editorial tool. Essentially, it is a reading of all the manuscripts simultaneously—an abstraction of a very high order. (But, as we shall see, it entails darkness as well as light—darkness of a very high order.)

The first division of the Variorum's 'Schema of Textual Relations' for this poem is at the celebrated variants for v. 46. For convenience, I will call them 'A' and 'B', and start my critique from this point. The Variorum projects a 'lost holograph' reading (p. 193):

A   There is no penance, **much less** innocence.

—which is represented by twenty-four subsequent manuscripts (listed just above on that page, p. 193), including the editors' copy-text, the Westmoreland Manuscript, 3171/NY3. The Variorum editors also project a 'lost scribal revision' (p. 194), with some variants of the two words in bold listed in parenthesis:

B   There is noe pennance **due to** innocence, (for pure   B8 B39
      CJ1 F5; for true   WB1)

—which is represented by thirty-seven subsequent manuscripts (listed just above). Evidently, Rosenbach MS 239/22 belongs to this line of transmission, and is thus a thirty-eighth member of Division B.

Note that there is something odd about the editors' styling of A and B. B is obviously in old spelling; and indeed a verse spelled and punctuated exactly like it can be found in the early manuscripts, specifically in the first of them listed above B on p. 194, 3192/AU1, from the University of Aberdeen; for citing the first manuscript in the alphabetical list is how the Variorum editors construct a lemma (if the lemma does not derive from the copy-text of the edition). I suppose they (reasonably) considered this arbitrary method impartial. A, by contrast, looks rather modern for a Renaissance text; and, in fact, it cannot be found exactly like this in any early manuscript—not in the first manuscript listed above A on p. 193, 3160/B7, from the British Library, which reads 'There is no pennance, much lesse Innocence', nor in the Variorum edition's copy-text, the Westmoreland Manuscript, which offers different spellings of 'There' and 'less': as 'Ther' and 'lesse'. So A and B, the editors' foundational distinctions, are curiously not on quite the same footing. Although this is indeed an old-spelling edition, modern spelling has somehow played an asymmetrical role in the editors' comprehension of the texts. In a moment, I will return to and amplify these small inconsistencies in a deconstructive reading of the editors' notes. For the present, however, let us pause in the textual argument in order to assess the literary consequences of these variants.

Helen Gardner had exploited a contradiction in Grierson's handling of this verse.[20] In his notes for the variant, he had suggested that the version he chose to print, 'no pennance due to innocence', was a 'softening of the original'. But he did not say who was the author of this softening. (Gardner assumed Grierson ascribed the softening to Donne himself; but his qualifications show Grierson was hedging his bets (as my italics will point out): 'The version in the text is a softening of the original to make it *compatible* with the *suggestion* that the poem *could* be read as an epithalamium' (Vol. II, p. 90). The Variorum editors, by the way, hold a scribe responsible for the change to 'due to'.) Nor did Grierson say why an editor should pass on to his critical text an *un*original reading in copy-text, as he did. (As we saw in the case of 'The Perfume', Grierson certainly could depart from copy-text—to add the couplet to it in this case, which couplet he must have deemed had been omitted from it or an ancestor.) In choosing instead 'no pennance, much lesse innocence' for her own edition, Gardner could present herself as triumphantly hard in her role as the restorer of the original reading—*and* with the implicit blessing of the flaccid former Oxford editor!

She could have stopped her triumph there. But, at the conclusion of her note in the textual commentary (p. 133), she characterizes the 'very expensively dressed' woman as one of the 'cities quelque choses' (a dismissive phrase she draws not from this poem, but from Donne's sardonic 'Love's Usury', v. 15). 'White, the colour of penitence and virginity', says Gardner, 'is not for her'. Here, bizarrely, the editor substitutes 'penitence' for 'pennance' and 'virginity' for 'innocence'. (The first requirement of an editor is to quote accurately.) Being a cognate, the first substitute is not problematic; but the second is wide of the mark. In saying that white, the colour of *virginity*, is not for her, Gardner seems out of touch with the erotic sophistication of the scene, for these scarcely seem like virginal players. (A critique of their *chastity* might be more apt.) But the seducer's radical claim in the version of l. 46 that Gardner rejects is that the solicited sex or the woman's body itself (be it virgin or not) are themselves as white as *innocence*, and hence need no covering of *penitential* white linen. 'Put off white linen, for you are white yourself.') (Only the man's clothing her with his own naked body, he tups his argument, answers need.) Gardner treats white as a badge of literal truth: it is not for naughty girls. And this interpretation functions well in the version of the line she has embraced. But in the amorous speech of the version she rejects, white is a colour of pure desire. With this editor, as with Grierson, it seems that emotion has somehow been at play, rather than pure textual science. Like him, Gardner seems to have had an investment in the ethical status of the sexuality of this poem. It seems to have made a difference to both of them whether the sex in the offing is a nuptial celebration or just raw fucking. Instead of seizing on these variants to show how volatile sex-talk can be, he cools it by institutionalizing it, while she heats it up by directing it toward the illicit. Grierson's way of dealing with the variant reading tends toward an Edenic view of male and female sex alike. Gardner's tends toward a negative judgment of just the woman's sexual behaviour—and makes no judgement at all of her John's! Grierson's edited view of sex is less sexy. Hers is sexy indeed, but at a cost, for—forget the thrill of undressing of the woman—it strips her of any pretence of dignity. It is sexy because it is sexist, and potentially cruel. And that can be *very* sexy indeed—but also very uncomfortable.

The ultimate point, of course, is not the editor's text, but Donne's. Neither editor answers the questions whether *both* versions of the verse might not be by the same author (as Gardner assumed Grierson assumed), and, if they are, which is earlier, and which later; and, indeed, whether the later cancels the earlier, or whether both options stand. Certainly, the Variorum editors are able to conceive of Donne as a revis-

ing author. (Apparently, the notion of a revising author is not as hereti-
cal in Donne studies as it has been in Shakespeare studies.) In their editing of 'Elegy 13. The Autumnall.', they allow for both a 'lost original
holograph' and a 'lost revised holograph' (not to mention a 'lost scribal
corruption'), p. 300. Curiously, however, the Variorum editors' tree does
not establish a 'vertical' relationship between the two holographs.

Now back to the Variorum editors' tree for 'To his Mistress going to
bed'. Their criteria for the division of the textual tree into 'two primary
lines of transmission' (p. 165) are problematic. At the start of their
'Textual Introduction' (p. 165) appear two more versions of v. 46,
supplementing A and B above, which I will call, respectively, A_1 and B_1.
By attending to further inconsistencies of detail, we can sense the
editors' difficulties.

A_1 Ther [or *Here*] is no penance, much lesse innocence

B_1 There is noe pennance due to [or *for pure / true*] innocence.

These two versions enlarge upon A and B with variants—and not only
those the editors added in square brackets, as the following collations
show.

A_1	A
Ther	There
[or *Here*]	
lesse	$\wedge$ **less**
innocence$_\wedge$	~.

B_1	B
[or *for pure / true*]	
innocence.	$\wedge$ ~,
$\wedge$	(for pure B8 B39 CJ1 F5; for true WB1)

Version A_1, exclusive of the information in brackets (which I will come
to in a moment), misquotes the edited text on the verso opposite it in
the Variorum edition, p. 164 (which accurately represents the
Westmoreland Manuscript):

Ther is no penance, much lesse innocence.

—for A_1 omits the terminal period found in both the copy-text and the
edited version of it. Version A does have the period; but, as we know, it
problematically offers modern spellings for two words of A_1, which are
also in the edited text: 'Ther' and 'lesse'.

Apart from the information in brackets, Version B_1, with its terminal
period, does quote the verse as it can be found in at least one manuscript, 3178/NY1.[21] But Version B offers a comma instead, and this

punctuation and spelling can indeed be found in 3192/AU1, which is the first manuscript in the list just above B, and the one we should have expected to be the editors' source. The likely explanation for the terminal period in B_1 is not that the editors wanted to quote 3178/NY1, but that, intending to quote 3192/AU1, they allowed the terminal punctuation of their own sentence to displace the final punctuation of the quotation. (This regrettable practice in quotation is, of course, widespread. Instead of printing

'~,'.

at the end of a sentence, which preserves the comma in the quotation, a conventional usage is often to print the following

'~.'

— in which the medium distorts the message.) As we observed before, the editors' formulations sometimes seem projected out of existing historical evidence, sometimes not.

My critique might amount to no more that an idle and petty demonstration of loose quotation—of 'Broken Telephone'—even within the same critical project, if only it had been confined to spelling and punctuation, both of which were highly unregulated in the early seventeenth century. But the matter in square brackets is substantive, and therefore more serious, even if it doesn't rival what the editors call a 'major verbal (and ideological) variant' later in the line (p. 165). Consider A_1, with its '[or *Here*]' as an option for 'Ther'. The lemma in the editor's 'Historical Collation' for this verse (p. 189) begins rather 'Heere', which is the spelling of this initial word in the verse in the first manuscript listed after it, 3202/B8,

Heere is noe pennaunce for pure iñocence

—but in its 'pure', this smacks of a B_1 reading. Well, the next text in the list (3173/B13) does offer an A_1 reading,

Heer is no pennance, much less innnocence

—but obviously its 'Heer' is not the source either. One may conclude that the spelling 'Here' in '[or *Here*]' is simply modern and does not have a specific source in the list (though the rest of the A_1 phrase is indeed old-spelling and is true to the Variorum copy-text). Evidently, the editors did not have a single criterion for generating the lemmata of the Historical Collation on the one hand and the textual reconstructions on the other. (The 'Heere' entry in the 'Historical Collation' is followed, by the way, with a list of seventeen extant manuscripts in many different spellings, and 'Here' can be found among them.[22])

But that is the least of the problems. These and other manuscripts show that '[or *Here*]' cannot be confined to A_I, in the 'much lesse' line; it should be in B_I as well, in the 'due to' line. And therefore it ought also to have been recorded in A *and* B. Simply put, for the sake of scholarly representation of the surviving evidence, the bracketed information should appear in all four of these hypothetical reconstructions. But the extensive omission of it is convenient, for this necessary term, 'Here', or 'Heere', or 'Heer', or however we spell it, threatens to uproot the editors' tree. The philosophical problem in A, B, and B_I seems to be one of circularity. (1) From the actual 'Ther' of their copy-text (and of many other manuscripts besides), the editors project hypothetical 'There' as the 'lost holograph', whereupon, (2) the hypothetical is allowed to beget the lost actual: 'There' > 'Ther'—and (3) this derivation confirms the authenticity of the Westmoreland Manuscript! The essence of the problem is that the Westmoreland Manuscript is just a single member of a class of derivatives. Its saying 'Ther' while the class to which it belongs equivocates between 'There' and 'Here' (as A_I alone reveals) is neither here nor there as a justification for the projection of 'There' as the exclusive reading of the lost holograph.

To probe deeper into this problem, let us draw a summary of information in the editors' 'Schema of Textual Relations' (pp. 192–97). According to the Variorum, two 'divisions' stem from a 'lost holograph', at the top of the tree, and from them descend six families (among which is the Westmoreland Manuscript, sole member of its family) and four subfamilies, comprising twenty-four extant manuscripts in all.

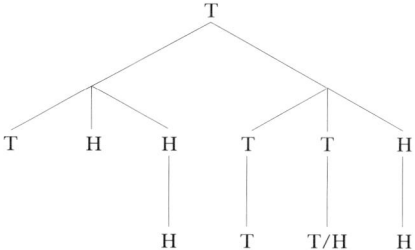

In each of the various units on this tree, the letters 'T' and 'H' stand for the substantives 'There' and 'Here' at the beginning of v. 46 in various surviving manuscripts (however these words may be spelled in those documents). As you can see, at the level of the family and the sub-family (*i.e.*, the two bottom rows), optional beginnings to the verse can be found, 'T' or 'H', which are deemed to stem ultimately from just the alleged 'T' in the lost holograph, above.[23] In effect, the editors imply that both extant 'There' and extant 'Here' derive from lost 'There'—or perhaps we should understand that this lost 'There' sometimes mutates into extant 'Here'. But would it be any less logical to suppose that both extant 'Here' and extant 'There' derive from a lost 'Here'—and that lost 'Here' sometimes mutates into extant 'There'? Certainly, each variant word makes various kinds of sense in context—in the *contexts*, rather, when you consider other variants in the verse (which I will come to in a moment); and neither variant, taken alone, seems deficient.

These realizations may tempt us (wickedly) to install a lost 'H' at the top of this tree, and consequently lead us to regard the actual 'Ther' of the Westmoreland Manuscript as a deviation from it, one which challenges the claim of that manuscript to authority, and suggests, therefore, the case for emendation of its 'Ther' to 'Here' (or is it to 'Heere' or to 'Heer'?), if the edition aims, that is, to represent the lost holograph, and not merely its reflection in the Westmoreland Manuscript. (Certainly, the editors do emend the Westmoreland Manuscript elsewhere, almost three-dozen times, in fact—most markedly in the title, as we have already observed, which they translate from Latin into English and supplement with the title from the 1669 edition. And so it is not as if they greatly respected the historical niceties of their chosen copy-text.[24]) Surely, if 'H' first appeared only in a sub-subfamily, one could argue strongly that it was a corruption of an original 'T'; but, as other witnesses at the same high level of the tree as that of the Westmoreland Manuscript challenge the projection of 'T' as the top of the tree, can we really be certain what the lost holograph read? The editors' bracketing of 'Here' in A implicitly does, of course, acknowledge the uncertainty I am encouraging; but the absence of the same bracketed material from B, A_1 and B_1, and especially, of course, in the edited text of the poem itself, which entirely excludes options, suggests this acknowledgment is reluctant. While the evidence of the manuscripts points to polyphony, the edited text is to be merely univocal.

The problem is somewhat like that faced by readers of Genesis 1 and 2. In the former chapter, female descends from male. Let's call this the 'There' text. In the latter, the 'Here' text, male and female are created simultaneously, neither sex from the other. The Bible seems a step ahead of the Variorum edition here, in that it merely presents multiple versions, rather than closing off further thought by allowing one of them (let's call it a 'patriarchal' scribal revision, shall we?) editorially to suppress the other (let's call it God's holograph)—to drive it into the apparatus. But in the Variorum edition, any doubts that come with variants are kept well away from the final edited text. After they have laboured with the variants, the Variorum editors deliver their text. But to my thinking, in the absence of Donne's holograph or holographs, our *struggle* for the text *is* the text. In this particular instance, by default, our struggle between 'T' and 'H' now is the text. (I am not here speaking of the Westmoreland text, which is, of course, merely 'T'. I refer rather to our projection of Donne's text from it.)[25]

I won't diagram the tree for the second of the editors' 'lines of transmission', that from the projected 'lost scribal revision'. But again they hold for two divisions of descendants, which result in five families, two of which mix 'T' and 'H'. From one of them descend two subfamilies, still mixing 'T' and 'H', and from one of them descends a sub-subfamily that does the same. So, the same 'Here'/'There' problem exists in both of the editors' primary lines of transmission. How do these two lines triangulate into the hypothetical spaces above them, the space of lost primary documents? What is at top? 'There'? 'Here'?

Now, we may trust that in the eye of God, every derivation of one manuscript from another can be placed unambiguously on a single tree—*His divine Ygdrasil.* But the twenty four manuscripts in this division are surely only a fraction of the original number, and therefore any tree we construct will contain gaps—gaps evident to God, we may suppose, but not to scholars. Items we place on the tree represent individual manuscripts as objects; but the lines of derivation (lines of *interpretation* to us), even if they should happen to be correct, do not necessarily connect them by direct descent, as mother to daughter, but rather may connect them less directly, merely as members of manuscript families, as aunt to niece, say. If a family of manuscripts shows 'T' here and 'H' there, and from them derive manuscripts with the same variety, no one should be surprised by the following formula for descent within the family: 'T/H > T/H'. But if only one 'T' survives from the parents and only one 'H' from the offspring, the scholar's derivation 'T > H' will look right, but, in The eye of God', is no more accurate a statement of *family* behaviour than 'H > T', even though surviving evidence does not at all prompt blinkered mortals to make this formulation.

In calling the text at the head of the second line of transmission a 'revision', the editors imply that there is a level of the tree above it. But they don't actually show one in their climactic diagram, on p. 197 (where 'lost holograph' and 'lost scribal revision' are ranged beside each other, their lines of transmission meeting only below). (The same problem was observed with regard to Elegy 13, 'The Autumnal', p. 103 above.)

Now, there is another tree in the textual notes, on p. 172, a tree for a single verse, v. 38 ; and this tree (the Variorum editors' 'Figure 1', reproduced here) also stems from the 'lost holograph'.

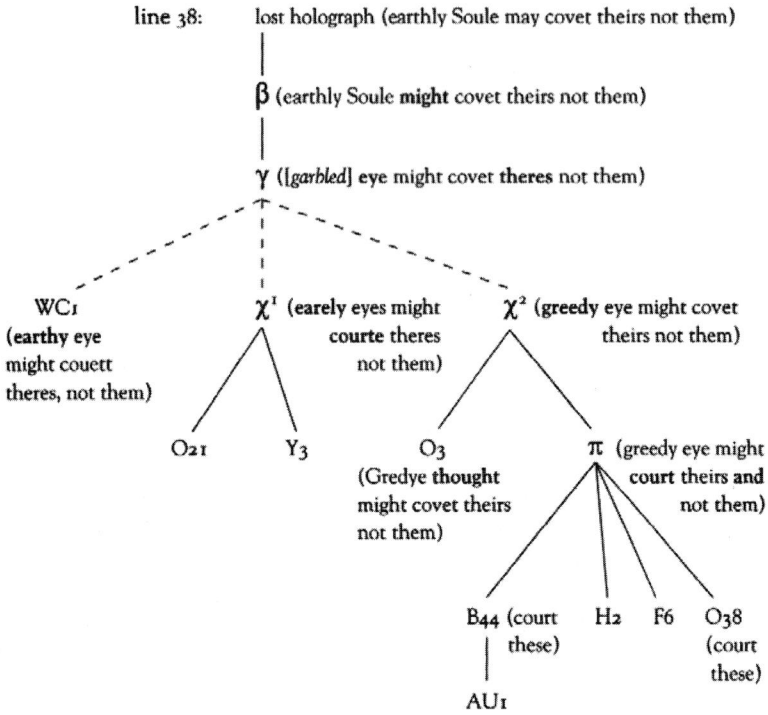

line 38:   lost holograph (earthly Soule may covet theirs not them)

β (earthly Soule **might** covet theirs not them)

γ ([*garbled*] eye might covet **theres** not them)

WC₁   χ¹ (earely eyes might   χ² (greedy eye might covet
(earthy eye   courte theres   theirs not them)
might couett   not them)
theres, not them)

                O21   Y3   O3   π (greedy eye might
                                        (Gredye thought   court theirs and
                                        might covet theirs   not them)
                                        not them)

                                                                B44 (court   H2   F6   O38
                                                                        these)   (court
                                                                                                        these)

                                                                    AU1

At the bottom of it are listed manuscripts from the line of transmission
that descends through the alleged scribal revision; but, strangely, that
revision is not actually named on the tree, and so, again, the editors
avoid stating a vertical relationship between their projections of holograph and revision, though they certainly imply one here.

It is not clear whether the editors think the main tree applies to
manuscripts as whole entities or whether individual verses from them
can have their own independent trees.[26] If the 'lost holograph' at the
top of each of these trees should be one and the same, the witnesses
from the 'lost scribal revision' multiply the confusing report of 'There'
and 'Here' in v. 46. If another lost holograph by Donne should stand at
the top of the second line of transmission—or, if a transcription of the
lost holograph by the author, rather than a revision, *per se*, stands there,
the editors' textual tree is fundamentally challenged. It may be, we can
speculate, that in one of his several supposed versions Donne wrote
'Here' and in another 'There', and that the variety of readings in the
witnesses at the level of the family may show complete fidelity to one of
these originals or the other, rather than variously manifest either fidelity
or corruption in the transmission of a single original. The editor's

impossible task would now be, centuries later, to figure out which word Donne had originally written, and which was the revision.

The editors' 'Textual Introduction' does indeed make ample allowance for 'collat[ion]', 'conflation' and 'contamination' (p. 174), 'missing exempla between the original prototype and the extant family representatives' (p. 170), 'genealogical interminglings' and the 'unusually protean nature' of this text 'while circulating in manuscript' (p. 174). The inconsistencies of the editors' own A, B, A₁ and B₁ run modestly parallel to the chaos of scribes and copyists whom they so patiently document, and they show how easy inconsistency is. Why don't they also allow for such protean qualities in the composition or authorial transmission of the poem? How is Donne's own art (or editing?) above the fray?

Let us pause again in the textual argument, for literary considerations. Does it really matter whether 'H' or 'T' is at the top of the heap with Dr. Donne? Indeed it does. Let us start with Line A from the supposed lost holograph, reading, 'much less'. (1) '**There** is no penance, much less innocence' can be taken, as an impersonal construction, meaning that these two qualities are fictitious: as if to say, philosophically, 'Mankind is certainly fallen and regrets it not.' (2) But in the demonstrative-adverb construction, '**Here** is no pennance much less innocence' can mean something like, 'You'll find no innocence in *this* bed—and no regrets either'. Should the speaker's finger touch his chest as he intones 'Here', he touches on his own morality. Should he point to her, he frames hers. Of course, the same range of reference also applies to 'There', when that word is taken as a demonstrative. Any part of her body he gestures toward could be idiomatically described as 'there'. We might expect the speaker normally to refer to his own body as 'here', but he could easily humorously disassociate himself from some part of it—guess which part?—by pointing: 'No innocence down there; no regrets.' Similarly, he could call her there 'here' if he were close to it. (And isn't the poem about getting close?) 'There' and 'here' navigate among four options of reference: all mankind, this couple, him, her.

Now for 'There' and 'here' in the other, 'due to', scribal line of transmission, Line B. (3) We can read '**There** is noe pennance due to innocence' as an impersonal construction pointing to a general truth: 'The innocent need not be penitent.' (4) In the demonstrative construction, '**Here** is noe pennance due to innocence,' one might understand that though the outside world may make one feel guilty about sex, 'Here, in love's hallowed temple, no one need apologize'.[27]

These various readings are all easy and plausible, and all are of literary consequence. If 'Here' and 'There' can possibly lead us to authorial variants, why cannot also 'much lesse' and 'due to', the variants with which the editors begin their textual tree? Or, to state the matter mathematically, why not all $2^2 = 4$ combinations of these variants? All four can indeed be found in actual manuscripts at the highest level of the two lines of transmission on the editors' tree, immediately below the hypothesized two lost versions, the author's and the scribe's. (In the references to the right of the following chart, I have indicated only a single extant manuscript in which each particular variant can be found.)

'lost holograph':	Heer . . . much less	3173/B13
	Ther . . . much lesse	3171/NY3
'scribal revision':	Here . . . due to	3186/F4
	There . . . due to	3169/H6

By bracketing off 'Here' in A_1, the Variorum editors imply that the only significant difference in this verse is that between 'much less' and 'due to', and that it is safe to ignore other variants in the verse. This approach leads to a simplified tree, one that grows by progressive bifurcations, marginalizing at each turn evidence that doesn't fit the logic of the tree-maker. The potential danger of such trees is that they force a narrow binary logic onto a very complex process, one for which we likely have, despite almost seventy manuscripts, only a fragment of the relevant evidence.

Now that we have returned to the major 'ideological' variants, let me refer to a similar textual problem in Donne's 'The Perfume', which the Variorum editors treat very differently. In v. 29 of this elegy there occurs a variant: 'dandled' vs 'ingled' (or 'nigled' or 'juggled' or 'iogled'). The Variorum editors chose 'ingled' for their text, following copy, the Westmoreland Manuscript, which they tentatively derive from a 'revised? lost holograph' (in contrast to the mere 'lost holograph', where 'dandled' is held to have originated). According to the editors (pp. 78–79):

> several considerations suggest that the revision [to 'ingled'] is Donne's. First the words do not resemble each other enough to lead one to suspect a scribal copying error; and, second, the change is unnecessary. Indeed, one sees nothing about 'dandled'—buried in the middle of a line in the middle of the poem—that would require metrical or conceptual improvement or otherwise attract a scribe's notice . . . . Finally, analysis of the variation throughout the entire corpus of texts indicates that this variant stands at the head, rather than somewhere further down the genealogical tree. . .

And so the Variorum editors regard 'ingled' as the prior (and therefore certainly authorial) reading (whereas the revision is less certainly his).

Now, cannot the same logic be applied to the variants 'due to' and 'much less' in v. 46 of our elegy? They also do not resemble each other, and so do not suggest a scribal copying error (as might the variants 'there' and 'here'). And no change in either reading is necessary. Neither reading is a metrical or conceptual improvement on the other. And the variants do stand at the head of the editors' tree. So—tell me —what makes the variant in 'The Perfume' seem possibly to originate in the author's revision (p. 94), but the rejected variant in 'To his Mistress going to bed.' to stem from a scribal revision (p. 194)?

****

To interpose a little ease, let us explore a parallel but much simpler universe, the early manuscript tradition of Keats's sonnet, 'On Sitting Down to Read King Lear Once Again'. There are four relevant documents, two in Keats's hand, whereas no manuscript of our Donne poem survives in the author's hand. One of Keats' drafts is on a separate leaf, D; the other is inscribed into his facsimile of Shakespeare's first folio, FC, and it is dated January 22, 1818. He also wrote a version of the poem into his lost letter to his brothers, dated January 23, 1818, a copy of which survives in the hand of John Jeffrey, JJ. And there is also W^2, a copy by Woodhouse of a lost transcript of some unknown Keats document in the hand of J. H. Reynolds.[28] All three copyists were devoted to representing Keats and may be contrasted with some of the scribes of Donne's poem, who presumably may not have known the author's identity and may not have scrupled to alter the poem as they transcribed it.

Here are principal variants among these four versions, two holographs and two transcripts.[29]

	D	*FC*	*JJ*	*W²*
4	⟨Books⟩ Pages	pages	volume	pages
6	Damnation	Damnation	Hell-Torment	Hell-Torment
7	⟨must I⟩ humbly	humbly	^	humbly
11	through...forest I am	through...forest I am	I am through...forest	through...forest I am
10	this	⟨this⟩ our	our	this
14	to	⟨to⟩ at	at	to

In D, v. 4, 'Pages' is written on the line, directly after deleted 'Books', and in v. 7, 'humbly' is written above deleted 'must I' . In FC, v. 10 'our' is written above deleted 'this', and, in v. 14, 'at' is reported to be written right on top of 'to'.

The relationship of the first two columns suggests that holograph *D* precedes holograph *FC*: in v. 4 in *D*, the original 'Books' gives way to the revision, 'Pages'; and this revised version advances to *FC*. The same holds true for the variant in v. 7. The *D* readings in vv. 10 and 14, 'this' and 'to' both appear in *FC*, but each is then revised there, to 'our' and 'at'.[30]

Now, is *JJ* before or after *D* and *FC*?—or perhaps between them? (The phrase 'this wintry day' in v. 3 of the sonnet makes the interpretation of the date, present only in *FC*, particularly important.) Of course, the date suggests that *JJ* is after *FC*, but the dating in *JJ* is certainly of the letter, but not necessarily of the draft of the sonnet it copied. Curiously, the date in the folio, *FC*, could be the date of original composition or the date of copying. In v. 7, the status of the *JJ* text is unclear; it may have omitted 'humbly' in error, for the verse is unmetrical without it. (It is now impossible to say whether Keats or Jeffries is responsible for the omission—or even whether the text descends from a draft in which the wording necessary to fill up the metre had not yet been composed, and was something like a desideratum rather than an actual omission.) But certainly, the readings deemed to result from authorial revision in *FC* are found in vv. 10 and 14 in *JJ*; and their presence might lead one to assume that *JJ* is the latest of these three manuscripts, and in a direct line of transmission, with no internal gaps. As there are readings in *JJ* that we have not seen before, 'volume' and 'Hell-Torment' in vv. 4 and 6, and the variant placing of 'I am' in v. 11, we might deem these to be Keats's latest evolution of the diction of the poem.

Finally for *W²*. In this version we also find 'Hell-Torment', and on this basis may consider *W²* to be another late version, after *FC* or even after *JJ*. But its readings of 'this' and 'to' in vv. 10 and 14 argue, to the contrary, for an origin before *FC*. It seems possible, therefore, that *W²* would be at home in several places along the time-line, here reverting to earlier readings, and there anticipating later ones.

The problem with placing *W²* in a time-line shows us that if we are partial in our selection of variants for the foundational differentiations of a tree, we can show that a given manuscript is early or late, just as we wish or as our unconscious assumptions dictate. Of course, it is also possible that the lost copy from which *W²* descends was not on the tree as we are constructing it, but rather before it, say—or even beside it, a sibling of *D*'s. What seems safest to say in the end is simply that in the readings of vv. 4, 6, 7, 10, 11, and 14 Keats made changes at various times. The readings in any particular later document may represent direct transmission of the reading of copy, or evolution of it, or even reversion from it to an earlier reading. Sadly, if we are editors in quest for the first or the latest thoughts of the poet, we may emerge from our encounter with these variants with no overall sense of the chronology of the various witnesses. But (and here is the consolation prize) in the aftermath of collation we certainly are left with a clear sense of problematic sites in the creation of the poem, sites where closure did not come easily, if it ever did. (Keats, like Donne, died before his poem appeared in print—though each poet had launched the circulation of his work, finished or not, in manuscript.) An editor's making of a tree to guide selection of copy for a single version of a text to serve as copy for an edition can easily prove a distraction both from this dynamic of poetic creativity and from the limitations of our own knowledge.

****

Appropriately, the Variorum editors do not use affective language to describe the variants, as did Grierson and Gardner. But no matter how well they may have devised their textual tree, it finally offers no evidence for assigning one variant to a scribe and the other to the author—and not of both to one, or both to the other—for no manuscript is in Donne's hand: simply there is no authorizing author in the known evidence. And even if one manuscript in his hand did exist, a clean copy, let us suppose, one unlike Keats's holograph manuscripts of 'On Sitting Down to Read King Lear Once Again', without any of its layers of revision, it would not prove that variant authorial versions did not once exist and that some of these variants are reflected in the readings of other manuscripts, those not in his hand. Face it: at some point, things are just not knowable. And here (or there)—I'll call it the McLeod of Unknowing—we will not be able to confront Donne (the giant for whom we may have climbed this textual tree), but will experience merely our own poor Jack-selves confronting choices. But whether the bifurcated top of an editorial textual tree precisely reflects the lost objects, it may be a telling map of our own overbearing subjectivity. At a moment like this, editorial styling, which may rest merely on an editor's social and sexual preferences before a polymorphous text, and not on science, is what we are relegated to: some editors are soft, it seems, and some are hard. Here and there, the history of editing records the ebb and flow of these stylings. At such an impasse, the main thing for me as a critical reader of Donne's wandering text—the *err*-text of this poem, not the *ur*-text—is that the evidence is multiple. There is ineradicable doubt as to what Donne wrote, as to whether he wrote once only or more often, as to whether he changed his mind or even changed it back.

Why do editors chose *between* the options, and not merely chose the options altogether? Why not embody uncertainty? Why chose? Chose? Some of the answer may lie in the €¢onomi¢$ of pub£i$hing. (The editor's verse line is shaped by the publisher's bottom line.) Some of the answer may lie in the supposed unpleasantness of uncertainty and ambiguity and doubt and skepticism and creativity and fecuntidy. For me, the main critical point to bear in mind is that when evidence runs thin, or is too abundant, the pressure on an editor to speak for the author may prove irresistible.

****

But though our constructed trees rooted in lost originals may not accurately reconstruct the past and may be philosophically biased, the manuscripts upon which they are based do constitute real evidence and may point to something generally useful in editorial trees—family resemblances. Let me now talk more about the problems associated with knowing a family, which is a loose association of manuscripts local-ized in the tree. But first, some more introductions are in order.

Low down on the line of the Variorum tree which grows through the 'lost scribal revision', appear these variants of v. 8, as the editors record them (p. 194):

That the eyes of busy fooles may be stopt there

—which is represented by ten manuscripts in this line of transmission (and by all of the manuscripts in the other line, which is deemed to stem directly from the 'lost holograph'); and (on p. 196)

That I may see my shrine that shines so faire.

—represented by eighteen. (To keep us humble, though, we should also note that there is one manuscript in addition, 3182/O34, which includes both variants—as part of a three-verse couplet! The editor's classify this manuscript as 'a lost scribal conflation?' (p. 197), and this anomaly in it challenges convenient arborifying.) Now, our Rosenbach manuscript reads with this latter division and is the nineteenth member. (I will iden-tify the rest of them in an endnote.[31]) All the members of this division read essentially

Ther is [or '*Thers*' (never '*Here is*')] no pennance due to innocence.

(The manuscript with the three-verse couplet, by the way, reads

Her is no penance dewe to ẏnnocens   3182/O34

—a verse the scribe omitted from the body, but added in the margin.[32])

Armed with this information, we can feel reasonably confident that v. 46 in the Rosenbach Manuscript, which also begins with 'Ther' (not 'Here') in this verse

Ther is no pennance [   ] to [ ]nnocence.   3214.5/R3

once read essentially,

Ther is no pennance due to innocence.

—and with improved infrared equipment, we might some day expect to *see* all the presently undetectable letters.

We have talked of some members of this family group already: all nineteen manuscripts except 3211/F12 have vv. 31–32 (numbered thus by the editors), after v. 46, so that they function as the penultimate couplet of the poem. With various spellings, most of these verses read essentially as follows.[33]

To enter into these bonds [or '*bands*'] is to be free
Then [or '*There*'] where my hand is set my seal shall [or '*should*'] be

But one manuscript in the family offers variants not included in this generalization.[34]

Then wheare my hand has felt my seed should bee   3193/O3

It is these nineteen manuscripts that represent the family group or 'division' from which I will select readings to insert, speculatively, in the bracketed spaces of my transcription of the Rosenbach Manuscript. This manuscript has several illegible stretches in v. 32, but I can read 'sett' and enough of '[   ]ale' to intuit 'seale'. But even if I could not read these determining words, the structure of the tree, we might hope, could lead us not to project 'felt' and 'seed' into the Rosenbach Manuscript because of the position and isolation of O3 within the group. The Variorum edition's 'Figure 1' shown above (p. 108) offers a tree for some of these nineteen manuscripts, a tree associated just with v. 38. The unique readings 'has felt . . . seed' instead of 'is set . . . seal' occur in a lone member of a subfamily, and their being remote and unique point away from their being Donne's. All the other manuscripts in our family read 'seal' (except F3, which shows 'selfe' altered to 'seal'). If, on the other hand, 'seed' had been reported at the highest level, above extant manuscripts of the supposed 'lost scribal revision', this F3 reading would stand a higher chance of being deemed authorial. But the imagery of the seal is so widely attested and is so appropriate to the literary context, which points toward a contract, potentially a marriage contract, that 'seed' does seem like a naughty scribal slip of the pun. Not that naughtiness is not an integral part of this poem. But if it were *authorially* naughty, we would expect to see this seminal joke at play higher in the tree. (By contrast, the cognate variants 'bond' and 'band' in v. 31 are all over the tree (like the variants 'Here' and 'There'), and either of them is plausibly authorial, and either is understandable intellectually or graphically as a spontaneous substitute for the other—by a scribe or by the roving, roaming, raving or waving, covering or wooing hand— *hands* of the author himselves.)

The potential practical usefulness of the Variorum editor's tree, here among extant witnesses, is that it means that, in projecting into the illegible gaps in the Rosenbach text, one is not wholly at the mercy of subjective aesthetics ranging among the options presented by all the known variants, but can hope to be guided by something more objective, by a sense of just the variants in manuscripts that bear a family likeness—which may be thought of as a function of historical dissemination.

But there do remain problems with trees in general and with this branch of the tree in particular, problems that will not go away in our attempt to use this tree for the purposes of projection into the gaps of the Rosenbach Manuscript. Verses 31–32 are the site of just such a problem. The fact that they are not 'repositioned' in one of the manuscripts of this family, in 3211/F12, may suggest that this manuscript stands higher on the tree than all the others in the division—is not yet 'corrupted' in its deemed authorial placement of this couplet, as were, we might suppose, every other manuscript in the family. And so, we could attempt to use this striking and concentrated variant as a criterion for constructing a tree. Now, in v. 17, F12 has a reading

17   ⌄ Off . . . so softly

that links it only with 3214/LA1 and 3217/Y1 among surviving manuscripts in the family, the rest of which read as follows.

17   Now off . . . ⌄ softly

It would seem that because vv. 31–32 are not 'repositioned' in F12, but they are in these other two with which it shares this variant, F12 should be higher on the tree than they. But the problem is that many of the other manuscripts in the family, all of which do have the 'repositioned' verses, show the normal 'Now off . . . ⌄ softly' for this variant, and this fact suggests, contradictorily, that they all lie closer to the source even than F12, and that the 'repositioning' of vv. 31–32 took place before F12, not after it. Confusingly, then, F12 would seem to be near both the head of the family and its tail—and that can't be.

One way a scholar might deal with a conflict like this is to assume that F12 and LA1 and Y1 are not direct ancestors of the other manuscripts with 'repositioned' verses, but are off on branchlets of the tree. The problem with this notion is that it implies that vv. 31–32 were independently repositioned to the same place (between vv. 46 and 47) in different lines of transmission. Surely, this transformation can hardly be explained as a spontaneous corruption of the text in different lines. Alteration of one or more of these manuscripts on the basis of collation elsewhere within the family (or even without) is implied. Other problems appear within this group of three manuscripts. F12 and LA1 share some unique variants, where Y1 has the 'normative' readings.

| 18 | Loue-hallowed | (F12, LA1) | vs | loues hallowed | (Y1) |
| 20 | Reuiew'd | (F12, LA1) | vs | Receiud | (Y1) |

This relationship implies that Y1 and both of F12 and LA1 had a close common ancestor high on the tree, with vv. 31–32 not repositioned. F12 descended from this ancestor without repositioning, but LA1, derived from it, or beside it, did reposition these verses, while other parts of the tree, including Y1 also did reposition. The same problem of identical spontaneous repositioning in different lines of descent is detected here, but with new precision as to where it took place. But the same illogicality prevails: some variations place a given manuscript high, others low—and that doesn't make sense.

Accordingly, one may speculate that the readings of a text are only partly the product of strict lineal derivation; they also can be altered by collation or conflation with other manuscripts, possibly with a text outside the division of this line of transmission, which is stipulated by the defining 'shrine' variant in v. 8. Accordingly, contradictory evidence like this (which is found wherever one turns in these many manuscripts) is of dubious value as a criterion for constructing the tree. But the daunting challenge of this evidence is to suggest that tree-building may not be the appropriate explanation for *any* variants. Even when they flow according to the logic of a tree, variants may do so only because of accidents of conflation. In fact, the chance that any manuscript or its ancestor could be the result of conflation or contamination or hybridization (call it by what prejudicial name you wish) or of spontaneous mutation (another not unprejudicial notion), sets a limit to the credibility of trees and to the resources I am using in my conjectures. If our trees reflect only a fraction of Ygdrasil, they can easily become tools merely of our self-congratulation.

A primary value to the exercise of trying to fill in the gaps of the Rosenbach Manuscript is that it challenges the Variorum tree, or trees.

His earthly sowle might couer theires not them:	3214/LA1
This earthly soule might cover theirs, not thẽ	3217/Y1
his earthly soul might cavell, those not ^{them}	3199/O36
his earthly soul may admier their's not them	3180/Y2
his erthly soule seeks after these not them.	3195/O13

The last three variants suggest that in some early version, the word 'cover' or 'covet' was 'garbled', to use one of the editors' terms ('Figure 1', γ). Some subsequent versions of these words may reflect repairs made with reference to various copies rather than direct transmission from a single source. It is not that the derivations in 'Figure 1' don't make sense. The problem is that there are other organizations of the information just as plausible—or just as implausible.

****

Nevertheless, guided by the family, I will finally offer the following conjectural text and notes on some of the controversial options and on the difficulties of weighing the evidence. And occasionally I will comment on variations within the family, even when there is no doubt as to the reading of the Rosenbach Manuscript—to stress that the family is not homogenous. Reference to the family serves as a check on wild speculation, but it brings its own chaos with it. I anticipate the day when the application of a more advanced technology to Rosenbach MS 239/22 may be able to test whether such informed conjectures are right or wrong. Since there is an actual object under discussion, objective readings may eventually be possible. When this day comes, it will perhaps serve to show that, though the Variorum editions' textual tree is philosophically problematic, it may (or might) have heuristic value anyway. After all, Ptolemy's model passed out of favour when physics challenged theology as the theoretical basis of science; but it nevertheless remained a practical tool for predicting eclipses. As we shall see, there are three unprecedented words in the Rosenbach Manuscript. If they had been illegible under infrared light, there would have been no way of supplying them from the family or from any other manuscript. The proposed method of supplying gaps in the Rosenbach Manuscript from the family of manuscripts to which the editor's tree assigns it has much to recommend it, but it is inevitably insufficient.

1   C̲om̲e Madam [c]o[m]e̲ all rest my powers d̲e̲f̲y̲e̲
2   V̲[n]till I la[bour] I in [l]abou[r] lye
3   The̲ f̲oe̲ o̲ft times hauing the foe in sight
4   [Is] ti[r]ed with standing thou[gh he neuer] fight.
                                thou[gh he do not]
5   Of with that gir[dle] l̲ik̲[e] heau[ens] zone glistering

1 One manuscript in the family addresses her as 'M:ʳˢ', another as 'Ladie'. One reads 'power' rather than 'powers'. In these notes, I will usually not specify manuscripts that can be identified through the Variorum notes. (In the note for v. 2, you will see that I do identify manuscripts; but that is because the Variorum is inaccurate or does not describe the subtle differences of spelling that concern me there.)

In the last word, 'defye', there is a strong blob of ink above the faint body of the second letter, which makes it look like an 'i'. However, I have read the blob as the separate top stroke of an 'e', because this letter links to the 'f' following from a middle position in the letter. (An 'i' would normally link from the baseline.)

2 Three manuscripts in this family say 'die' instead of 'lie'. Outside the family, four manuscripts read 'die', and one (3180/Y2) equivocates (though the Variorum regards it simply as 'die').

It may seem common sense to use the complimentary non-defective parts of words repeated in the same line to repair each other. But the matter is not so simple. Of the eighteen manuscripts in this family, three of them vary the graphics or spelling of such a word: 'laboʳ' *vs* 'labor' (3181/Y3); 'labour' *vs* 'laboure' (3193/O3); 'labour' *vs* 'labor' (3207/F3).

3 There is some difficulty reading the end of 'hauing'. In this period, present participles often end in '-inge'; but all legible examples of the ending in the manuscript of this poem are '-ing'; and so I read 'hauing'.

The Rosenbach Manuscript is clear on the repetition, 'The foe . . . the foe', but 'The foe . . . his foe' is more common in the family.

4 A common reading out of this family is 'though they neuer fight', but within it the options I offer are the only two. 'though he do not fight' appears only twice in the family.

5 'glittering' appears only once in the family, and only slightly more than half a dozen times in all the surviving manuscripts. (Poor legibility of the end of the line means it cannot actually be ruled out as a reading of the Rosenbach Manuscript.)

In the family, 'like to heav'ns' appears once and 'like the Heauens' twice. The spelling 'hauens' also occurs, and it suggests that the different words we now spell as 'haven' and 'heaven' (which are not cognates) were not easily differentiated in the seventeenth century by spelling or by pronunciation. (Where the 1609 Q1 text of Shakespeare's Sonnet 129 concludes 'heauen . . . hell', the next two (modernizing) editions, Benson's (1640) and Gildon's (1710), read 'Haven . . . Hell'.)

6   [But a] farre <u>faire</u>[r] wor[ld] encompassing
7   [Vnpin] y^t <u>spangled</u> brestplate y^t you <u>weare</u>
8   That I may see [my s]hrine that shines so faire
         [the s]hrine
9   Vnlace yor selfe for that harmonious chime
10   [Te]ls me [from you] y^t now tis yor bedd time
11   <u>Of</u> with that happy buske that I enuy
12   <u>T</u>[h]at still will be and still can stand so nigh

6 There is an interesting lexicographical problem in many manuscripts within this family as well as without. Is there one word here, 'incompassing' or 'encompassing'—or two, 'in compassing' or '⟨i⟩en compassing'? (This last, appearing in 3214/LA1, seems to change the phrase to a single word (for 'en' is not a recognized word), though graphically asunder. My field notes suggest that, missing the revision of 'i' to 'e' by ink of a different colour, the Variorum reports it merely as 'in compassinge'.) And for something more beautiful still, consider the medial capital in 'InCompassing' (3193/O3); it exposes the etymological roots of the single-word form in a prepositional phrase. (Compare *on wake* > *awake*, or *on sleep* > *asleep*, etc.) All these variants are present in the family of the Rosenbach Manuscript as is also the deficient '∧ compassing' (3198/O23). Outside the family, we see a similar range: 'en compassing', 'in Compassinge', and 'enCompassinge'.

7 Five manuscripts in the family read 'spangling'; nine others offer 'which' instead of the second 'y^t' seen in the Rosenbach Manuscript. In the family, two other manuscripts read 'spangled . . . that'. None has that reading outside the family.

8 'my shrine' appears in eleven manuscripts in the family, 'the shrine' or 'y^t shrine' in four. One reads 'That I may shrine'. One reads 'throne' for 'shrine'. And two do not have the verse at all. (See 'Thy' / 'A' / 'My', in the note for v. 28.)

9 One manuscript in the family reads 'Vntie' for 'Vnlace'. Another, 3172/O21, originally commanded the mistress to unlace herself 'from that harmonious Chime', though 'for' was eventually substituted for 'from'. (The Variorum does not record the 'from' or the presence of a substitution.)

10 Three times, 'its' or 'it is' appears in the family for 'tis'.

11 One member of the family reads 'Bushe' instead of 'buske'.
    The Rosenbach Manuscript is unequivocal in the third to last word, 'that'. The members of the family are evenly divided between 'that' and 'which'. A very common reading outside the family, including the Westmoreland Manuscript, is 'whom', which occurs once in the family.

12 The Rosenbach's 'will . . . can' is the commonest reading in the family, but there are also multiple examples of 'will . . . will' and 'can . . . will'. There is even one 'can . . . can', which is the reading of the Westmoreland Manuscript, and is dominant outside the family.

13   Y[our] gowne going of such b[eauteous] state re[ue]<u>al</u>[es]
        Y[ᵉ]   re[ue]<u>al</u>[e]
        Y[ʸ]
14   A[s] when from flowery meads hills shadowes ste<u>al</u>[es]
                                                    ste<u>al</u>[e]
15   [Of with y]<u>oure</u> [wiry coro]nett an[d] show

13 'Your' is the majority reading for the first word of this verse. The family offers
'The' once, and outside the family 'Thy' occurs once. In reading this hand, it is
hard to differentiate capital 'Y' from small 'y'; and so my use of a capital at the start
of the verse is arbitrary. See the unobliterated 'You' or 'you' at the start of the seventh verse on the verso page, and judge for yourself. But 'Y' can also be the letter
thorn—and so I must offer 'Yᵉ' and even 'Yʸ', as optional readings. (I have never
seen 'Yʸ', but I suppose it exists somewhere in contemporary mss.)

My earlier, Swiss-cheese, version of this text showed an unread space at the end
of this word: 'gowne[ ]'. I had put it there because I was aware that some texts read
'gownes' here or 'gowne's'; but the square brackets are gone in the second version,
because none of the texts in the present family reads so. This is an example of how,
through the help of the tree, one may come to *some* degree of conviction about what
the text likely reads, although the manuscript remains obscured.

13, 14 In the infrared image, the exact spelling of the rhyme is obscured by curva-
ture into the margin. The rhyme 'reueales' | 'steales' may seem common sense to
us on the basis of grammar in the standard text, where 'state' governs 'reveales' and
'shadowe' governs 'steales' (as they do in the Westmoreland Manuscript); but most
of the members of the family say 'shadowes <u>steales</u>', though one obeys grammar
like this—'shaddow steales', and two like this—'shadowes steale'. The latter solution transfers the grammatical problem back to v. 13, where both manuscripts in
question now read 'state reueale', which is bad for grammar but good for rhyme.
One member of this family (3200/O38) records 'state reveals' and 'shadow's steale',
and so preserves grammar, but at the expense of rhyme. Here, curiously, a
knowledge of the diverse readings of the family does not deliver one to relative
certainty about a reading, as did the crux about 'gowne' earlier in the verse.

15 'youre' is the necessary reading here, but it is found in only one other manuscript in this family—as 'yʳ'; fifteen others read 'that' or 'yᵗ'. The latter could easily
be misread as 'yʳ'. It is sobering to think that if the following words pass through
standard abbreviations, they can easily be confused with one another: *your, that, thee,
the, thy, it* (i.e., '*yt* '').

Almost all manuscripts read 'wiry', but 'rich' and 'wiers' occur once each outside the family, and 'uery', 'v⟨i⟩erie', and 'Iuorye' once each within. More to the
point, these two family members read 'yᵗ uery', 'that v⟨i⟩erie', and 'that Iuorye';
and, because of the common 'that', I tend to reject the nouns in these phrases as
possible readings for the Rosenbach Manuscript; and so I adopt 'wiry'. Here again,
I find the tree helpful in limiting conjecture.

16   [The hairy diadem th]at on you doth grow
        [The hairy dyadems th]at
17   [Now off with those shoes] and then softly tread
                [these]
18   In this [loues] hallowe[d] temple th[is] soft bed.
                [loue]   *[end of 52v]*

19   In such white robes heauens Angells vse to bee   *[start of 53r]*
20   Recea[ued] of men t[hou] Angell bringst with thee
21   A heauenly Maho[m]etts Pa[ra]dise a[nd] though

16 The second option I list for the start of this verse, 'dyadems', is found once in the family. 'That happye diadem; that there doth growe' is another one-time reading in the family. I reject taking parts of the latter to restore the Rosenbach Manuscript because the words which can be read in the Rosenbach Manuscript do not match its 'that there'.

17 To judge by the illegible space at the beginning of the line, this verse begins with 'Now off'; but six members of the family begin 'Off'—and one begins 'Of now'.
     'these' is found only once in the family, but more commonly without.
     Instead of '[sof]tly', one manuscript in the family reads 'safely', a reading common outside it. (One member of the family reads 'then ∧ treade', omitting either variant.)

18 Where the Rosenbach Manuscript reads 'hallowe[d]', two members of the family have 'Hollowed' (a reading not uncommon outside the family). The word before this is hard to read in the Rosenbach Manuscript, and its identity is unsure. Two other texts in the family read 'Loue-hallowed temple' or 'Loue Hallowed Temple', and outside the family occur several similar examples, and also two examples of 'loue hollowed'.

19 In the family, there are two examples of the past participle, 'vs'd', a common reading throughout the manuscripts (including the Westmoreland Manuscript).

20 There are two 'Reuiew'd by men' in the family, but the legible beginning of the verse in the Rosenbach Manuscript, 'Recea[   ] of men', precludes this reading there. The preposition 'of' is unique, not only in this family, but also among all the manuscripts. (This unanticipated diction points to the limits to restoration of the text of the Rosenbach Manuscript from other members of the family—or from any other manuscript.) 'Recciucd by men' is the all-but-universal reading. There is one 'receau'd w^t men' (3195/O13), however, outside the family. And in the 1669 edition, there is the unprecedented but influential 'Reveal'd to men'.

21 The Rosenbach Manuscript is unequivocal: 'heauenly'. But both in the family and without occur these three variants: 'heauen like', 'heauenlike', and 'heauenly'. To modern eyes and ears, the first suggests that the woman brings a heaven that is

22   All Spirits walke in white we easily know

23   By this t[hese] Angells from an euill spright
              t[hose]

24   They set o^r hair[es] but these o^r flesh vpright
              hair[e]

25   Licence my rouing han[ds] and lett th[e]m goe .

particularly like Mohammed's; the second suggests that Mohammed's paradise is like heaven; and the last, that his paradise is heavenly. 'Like' and '-ly' are cognate, and so the latter two variants show a compound at different stages of evolution, where it offers itself as two discrete words. Both of the variants 'like' and '-ly' function as adverbs. However, 'heauen like' potentially offers a combination of noun and adjective. I say 'potentially' because, in the early seventeenth century, the presence of a space between 'heauen' and 'like' did not preclude their being taken as a single word, an adverb. (In modern English, we can write either 'cannot' or 'can not'. The two formulations have overlapping ranges of pronunciation and of stress; they are not as far evolved as 'Off' and 'Of', which no longer mean or sound the same.) It is not clear that in the early seventeenth century the differences among these three graphic readings would have been able to discriminate among the three interpretations offered. It may be that contemporary pronunciations of the variants could have stipulated different grammatical structures, but graphics could not.

Atypically for the hand in this manuscript, the 'h' in 'Maho[ ]etts' is italic. Use of italics for the styling of proper names is common in contemporary manuscripts.

22 The first word in the verse in all members of the family is 'All', and therefore seems not in doubt in the Rosenbach Manuscript. But both 'Ill' and 'All' are very common outside the family, 'Ill' being the reading of the Westmoreland Manuscript. (I do not offer it as an option here, however, because of unanimity in the family.)

23 There are three examples of 'those Angells' in the family, and one each of 'an Angell' and 'all Angels'. 'an' is an unlikely candidate for reading in the Rosenbach Manuscript because of grammar ('Angells' is plural), and it and the 'all' are both unlikely spatially, for the presence of a longer word is suggested, either 'these', by far the more common, or 'those'. The family once offers 'Angells by'.

24 'haire' is the reading of five members of the family, and it is also found outside. The second 'o^r' reads 'the' in a small number of manuscripts outside the family, including the Westmoreland Manuscript.

25 'rouing' is clear, but the family includes 'roaming' three times and 'rauing' once. As noted above, p. 98, the period may be stray ink; it sits high and far off the last word.

26   Be<u>hin</u>d before [a]<u>bo</u>ue betweene belo<u>w</u>

26 The itinerary of the licensed hand is not in doubt in MS 239/22;

Behind before aboue between below

—but in the family there are three other routes, which bulk large.

Before, behind, aboue, betweene, belowe.
Behinde, before, betwene, aboue, below.
Before, behind a boue beneath, belowe

(These are used twice, thrice and once, respectively.) If in the Rosenbach Manuscript several of the terms had been illegible, it would have been very difficult to practice safe projection of them or their sequence from other manuscripts in the family: in this verse, one's projections would inevitably declare something about one's own sexual fantasies. Manuscripts outside the family are no less restrained than those within:

Aboue, behinde, before, beneath, belowe.	3167/B46
Before, behinde, betweene, above, belowe.	3176/HH1
beetweene, before, beneath, aboue, below	3190.5/WB1
Behinde, Before, Above, Beneath, Below.	3197/O22
Betweene, before, aboue beneath, below	3203/B39
Before, behinde, ⟨betwene⟩ beneath, aboue, below,	3204/B43
Behind, before, aboue, betweene, belowe.	3155/O20

(Most examples of this grateful vicissitude occur more than once, but I have listed only a single manuscript for each.) The hands' *first* destination can be behind, before, above, or between; the *second*, before or behind; the *third*, above, between— on second thought (and, effacing 'betwene' in a different roving hand) *beneath*—or before; the *fourth*, between, above, or beneath; and the *fifth* merely below. (The last position is the rhyme word, of course; lack of variation here should not be taken as a failure of erotic imagination. And, indeed, 'below' is a very handsome cul mination.)

All this is the stuff of the funniest collational note in English literature, a *Kama Sutra* in miniature. But, if you are looking for a tip or for a laugh, don't try reading the textual notes of any of the editors: for the work there is textual, not sexual. Grierson's and Gardner's listings of variants for this verse are meagre indeed. And though the Variorum's is full, it collates haltingly, one word at a time, so that the feel of the verse is beyond one's grasp. You will see what I mean by looking at the note for the first of the five words in the verse:

26 Behind,] Betweene,   B8 B39 CJ1 F5 WB1 Y6; Before,   B43
F4 F12 HH1 LA1 Y1 G; Aboue,   B46; ~‸   H3 NY1 P1 TT1;
~.   TT2.

(Not *quite* a turn-on, is it?)

Why should this verse be so variant? In the tightly organized dissemination of text that constitutes the Variorum editors' tree there is no allowance made for

27   Oh my Ameri[ca] my new found [l]and
28   Thy kingdome [i]s safest when with one man m[an]d
            [ti]s
29   My Mi[ne] of precious stones [ ] my Empery

authorial variants at the top of the tree. If, therefore, it is those who transmitted the
text that are responsible for the variant, we might suppose the lack of syntax binding these five disyllabic words made them prone to being reorganized in the memory. But faulty memory is not the only explanation. It may be that those who
copied out the poem felt free to participate in it, not just to recreate it by copying.
Certainly, since the right rhythm is guaranteed in all arrangements of the words in
the line, they could indulge themselves. Having constructed the line as a sequence
of appositive disyllables, Donne could well have imagined that he might provoke
readers not only to read the verse, but also to toy with it. Is authority, then, to be
limited to the author?

27 Two family texts repeat the 'o' before the second 'my', but there doesn't seem
room for this word in the Rosenbach Manuscript.

28 'Thy' (which mitigates the speaker's egotism) is unique among all reported
manuscripts. No amount of comparison within the family of the Rosenbach
Manuscript or beyond it would ever have brought one to surmise this word. Only
seeing is believing. (There is one 'A' outside the family. All other manuscripts read
'My'. The first printed edition reads 'The'.)

    With some reluctance, I read 'kingdome is', but not because I can actually find
'is' in the family, where the readings are 'kingdome's safest', 'kingdomes saffest',
'Kingdoms, safest', 'kingdome safest', etc., but because there is an unexpectedly
large space between 'kingdome' and 's'. The 's' is clear, but the space before it is
foggy. One might suppose it contains 'ti' (for there is a suggestion of a 't'); however,
'tis' is not a reading in any of the other manuscripts. Outside the family, there is
only one occasion I see 'is' used (in 3182/O34, a 'lost scribal conflation'), and it follows 'Kingdome⟨s⟩' (that is, 'kingdomes' with its final letter deleted). The problem
is whether 'kingdomes' is subject and verb or a possessive noun.

    Three members of the family read 'with one t'is mand'. Another did read this,
but has been altered to read 'with one man man'd'. Conversely, one manuscript
that originally read 'with one man mand' has had a 'tis' inserted after 'man'. The
presence of a third-person, singular pronoun near the end of the verse renews
thought that 'tis' might be found in the illegible earlier part of the Rosenbach version of the line.

29 One manuscript in the family reads 'stone'.

    There is a rather large space before 'my', and there may be some oblique stroke
there running from lower left to upper right. In some manuscripts there is punctuation there. I have not speculated how to fill this space.

30   [h]ow blest am I in this dis[couering thee]?
33   full nakednesse all eyes are due to thee
34   As soules vnbodyd bodyes vncloathd must bee
35   To tast whole ioyes gemmes that you weam[en v]se
36   Are as Atlantas bals cast in men[s] views
37   That when a f[ooles] ey[e] lighteth on a gemme

30 In some manuscripts, the last word is 'discouery'. That seems not the reading of the Rosenbach Manuscript, because the illegible characters there extend over more space than that word alone would take up. In any event, the punctuation at the end of the verse forbids enjambment into the traditional v. 33 (not v. 31, for vv. 31–32 are 'repositioned' after the traditional v. 46) also offers 'discouering the' (read either modern 'thee' or modern 'the') and 'discouering thy'. The legibility of 'dis' forbids the reading found once in the family, 'thus receiuing thee'. See pp. 90–91 above for further discussion of this line, especially in light of the frequent repositioning of the next couplet, the traditional ll. 31–32.

33 'ioyes' is the more common reading here, but 'eyes' is also found, four times, in this family alone.
    In the fog, 'nakednesse' seems to terminate with a double Greek-style 'e', but, as this spelling is so unusual, I have thought to take the first of them to be a round 's'. (A round 's' directly after a long one is a familiar graphic convention, but there are no (other) examples of it in this poem in the Rosenbach Manuscript.)

34 Within this family, the variants for this verse are numerous; but, as it is mostly legible, they are therefore of only academic interest. The first word is variously 'As' or 'All' or may be eliminated; 'vncloth'd' is once 'clothd'; 'must' can also be 'would' or 'should'.

35 In this family, 'you weamen vse' is once 'youre women chuse'. Instead of 'you' 'yee' appears twice, and 'y^e' once.

36 'Atlanta[ ]s' in my Swiss-cheese version is replaced by 'Atlantas' in the second, not because I can actually see that the apostrophe sometimes found here in the manuscripts of this poem is not present, but because the loop of the 'y' in 'ioyes' in the line above, fills the space between 'a' and 's' where the last letter of 'Atlantas' would normally go: evidently the terminal 's' was spaced off the word so as to dodge the tail of the 'y'.
    In the family, 'as' reads 'like' five times, 'of' once.

37 In the family, 'lighteth' is once 'lightneth' and once 'lightining' (in the phrase 'That ^a_∧ fooles eye lightining') or 'lightn⟨eth⟩ing', once 'ligthteth', and so on. There seems confusion whether the word is derived from 'alight', 'lightening' or 'lightning'. In the family, 'eye' is once 'sight'.

38 See the editors' extensive tree for this notably corrupted verse, their 'Figure 1' (p. 108 above).

38   his greedy eye must cou[e]tt th[eres not] them
                       cou[r]tt th[eres not] them
                                th[ese and not] them
                                th[es not] them
                                th[eirs & not] them
39   Like vnto bookes with gaudy couerings made
40   ffor lay men [are a]ll weomen [th]us arraid?

The Rosenbach Manuscript's 'must' is unprecedented in the family—and beyond. (The others in the family read 'might', except once 'may', a reading common outside the family, where it is the reading of the Westmoreland Manuscript.) If this area of the Rosenbach Manuscript had proved illegible, nothing on the Variorum tree would have led us to the true reading.

How to fill in the gap in 'cou[ ]tt' in the Rosenbach Manuscript? The clear presence of 'greedy eye' in this manuscript (the reading 'eye(s)' is found some five times in the family, and never outside it) might lead one also to read 'court' (which always accompanies it in these five manuscripts). A non-candidate from the family is 'couer', which occurs only with 'earthly soule', twice, and only within the family. Within the family, 'couet' occurs only with the variants 'Gredye thought', 'earthy eye', and 'earthly soule', but outside the family it is dominant (though 'court' is also found), and is the reading of the Westmoreland Manuscript. The variation of diction 'covet' vs 'court' depends on the letters 'e' and 'r'. 'e' connects to the letter following from its mid-point or lower (see 'Princes', l. 3 of 'The Perfume' on 52v of the Rosenbach Manuscript), whereas 'r' connects from the top in one of its shapes (again see 'Princes') or with a rising stroke from the baseline in another (see 'coarse' in the last line of 'The Perfume'). But the shape of the letter is hazy in the Rosenbach Manuscript, and the only certainty is that a single small letter is lacking. The seeming double 't' at the end of the word in the Rosenbach Manuscript may be thought to rule out 'couer'. (I say 'seeming' because one of the vertical strokes is so faint, I cannot be sure it is not paper texture rather than ink.) But this exclusion does not help decide between 'court' and 'couet', which can look alike in secretary hand, though the spelling of 'courtt', with two t's, looks odd, and is not found in any other manuscripts, whereas 'couett' is .

39 According to the Variorum editors, the 'lost scribal revision' has two divisions, based on v. 8. The division that includes the family divides again, into two branches, characterized by the readings 'Like pictures or like gay bookes coverings made' and 'Like unto bookes with gaudy Couerings made' (in the branch where the Rosenbach Manuscript belongs).

40 Five members of the family read only '‸ women are' instead of 'are all women' (or 'are oͬ women', which appears once), but the gap in the manuscript is large enough for the usual 'are all'. Also found are 'are like women'. 'when thus arrayde' appears once in the family, 'should bee thus arrayd' three times.

41   <u>T</u>hemselues are musick bookes [which] only wee
42   (<u>W</u>hom th[eir] impu[ted grace] will dig[ni]fye
43   <u>M</u>ust bee reuea[l]<u>d then</u> S[weet that I may]<u> know</u>
44   <u>A</u>s liberally a[s] to a <u>m</u>idwife [shew]
45   Thy [s]el[fe] cast all <u>yea thi</u>[s wh]<u>ite linnen</u> [henc]e
46   Ther is no pennance [due] to [i]nn<u>oce</u>nce.
31   [To] enter in [those bonds is] to be free
          [these bands is]
          [those bands is]
          [these bonds is]

41 'musick' outnumbers 'mystic' twelve to five in this family—the only place it occurs. One member begins 'No they are musik bookes'. Outside the family, 3204/O43 originally read 'mislikt'; it was altered to 'misticke'.

42 I see no evidence of a closing parenthesis for this line. In the family, 'would' appears once for 'will'.

43 In the family, most examples of v. 43 begin 'Must see', but there are three examples of 'Must haue' and one of 'Must bee', the Rosenbach reading. The only other occasion in the family in which the verse begins 'Must bee' provides my reading for the gap at the end of the verse, 'S[weet that I may]'. The other contender from the family is 'sure that I may', but on the two occasions in which it occurs, the verse begins 'Must haue', which does not match the Rosenbach Manuscript. 'Sweet' (and even once 'sweet duck') can be found occasionally outside the family, but it is the main reading within it. The Westmoreland Manuscript reads 'Must see reuealed. Then since I may know'.

44 The substantive readings in the verse are not in doubt. But elsewhere in the family there are two examples of 'as to thy midwife' (which is found in the influential 1669 printing) and one of (the rather comical) 'As a Midwife' (3193/O3).

46 The Variorum's test for the 'lost scribal revision', 'due to innocence', cannot be fully made out here, but is not in doubt. All members of the 'family' substantively read 'There' or once 'Thers'.)
    One manuscript, 3211/F12, reads 'ignorance', but it was altered to 'innocence' by the same hand.

31 The cognates 'these' and 'those' (like 'There' and 'Here', discussed above) are options found throughout the full range of manuscripts, not just in the family. Furthermore, inside the family and outside, either word can be preceded by 'in' or 'into', and so I can't rule out the possibility of either 'those' or 'these' in my reconstruction of the Rosenbach Manuscript. 'these' and 'those' seem able to be spontaneously substituted for each other, like 'bonds' and 'bands', each of which can also follow 'in' or 'into'. Thirteen family texts read 'into', two read 'to', and three read 'in'.

32 'should' is a common variant of 'shall', but it can be ruled out here. I have chosen 'hand is' before 'set', but in the family there is one 'hand shall set', one 'hand

32   There wher my [hand] is sett my [se]ale [sh]<u>all bee</u>
47   To teach the[e I am] nak[ed] f[irst why] <u>than</u>
48   What needs [tho]u [haue] more c[o]ue<u>ring then a man</u>

it self' and one 'hands are sett'; this latter I especially reject because it also originally read 'selfe' (later altered to 'seale', possibly in the same hand). But all these
rejected readings are spatially inappropriate.

47, 48 The two modern words 'than' and 'then', which are cognates, were not to
be distinguished in early seventeenth-century spelling. Some texts have the same
spelling in both verses (either 'then' or 'than') and some have different spellings,
either 'then . . . than' (the usage in the Rosenbach Manuscript and the Westmoreland Manuscript) or 'than . . . then' (the modern usage).

   Often in contemporary hands, no difference can be detected between 'W' and
'w'. I have arbitrarily reported 'What', merely because the verses in this hand usually start with a capital.

****

As this reconstruction is merely a first stab in the dark of these letters, it
may be best to leave weighty conclusions (and revisions) till later,
especially if there might soon be more sophisticated infrared equipment
by which to read the manuscript and evaluate my representation of it.
In the meantime, however, for good reasons we can conclude that the
experience of peering into obscurity with this invisible wavelength of
light has not entirely wasted our time. In general, the essay demonstrates a new and useful tool, infrared reflectography, to all those trying
to read obliterated texts. In particular, it demonstrates, with qualifications, the usefulness of the highly elaborated tree of transmission proposed by the Variorum edition of Donne's elegies. The recovery of
some of this censored text in the Rosenbach MS 239/22 offers three
unprecedented readings for Donne's elegy—'of' in v. 20, 'Thy' in v. 28
and 'must' in v. 38 (the last two being of aesthetic consequence).

   In the place of ineffable darkness, technology offers us some chaotic
legibility.

NOTES

1 The manuscript is identified as item 3214.5 in Peter Beal, *Index of English Literary Manuscripts*, Vol. I, Part 1: 'Andrewes–Donne' (London & New York, 1980), pp. 497–567. Hereafter, the Beal numbers of manuscripts newly referred to will be given in the body of the essay, often along with the sigla of the Variorum edition, for which, see n. 2. I am grateful to the Rosenbach Museum & Library, Philadelphia, for permission to reproduce photographs of its holding, 'Commonplace book MS 239/22', and especially to its Curator, Elizabeth Fuller for her kind and practical assistance, including arranging and funding transportation of the manuscript for photography. I am also grateful for the expert technical services of Joe Mikuliak, Conservation Photographer, Philadelphia Museum of Art. Thanks as well to my colleague Jerry Melbye and his former student, Christine Warias, now a forensic document examiner, for their early guidance in my quest for information about infrared technology.

This essay was written during my tenure of a Mellon Fellowship at the Folger Shakespeare Library. My deepest gratitude for this wonderful experience to the Foundation and the Library, and to David Kastan, Stephen Orgel and Peter Stallybrass for their support of my work on Donne. I am also indebted to Erindale College, University of Toronto for an internal SIG grant (from funds allocated by the Social Sciences and Humanities Research Council of Canada) for photography of the manuscript. At my college, I am indebted to Brandon Besharah, Alison Dias and Steve Jaunzems for support in graphics, and to Rishi Arora and Stefan Neuffer for computer support.

My essay is greatly enriched by the discovery of a new excerpt from Donne's 'To his mistress going to bed' by Mark Bland, which he has kindly allowed me to announce here, along with his identification of the hand and of the probable date.

2 Gary A. Stringer (gen. ed.), *The Variorum Edition of the Poetry of John Donne*, Vol. 2: *The Elegies* (Bloomington, Indiana, 2000), pp. 175 and 178. (The Variorum siglum for this manuscript is 'R3'.) In this essay, I will often designate manuscripts with reference first to the number in Beal's catalogue, then to that in the Variorum. Thus, Rosenbach MS 239/22 is '3214.5/R3'.

3 A note on transcription: An '-s' that is a counter-clockwise circle, with a finishing stroke downward (and often to the right), below the base line, as in 'things' in v. 8 (to which we may contrast the shape of the '-s' in 'things' in v. 4, a clockwise circle finishing upwards, above the x-height) is often transcribed as '-es' in English, or also as either '-es' or '-is' in Latin, even though there is no graphic evidence of two separate letters. The projected vowel was grammatically functional in Latin, but I am not convinced it is justified in such a late period of English as the early- and mid-seventeenth century. In my work on Donne, I have encountered this same down-turned terminal 's' directly after an 'e', and it would be very strange to transcribe the word in question, as 'meade[e]s' or 'meadees' (see v. 14 in 3182/O34, Bodley's MS Rawl. poet. 117, where the poem is located by three different references: 58r & 59v [*sic*], or 222v & 221r rev. [*sic*], or 213v & 212r [*sic*] (in pencil)). This experience has now made me reluctant to project the '-e-' anywhere in my readings of such an '-s' in any of the manuscripts of this poem. (Elsewhere in this Bodleian manuscript, this counter-clockwise '-s' is found in 'Mahometts' (v. 21) and in 'needs' (v. 46), which is overwritten as 'needst'. The form of the letter in the revision is a common round 's', untied to the following 't'.)

4 This, along with 'The Perfume', is one of five Donne texts noted by Edwin Wolf 2nd in this manuscript, who, while an employee of Rosenbach's (before becoming the Librarian of the Library Company of Philadelphia), made a first-line index of all the manuscripts that came through Rosenbach's hands (whether they stayed in his collection or not). On 7v and on 8r appear epigrams: 'A lame begger' and 'A licentious person'; and on 44r–45v and on 51r, two elegies: 'The Bracelet', and 'Natures lay Ideot'. (I have used Grierson's names and spellings of these texts.) As with 'The Perfume', the author of these last two is identified by (Donne's) initials. (See Beal's *Index* for the actual titles in the manuscript.)

5 *Variorum*, 75, 94–95. As both vv. 7 and 9 in the full text begin with 'Though he ha', one surmises that the couplet was dropped through eye-skip in the manuscript line of transmission from which *1633* descends.

6 Herbert J. C. Grierson (ed.), *The Poems of John Donne, edited from the old editions and numerous manuscripts*, 2 vols. (London, 1912); Helen Gardner (ed.), John Donne, *The Elegies and The Songs and Sonnets* (Oxford, 1965).

7 The dating comes from Peter Beal's *Index*, item 3214.5. I see this date also on the back of the photo of opening 52v–53r provided by the Museum. If the dating after 1638 is correct, it demonstrates how, with regard to the text of 'The Perfume', the readily available printed editions of 1633 and 1635 did not supplant handwritten copy in the preparation of the Rosenbach Manuscript.

8 Unfortunately, these effects of reversed values of light are not visible in this reproduction, since, for publication, I have heightened contrast to increase legibility of the uncensored text.

9 Beal's eleventh-hour identification is in the Addenda to his *Index*, item 3214.5.

10 The entry is transcribed from Edward Arber, *A Transcript of the Registers of the Company of Stationers of London* (London, 1877), Vol. 4: 1620–1640. The Register for October 31, 1632 records that John Marriott entered for his copy '*The five Satires* written by Doctor J : Dun these being excepted in his last entrance' (and Marriott paid another sixpence).

11 Geoffrey Keynes, *A Bibliography of Dr. John Donne, Dean of Saint Paul's* (Oxford, 1973); see item 107, 'Poems not previously printed'. The footnote to that entry misleads one to think our poem also appeared in *Wit and Drollery*, London, 1661. (But it is the other subject he discusses under '*Poems previously printed*' that appeared there, 'Loves Progress'.)

12 This has now been reproduced in facsimile in *The Harmony of the Muses by Robert Chamberlain 1654: A facsimile edition with introduction and indexes by Ernest Sullivan, II* (Aldershot, 1990).

13 For examples, C. A. Patrides (ed.), *The Complete English Poems of John Donne* (London, 1985), p. 183; and T. W. and R. J. Craik (eds), John Donne, *Selected Poetry and Prose* (London & New York, 1986), p. 86. Nor did I hear the good news myself until recently; after I had confidently referred in lecture to the 'first printing, in 1669', Paul Parrish, one the Variorum editors in the audience, discreetly pointed out my error to me.

14 The Variorum records 72 manuscripts for 'The Anagram', 63 for 'The Bracelet' (which was first printed in *1635*), 50 for 'The Perfume', 48 for 'The Autumnall', and so on in diminishing numbers. (See the beginning of the 'Textual Introduction' to each elegy for tallies for the other titles.)

15 In support of a dating *c*.1640, Bland points to Stanhope's note on 2M3r: 'Sr Thomas Edmonds is today dead by whose death sr Thomas Iermane ye now Controller getteth 800 ls an year at ye least'. (This reference, Bland concludes, points to

September, 1639.) Furthermore, he reports, Stanhope's hand was larger and less controlled in the 1650s than in the recent example. At that time, the nib was also wider and the ink darker.

I am grateful to the Bodleian Library for permission to publish this image of page Ss1ᵛ (p. 314) from Selden's *Mare clausum*.

16 Contrast 'Atlanta's balls' in v. 36. A reading of Ovid leads one to expect 'Hippomenes' balls'.

17 'They are the parents of whom we are the seed of their seed, the blood of their blood, the flesh of their flesh. . . . You must not pound your Prick it causeth Frenzyes . . .'. Thanks to Laetitia Yeandle of the Folger Library for help with the Latin. (I needed no help with the—I handled the French myself.) My thanks to University of Toronto colleagues Edward A. Heinemann and Russon Wooldridge for advice about the unhistorical ('epithetic') 's' in 'bransler'.

18 There are other telling fulminations elsewhere in this book. The following struck my eye as I paged through it: 'Jhon | Dunne, | Anne | Dun | ne | un | done' (b4v); 'I loue gold better then syluar. | yet I had rather my mother | had ten thousand ls in syluar | lyinge by her then one in Gold soe shee would | giue it mee all.' (p. 62); 'a rape upon | myne honour | I would haue | rapd Sodomy | & rapd in | cest eeuen | in Cleargy | men death | without yᵉ | redemption | of readinge | or by yᵉ booke | legit, aut non legit? | Legit ut Clericus.' (p. 254).

19 The Variorum lists the verses in this manuscript as 9–12, 16, 17b–18, 22–28, 31–32, 34–35a, 45–48 (p. 178).

20 Gardner (ed.), *The Elegies*, p. 133, note for v. 46.

21 The Variorum Donne does not offer information at this level of detail; I am drawing on my photographs of the manuscripts.

22 Of course, the dozen-and-a-half manuscripts evince many spellings of this word besides 'Heere': 'Heare', 'here', 'Here', 'Heer', 'heer', 'Her', 'heere', but none of them is actually spelled out in the Historical Collation. The reason for this lack of representation is that the lemma is constructed either from the (emended) copy-text, when possible, or from merely the first document listed after the lemma, if it is not. (This list is organized alphabetically by siglum, without reference to position on the tree.) In this case, 'Heere' is the spelling of 3202/B8, first in the list of manuscripts for this particular collation. This arbitrarily-chosen manuscript happens to be at the very bottom of the tree—the lone inhabitant of the editors' only 'sub-subfamily', a category below subfamily, family, division and line. Instead of quoting this most distant descendent for the bracketed variant in A_1, the rest of which derives from the manuscript that the editors regard as closest to Donne, they offer a modernization, and so end up with an incongruous pair, 'Ther' and 'Here'.

Note that options B and B_1 ('[or for pure   B8 B39 CJ1 F5; for true   WB1]' and '[or *for pure/true*]') neglect 'due for', found in 3196/O19. (The editors' collation on p. 189 does, however, record this variant.) 'due for' occurs once, as does 'for true', whereas 'for pure' appears four times. As I go on to say in the body of the essay, if details of all the variants were introduced into the textual argument they would threaten to overwhelm the neat formulations of A and A_1 and of B and B_1. Yes, they would; but that is what evidence is for.

23 In this range of manuscripts, by the way, there are five texts that read 'H' and nineteen that read 'T'. But the identity of what lies at the top of the tree is not necessarily to be decided by majority vote. The important fact, rather, is that many witnesses of the conjectured top of the tree are in conflict. And this realization leads one to doubt the idea that this tree leads to a single source.

24 Their most repeated 'emendation' (five times in this poem) is of 'Of' or 'of' to 'Off'
   or 'off': "we have expanded to 'off' his characteristic but frequently misleading spelling
   of the word as 'of.'" (p. 177). The old-spelling editors seem unaware that modern 'of'
   and modern 'off' are cognates. (Their Indo-European cousins are German *ab*, Latin
   ab, and Greek απο.) The editors' emendation has actually mislead readers to an unhistorical disambiguation. In Late Medieval times, it was absurd to confuse one word with
   the other, because they were one and the same. Like 'travel' and 'travail', or 'busyness'
   and 'business', or 'holiday' and 'holy day', or 'metal' and 'mettle', or 'essay' and 'assay',
   or 'stationary' and 'stationery', or 'antic' and 'antique', or 'to' and 'too', or 'courtesy'
   and 'curtesy' and 'curtsy', their separation into different words, with different spellings,
   and often with different pronunciations and stresses is a late phenomenon, and was not
   confirmed in John Donne's time—or in the time of his friend, Rowland Woodward,
   the scribe of the Westmoreland Manuscript (see the Variorum edition, Introduction to
   Vol. 2, p. lxviii.) The editors' emendation is geared to the audience that speaks Modern
   English; it therefore patronizes readers who come to an old-spelling edition for historical linguistic and textual evidence. By the way, the editors leave alone the spellings of
   'than' and 'then' in the last two lines of the poem, though, by their own standards, they
   thus 'misleadingly' reverse the modern spellings of these cognates.
   See also the differences among 'newfoundland' (v. 27), 'new found lande', 'New-
   found Land', 'New found-land', and 'New-found-Land', *etc.*

25 It should be pointed out that the Variorum scrupulously offers *three* texts of 'Elegy
   15. His Parting from Her.'.

26 If these two trees are simultaneously true, one can deduce something of the period
   of transmission of the text before the primary division into lines that the editors have
   announced—'much less' or 'due to' in v. 46. In the tree for v. 38 on p. 172, the editors identify a hypothetical stage, β, just below the 'lost holograph', in which 'might'
   appears for the supposed original 'may'. Now, most of the extant manuscripts that
   read 'might' are in the line that reads 'due to' in v. 46; but two of them, B13 and B46,
   appear in the other line, 'less than'. Why is the distinction between 'may' and 'might'
   not therefore the primary division of the Variorum tree into lines? A plausible
   answer to this question, is that some words, like 'There' and 'Here' or 'bonds' and
   'bands'—or 'may' and 'might'—may be prone to spontaneous substitution, one for
   the other. In the case of v. 38, it may be their both being modal verbs that facilitates
   substitution. Or it may be the lack of consequence to the meaning of the line. These
   are not bad arguments, but the editors need to make one or the other, and see where
   it leads them. One place it could lead them, uncomfortably, is to defining a large
   vocabulary which cannot be trusted for making trees, and which, in their edited
   texts, cannot be trusted to represent what Donne wrote.

27 There is another 'due to' construction, in v. 33: 'Full Nakednes, all ioyes [or 'eyes']
   are due to Thee'. Different meanings of 'due to' pertain. For examples, Nakedness
   ought to be the *object* of every gaze; nakedness is the *cause* of every joy.

28 The sigla and collations derive from Jack Stillinger (ed.), *The Poems of John Keats*
   (Cambridge, Mass., 1978); from a facsimiles of *W²*: Stillinger (ed.), *Poetry Manuscripts
   at Harvard: John Keats* (Cambridge, Mass., 1990); and from the originals of *D* and *FC*
   and *JJ*. Stillinger's collations aim for accuracy in substantives, but not necessarily in
   accidentals. See also Stillinger, *The Text of Keats's Poems* (Cambridge, Mass., 1974),
   pp. 159–61, where he sets out a tree.

29 The holographs certainly reveal the text in layers. The transcripts do not; nor can
   they be relied upon to show any layering that may have existed in copy. We are thus
   on unequal footing when we compare documents of these two classes.

30 In *FC*, if 'at' should prove to have been written over by 'to', the case would change entirely.

31 3172/O21, 3174/H3, 3181/Y3, 3183/B16, 3189/PM1, 3191/WA1, 3192/AU1, 3193/O3, 3200/O38, 3205/B44, 3206/WC1, 3207/F3, 3209/F6, 3210/F9, 3211/F12, 3213/H2, 3214/LA1, 3217/Y1.

32 Verse 46 is written vertical in the margin in small letters, seemingly by the same hand. The first letter of 'ynnocens' is dotted, like an 'i'. (For dotted 'y' see the head-note for 'Y' in the *OED* entry.)

33 The editors claim that these verses 'reinforc[e] the innocence ascribed to the lovers in the (revised) "due to" version . . . by suggesting that they have recently entered the bonds of marriage', pp. 167–68.

34 The Variorum edition reads 'has sett' where I read 'has felt'. (This manuscript, 3193/O3, by the way, is the only one to read 'has'.) Contrast 'felt' (v. 32) with 'sett' (v. 24) in this manuscript. The resemblance of 'f' and 'long-s', and the routine non-crossing of 't' in this hand (and therefore its looking like 'l'), lead to ambiguity; these resemblances may account for the difference between my reading and the Variorum's.

35 However, the listings of the holograph *before* the revision in a summary of the larger tree, p. 192 of the Variorum edition, and also in that tree itself, pp. 193–7, imply the primacy of the holograph. One might say the same even for the listing of the holograph and the revision on the same level (contrary to my suggestion that they were equal), because the holograph is listed at the *left* (where the eye falls first). In the 'much lesse' line of transmission, 'might' occurs in 3167/B46. (As this ms resides in a sub-family, the editors might well dismiss its reading as a result of conflation.)

36 In O3, the editors render the old-fashioned 'Gredye' exactly, including its capital letter; but they present the manuscript's 'thought, may Couett theirs,' in modern spelling, as 'thought might covet theirs', without the initial capital in the verb, its round-u, or its double final consonant. Nor do they quote the two commas, the first of which, at least, was necessary, being internal to the quotation.

37 See the collation for v. 38 on p. 187: 'not] and ~ . . . B44 (>&<)'.

Francis Beaumont's Verse Letters to Ben Jonson and 'The Mermaid Club'

Mark Bland

I

Jonson understood the importance of patronage, and it has long been appreciated that his social verse served both ethical and financial ends.[1] His praise elevated the moral stature of the recipient, and was in turn remunerative in coin and kind to himself. Rather less attention, however, has been paid to the poems that Jonson received from others, and how his reputation was shaped by such estimates of, and tributes to, his worth. Yet in the first decade or so of the seventeenth century, Jonson was addressed in a large number of poems, including four major verse letters from Francis Beaumont and Sir John Roe, and a long satire on travel by Sir Edward Herbert. It was only in the 1630s that he received anything like the same kind of attention again, and by then the reasons for seeking his patronage were more predictable owing to his fame. It was during these later years that the earlier verse letters of Beaumont and Roe began to circulate more widely, the latter sometimes wrongly associated with John Donne.

In particular, Beaumont's verse letters to Jonson have been a source of biographical and bibliographical conundrums; their authorship, date, text, and context, all being subject to speculation and error. As these poems were circulated in manuscript, they offer an insight into the connections between a group of verse miscellanies; and they are informative of the complexities that the analysis of such documents offer. If various studies of early modern manuscript texts, over the last fifty years, have tended to emphasise the levels of uncertainty in the transmission history and the effect of contamination across traditions, the more significant aspect of such problems that this study reveals is their insignificance.[2] Certainly, with one poem, it is possible to establish that contamination between traditions did take place, but equally that insight does not prove a necessary pre-condition for determining the early history of the text.

II

One of the initial problems in determining the transmission history of any text in manuscript is to establish the direction in which the variants occur and, thus, how the individual copies became different from one another. In some instances (as with Jonson) a printed text or autograph manuscript offers sufficient information for a premise to be established. In other instances, as with Beaumont, no such assumption can be made, and other factors need to be taken into account where possible (such as the omission of words and lines). Details such as known dates or associations may also prove useful. Another important starting point is to look for obvious familial groups (often these stand out during collation), even if the analysis derived from such initial assumptions requires modification when the variants are studied in greater detail. There is, in fact, no ready and easy way to render the distinctions between the surviving texts of a poem without offering a close analysis of the variants. As one purpose of this article is to establish an accurate text of Beaumont's poems (in as much as this is possible), an edited version of the texts, with line numbers, is appended. In what follows, it is assumed that the reader will consult these texts as necessary. When sigla are used, these follow the proposals put forward by Harold Love.[11]

The first verse letter from Beaumont to Jonson, which begins 'The Sun (which doth the greatest comfort bring . . .)', survives in nineteen currently recorded early copies—seventeen in manuscript, and two non-authorised printed texts.[12] Of these, only one version is complete (San Marino, Huntington HM198 part 2). The remaining eighteen copies can be sub-divided into five groups. First, three manuscripts omit line 80 (Washington, Folger V.a.96, Cambridge, Mass., Houghton English 626, and Huntington HM172), whilst a fourth replaces the line with another verse (Cape Town, South African Library Grey 7.a.29).[13] Second, two manuscripts (Huntington HM198 part 1, and the fragment British Library Egerton 2421) re-order lines 9–18, with HM198 part 1 omitting lines 39–40. Third, three manuscripts (British Library Additional 30982, St John's Cambridge S.23, and Folger V.a.170) move lines 55–60 to lines 65–70, and omit lines 71–74. Fourth, three manuscripts (Oxford, Bodleian English Poetry e.97, British Library Sloane 1792, and London, Westminster Abbey 41) omit part of line 53, lines 54–56, and part of line 57, and the latter two omit part of line 23, line 24, and part of line 25. Finally, four manuscripts (Bodleian Malone 13, Houghton English 966.3, and the two copies in Trinity College Dublin 877) as well as the two printed texts (hereafter, *1640* and *1647*) lack part of line 23, line 24, and part of line 25, but retain the text at lines 53–57. Further, the four manuscripts (but not the printed texts) at line 16 all read 'marr'd' instead of 'spoil'd'. Given the significant structural differences between the various groups, the question arises as to whether such modifications happened as a consequence of textual deterioration, or whether they derive from authorial revision. In order to determine which of these outcomes is the correct one, each group will be analysed separately and then the information assembled as the discussion evolves.

The first group of poems, that either omit line 80, or substitute a new verse, may be considered alongside HM198 part 2. The omission of this line cannot be the consequence of revision, but rather must have been caused by 'eye-skip' at an early stage in the copying process. The line in HM198 part 2 and the twelve other non-fragmentary manuscripts reads 'Who have no good in me but simplicity', as does *1640*. Grey 7.a.29 reads 'in spite of fortunes, friends, and destiny', whilst *1647* has 'Who have no good but in thy company'. Thus, the version found in Grey 7.a.29 has no relationship with the version found in *1647*, and the latter (with its other variants) must be considered separately. The three manuscripts with the missing line, Folger V.a.96, Houghton 626, and HM172, are from a family that more broadly includes Bodleian Don. c.50 and Philadelphia, Rosenbach 239/23:[14] that these particular manuscripts are linked is not unusual. In fact, the texts of Houghton 626 and HM172 are almost exact copies of one another and must derive from the same underlying exemplar.

The first difference between HM198 part 2 and the four 'line 80' manuscripts is at line 5, where (in common with all other copies) HM198 part 2 reads 'Countrie stile': the four manuscripts (including Grey 7.a.29) read 'Country talke'. Similarly, at line 6, HM198 part 2 reads 'yor full Mermaide wine' against 'the full'; at line 45, HM198 part 2 reads 'saw you' against 'saw thee'; and at line 63, HM198 part 2 reads 'then I needs must cry' against 'then forc'd [do] I cry'. Finally, at line 71, HM198 part 2 reads 'fellows that show' against 'fellows that [do] know'. The number of agreements confirms that Grey 7.a.29 is from the same family and, therefore, that its alternative line 80 is an interpolation made by someone who realised that a line was missing.

The next stage of the problem is to determine the relative position of Grey 7.a.29 and Folger V.a.96 in relation to HM 198 part 2. Of the five manuscripts, only Grey 7.a.29 and HM198 part 2 have titles, with Grey 7.a.29 signed 'finis. ffr. Beaumont'. Thus, either the manuscript from which HM 198 part 2 was copied, or its parent, must have carried the attribution. Grey 7.a.29 agrees with HM198 part 2 at line 82 with the correct reading 'T'acknowledge' rather than 'To acknowledge'. At line 17, these manuscripts read (in error) 'sutlest' (in Grey, 'subtlest') for 'Sutcliffs', indicating that palaeographical confusion combined with a mis-understanding of the text was the source of that particular error. At line 33, HM198 part 2 reads 'He doth consider'. In Folger V.a.96 this becomes 'One doth consider', whereas Grey 7.a.29 and the other two manuscripts read 'We do consider'. At line 68, Folger V.a.96 gives both the subgroup reading 'of my mind' and the correct reading in common with HM198 part 2 of 'with one wind'. Further, at line 18, Folger V.a.96 agrees with HM198 part 2 to read 'write worse yet', whereas Grey 7.a.29 and the other two manuscripts read 'more yet'. The problem, therefore, is that both Grey 7.a.29 and Folger V.a.96 have separate specific associations with HM198 part 2.

For reasons that will become apparent when the full stemma of the poem is presented, the lost parent manuscript that omitted line 80 will be called *MS* 5. This manuscript was probably written in a mixed hand by a scribe with a tendency to drop the terminal e. Thus, at line 18, the scribe may have written 'wors yet', a variant that could have been read by the source of Grey 7.a.29 as 'more', and repeated by the source for Folger V.a.96 as 'wors', with the source of Houghton 626 and HM172 to mis-read, independently of Grey 7.a.29, 'more': the point being that there is a simple explanation as to why independent variation may have arisen, and it is not necessary to assume that the variant derives from another lost exemplar. Clearly, at line 33, *MS* 5 also introduced the reading 'One doth' for 'He doth': this, again, seems to have led to the variant reading 'We do' in Grey 7.a.29, and the HM172-Houghton 626 pair, as they independently attempted to make sense of the passage. Similarly, at line 68, the lost *MS* 5 must be the source for the variants 'of my mind', which is found in all of the sub-group: whether the emendation in Folger V.a.96 of 'with one wind' indicates access to another copy, a fortunate guess, or simply a correction in the underlying document is unclear.

The problem of different scribes arriving at the same mistake by independent means would appear to occur as well in Grey 7.a.29 and HM198 part 2, as both share the same error (line 17, 'sutlest' for 'Sutcliffs'), although demonstrably Grey 7.a.29 does not descend directly from HM198 part 2 (the former sharing the main errors of the sub-group): the likely cause of the error being a failure to understand the allusion. On the other hand, whilst the shared reading at line 17 is not the product of a common source, the retention of the contraction at line 82, the fact that in Grey 7.a.29 the poem has both a title and an attribution (whereas the other three manuscripts do not), and the common textual association of Folger V.a.96, Houghton 626, and HM172 with respect to other poems as well, all suggest that Grey 7.a.29 belongs to a different line of descent within the group than Folger V.a.96 and HM172-Houghton 626. To a certain extent, this conclusion is a matter of conjecture and judgment made according to the balance of probabilities: however, as both manuscripts are the best representatives of the lost *MS* 5, they are of equal relative value as secondary witnesses to that text. This is particularly true as it is unlikely that Grey 7.a.29 is as close to the lost *MS* 5 as the stemma indicates, owing to a number of variants that are not found in any other manuscript.[15] A lack of evidence in the form of a further intermediary, however, restricts the possibility for conjecture. Thus, with the caveat that we might expect there to have been at least one further manuscript that once existed between *MS* 5 and Grey 7.a.29, the first stage of the reconstruction may be drawn.

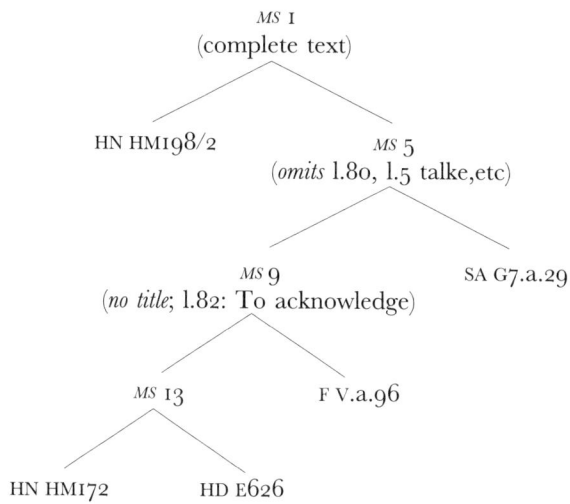

The next stage of the recension can be developed with reference to Huntington HM198 part 1 and British Library Egerton 2421. These two texts are united both by their re-organisation of lines 9–18, and the readings of 'frights' for 'fights' (line 25) and 'herein their wit' (line 32). HM198 part 1 reads 'stile', 'your full', 'saw you', 'need must cry', and 'show' (lines 5, 6, 45, 63, and 71), establishing that its relationship is not with the Grey-Folger sub-group, but HM198 part 2; Egerton 2421, being a fragment that lacks half of line 4 and half of line 5, as well as ending at line 32, shares only the second of the five variants. At line 21,

Egerton 2421 agrees with HM198 part 2 in reading 'but yet' against HM198 part 1 'and yet'; and at line 31, it reads 'all are' with HM198 part 2, against HM198 part 1 'are all'. Like HM198 part 2, HM198 part 1 retains line 80; however, it lacks lines 39–40, and has a further substantive variants.[16] Importantly, the title for the poem agrees across the stemma with Grey 7.a.29, which would tend to confirm the placement of that manuscript in the stemma of its group.

Owing to the fragmentary nature of Egerton 2421, it is impossible to know whether the omission of lines 39–40 occurred in the same manuscript as the one in which lines 9–18 were re-ordered, although this seems likely. Perhaps, the most significant variant recorded by Egerton 2421 is its title which reads 'A letter from S^r francis Beamont To Dr Donne'. This is the only text which suggests that Donne was the recipient and not Jonson. The title is clearly a later interpolation, and without authority, but it does indicate that the manuscript is probably at least at one further remove from the document that re-ordered lines 9–18—a conclusion that is reinforced by the truncation of the text. Structurally, it seems probable that the document underlying Egerton 2421 was either a booklet in which the first 32 lines were written on the final leaf of a quire (with the loss of the next quire giving rise to the note at the end of the copy, 'cætera desunt'), or that it was a separate of three half-sheets written on one side only. On balance, the former is more likely, although both explanations are possible. As a consequence, the next stage of the stemma may be constructed as follows:

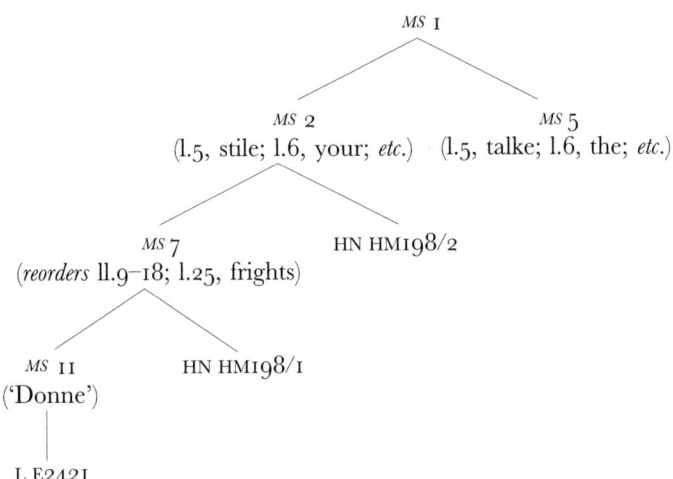

Thus, there are at least two distinct traditions of the poem, with which the next group of St John's S.23, Folger V.a.170, and British

Library Additional 30982 may be compared. These manuscripts are united by the omission of lines 71–74, the transfer of lines 55–60 to lines 65–70, and the readings 'lies' for 'is' (line 32), 'we are none that can beare' for 'here are none that make' (line 37), and 'right Cockneys' for 'downright Cockneys' (line 60, but line 70 in the manuscripts).

With the Grey 7.a.29-Folger V.a.96 group, the St John's S.23-Folger V.a.170 manuscripts share a number of common readings.[17] Thus, as well as preserving their own distinct traditions, the two lines of descent must be related through a common ancestor. On the other hand, like the HM198 parts 1 and 2, the St John's S.23 group preserves the parentheses in lines 1 and 3, and the phrase 'then I needs must cry' (line 63). This indicates the antecedent manuscript (MS 3) that gave rise to the Grey 7.a.29-Folger V.a.96 group (MS 5) and the St John's S.23 group (MS 6), introduced most, but not all of the variants; and, further, that it was textually complete (as the MS 6 line of descent retains line 80, despite the other alterations to and omissions from the text).

Within the St John's-Folger group, it is possible to make some further distinctions. Although all copies have variants, and Additional 30982 is a poor copy that probably derives from a further lost intermediary, it is demonstrable that it is linked to St John's S.23 at line 12 with the reading 'will' for 't'will', and line 82 with 'to acknowledge' for 't'acknowledge'. At line 62, the readings 'with one winde' (St John's S.23), 'with our winde' (Additional 30982), and 'with our minde' (Folger V.a.170) are probably independent, reflecting u/n, w/m, and secretary e/r mis-readings, the last being possible if the bowl of the 'e' was not

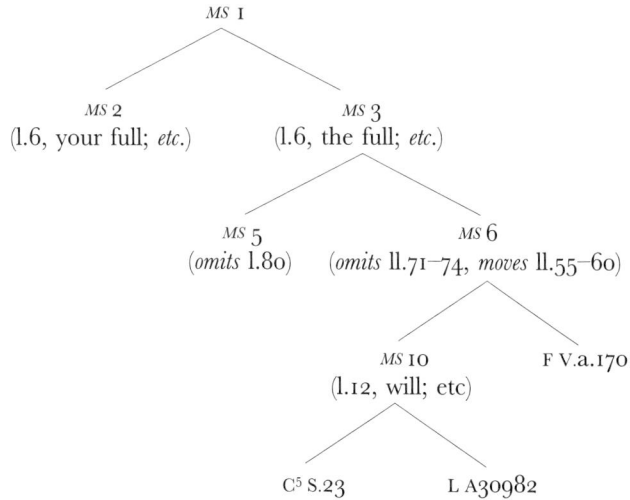

well formed. What this does help to confirm, however, is that the cause of the common mis-reading in the related *MS* 5 tradition was the result of a lack of scribal clarity in *MS* 3. With this information, therefore, it is possible to establish the next stage of the reconstruction.

What is emerging, at this stage of the analysis of variants, is that all the surviving witnesses are at some distance from the original source document. That perception will only be confirmed, and the evidence complicated further, in what follows. Second, it is evident that the primary cause of variation in the texts is usually a result of mis-reading the script of someone else, with certain kinds of confusion being common (for instance, w/m, u/n, e/r); the substitution of synonyms is less frequent, although present in all traditions. What is surprising is how early the loss of lines through eye-skip is, and how early readers (not Beaumont) restructured the text; for the stemma indicates that the copies that gave rise to the omissions were already at several removes from the author. Although the stemma is far from complete, at this point it is also helpful to establish a first summary of the information, so that what follows has a context.

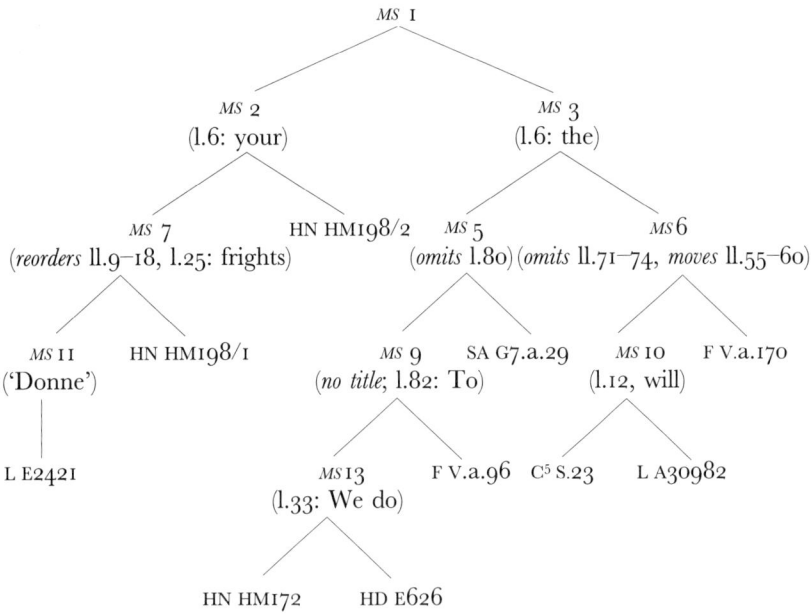

The stemma of the manuscript, as illustrated, is straightforward; from here on, the right hand side is complete; the problem is with the left hand side, as all the remaining versions are linked with HM198 part 1

in reading 'are all' (line 31) rather than 'all are', and all but one (English Poetry e.97) lack part of lines 23 and 25 and all of line 24. Four of the manuscripts that lack part of lines 23–25, read 'marr'd' for 'spoil'd' at line 14—with Trinity College Dublin 877*b* agreeing with HM 198 part 2 on several occasions,[18] and Bodleian Malone 13 agreeing mainly with Trinity College Dublin 877*a* and Houghton 966.3, but with Trinity 877*b* and HM198 part 2 twice,[19] indicating that it is antecedent to the text that gave rise to Trinity 877*a* and Houghton 966.3.

The problem emerges when *1640*, *1647*, and English Poetry e.97 are introduced. Strictly speaking English Poetry e.97 must belong to a line of recension that began prior to the omission of the material at lines 23–25; however, it agrees predominantly with the Trinity *877a-1647* group. Similarly, the two printed texts agree largely with Malone 13, Trinity 877*a* and Houghton 966.3, reading 'Lye where it will' for 'Where ere it lies' (line 18) and 'perchance' for 'perhaps' (line 42); however, they read 'spoil'd' in common with HM198 part 2, and its variant 'spilt' in English Poetry e.97 (which omits line 18). Logically, therefore, one would expect a stemma in which certain variants were introduced by the ancestor (lye where it will; perchance; etc) before the material was omitted from lines 23–25, giving rise to the Trinity *877a-1647* group on the one hand, and the English Poetry e.97 group on the other. Next within the Trinity *877a-1647* group, we would expect one line of recension for the printed texts in which certain original readings were retained (spoil'd), with 'marr'd' as the variant of the other group.

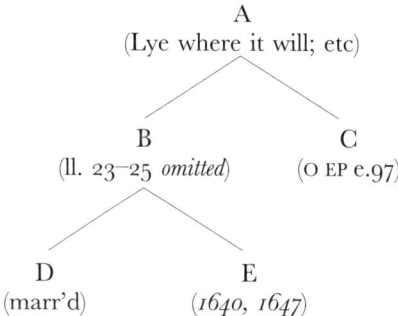

A
(Lye where it will; etc)

B   C
(ll. 23–25 *omitted*)   (O EP e.97)

D   E
(marr'd)   (*1640*, *1647*)

The first problem with this reconstruction is that, while it explains the Trinity 877*a* group, Trinity 877*b* reads (correctly) 'Where ere it lies' and (incorrectly) 'marr'd' as well as omitting the material from lines 23–25. In fact, most of the readings in Trinity 877*b* indicate that it derives from a manuscript prior to A (see footnote 16). Thus, Trinity 877*b*, *1640*, *1647*, and English Poetry e.97 are in conflict, and the source for one or another must have been contaminated.[20] As Trinity 877*b* is in the same volume as Trinity 877*a*, and as Trinity 877*a* reads 'marr'd' and omits the material from lines 23–25, it is more likely that the source for Trinity 877*b* was modified, for although it is a superior manuscript, a reading like 'marr'd' may have seemed more satisfactory, and thus have been adopted. For the moment, therefore, Trinity 877*b* will be removed from the reconstruction, until the remaining elements are resolved.

The next stage of the problem involves English Poetry e.97. This is manuscript lacks lines 17–18, 33–34 and half of line 35, as well as part of lines 53 and 57, and all of 54–56. Two other manuscripts, Sloane 1792 and Westminster 41, share the omission of material between lines 53 and 57 with English Poetry e.97, as well as the common reading 'three ways' at line 39. Like the Trinity 877*a-1647* group, these manuscripts read 'and yet' (line 21), 'are all' (line 31, with Sloane 1792 simply reading 'are'), 'perchance' (line 42), and 'every one' (line 48).[21] Separately, Sloane 1792 and Westminster 41 read 'lie where it will' at line 18, and 'gravest' at line 34. Thus, given the common links between the Trinity 877*a-1647* group and the English Poetry e.97 group, there must have been a complete copy of the poem containing all the variants listed, that then gave rise to two imperfect copies, one lacking material from lines 23–25, and one lacking material from lines 53–57.

The problem, however, does not end there, for there are further signs of contamination within these groups. As is revealed in the reconstruction below, the theoretical manuscript *A* is the lost MS 12, *B* is MS 14, and so on. The significant fact about MS 15 is not only that it lacks material from lines 53–57, but that it has the variant reading at line 39, 'three ways to grind'. This reading is present in *1640* and Malone 13. On the other hand, Westminster 41 reads 'marr'd'. Otherwise, these texts clearly belong within their groups. It is possible, therefore, that at some stage two manuscripts, perhaps MS 16 and MS 18, were compared by different users and some mild contamination across the traditions took place. (Perhaps fortunately, this insight is not a necessary precondition for the establishment of a copy-text). It is also likely that the editor of *1640* compared at least two copies of the text and adopted the 'three ways' reading, otherwise retaining the better text.

On the other hand, the editor of *1647* (presumably the publisher Humfrey Moseley) completely rewrote the ending of the poem, changing the second half of line 80, and adding an extra couplet. The gist of the change was to replace Beaumont's modest deferral to Jonson with a coarser sense of their conviviality. The point, in the political context of the Civil War, is that their friendship might be contrasted with the divisiveness of England in 1647. For Moseley (and the theme recurs in the collection of Cartwright's plays and poems),[22] Jonson is symbolic of another more amiable time. That the change weakened the ending of the poem, shifting the emphasis from Beaumont's modest gratitude, is in hindsight obvious, but Moseley's purpose was to reinforce the contrast with times past to an audience that would remember its difference from the present. Interestingly, the source that he modified in *1647* appears to have been that used for *1640*.

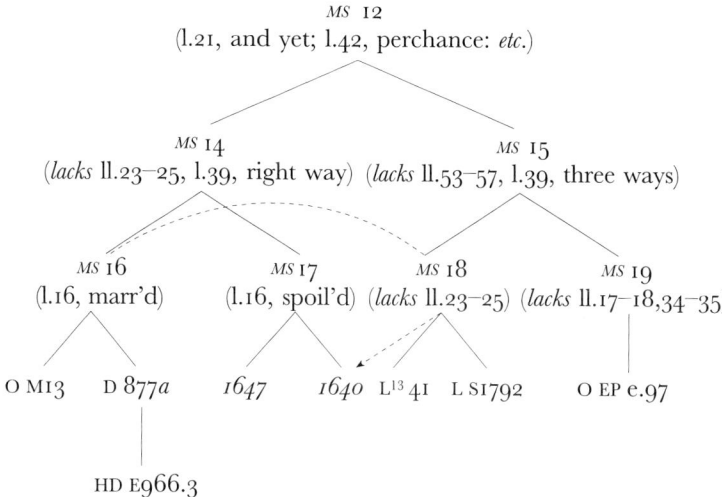

The final problem is to link and explain the connections between *MS* 2, HM198 part 2, HM198 part 1, Trinity 877*b*, and *MS* 12. Earlier, it was established that the source readings for *MS* 2 were 'stile', 'your full', 'saw you', 'need must cry', and 'show' (lines 5, 6, 45, 63, and 71). As well, *MS* 2 must have varied from *MS* 3 in reading 'haue no good' rather than 'know nothing' (line 80). Some other features of this document include the presence of an opening parenthesis in the first line ('The sun (which doth . . .') which is found in both HM198 part 1, and in the *MS* 3 tradition in Folger V.a.170; and line 80, which HM198 part 1 records as enclosed in parentheses. It is also possible that *MS* 2 read 'Sutclifs' or 'Sutlifs', whereas *MS* 3 read 'Suttcliffs' (line 17): the difference resulting in the misreading in HM198 part 2 'sutlest' which is less likely to have occurred if there had been the double 'ff'. There can be little doubt that there was an intermediary between the autograph and HM198 part 2: the punctuation of the surviving manuscript is simply too poor to have come from the original, and it is far more likely that there was a further lost intermediary than that there was none at all.

When Trinity 877*b* is introduced into the stemma, several further details are clarified. Like HM198 part 2, Trinity 877*b* reads 'Where ere

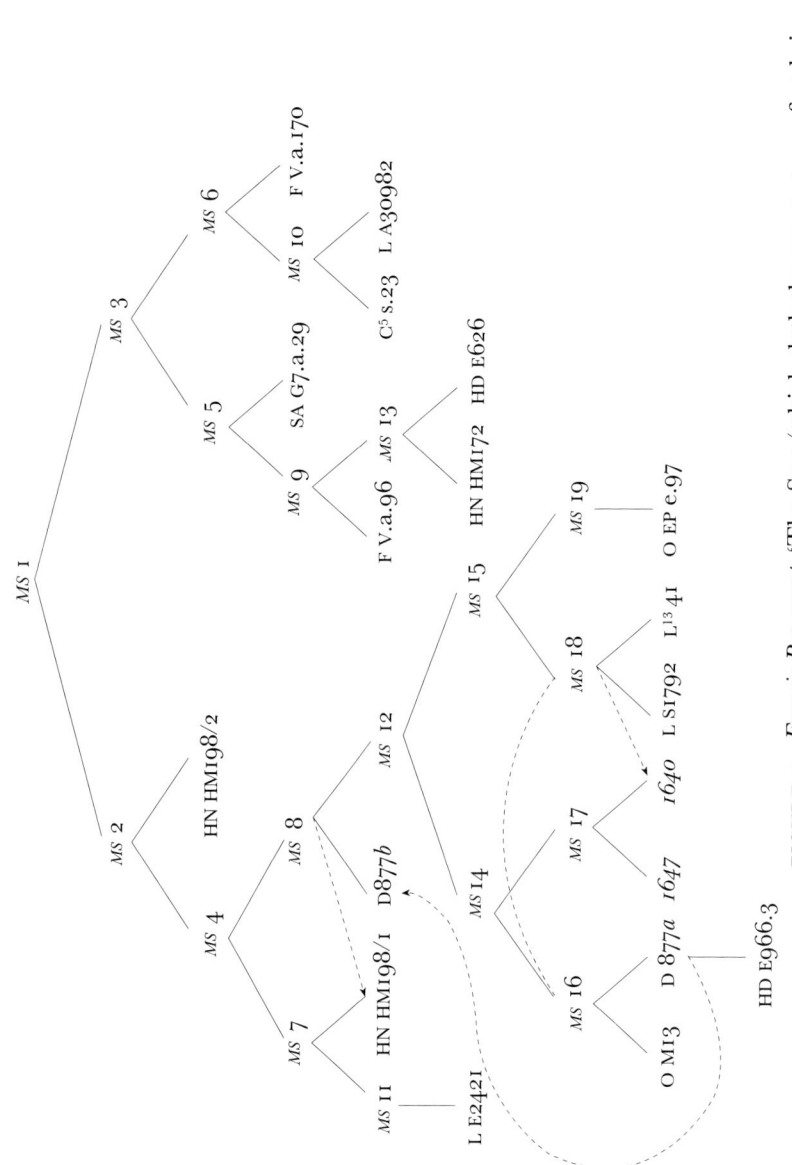

FIGURE 1. *Francis Beaumont*, 'The Sun (which doth the greatest comfort bring . . .)'.

Obviously, it is possible to modify the data (in particular, to adopt uniform spelling and remove all punctuation), or weigh the variants; however such an approach involves a degree of mis-representation, not least when one tries to analyse the distance between copies rather than their relationship. Based on genetic analysis, the selected copy-text would, in fact, have been Trinity 877b (admittedly a better choice than Simpson's Trinity 877a). More problematically, the two most distant manuscripts (that also formed a pairing) were the fragment Egerton 2421, and the copy-text HM198 part 2. In the former case, the fragmentary nature of the text may explain why the manuscript was perceived as significantly different, but with HM198 part 2 what the distance appears to have identified is that the text is more closely related to the ancestor—a reading of the diagram that is counter-intuitive.

The point of these comments is not to repudiate the methodology (the techniques involved were valid and the data were of real use and interest), but to emphasise that the results can be counter-intuitive, and that they need to be combined both with traditional Lachmannian analysis, and an understanding of the material evidence, to be of genuine use—at least as far as early modern manuscript studies is concerned.[27]

One of the more interesting results of the genetic analysis was to suggest that Additional 30982, HM198 part 2, and Folger V.a.96, were the most distant manuscripts from each other for the purposes of textual analysis, whereas a Lachmannian analysis groups them more closely together. These manuscripts, along with the Holgate miscellany (New York, Pierpont Morgan Library 1057) are the four sources for Beaumont's second verse letter to Jonson, 'Neither to follow fashion . . .', the text of which was first printed by E. K. Chambers, who knew only of the Holgate miscellany and Additional 30982.[28] Simpson took his text directly from Chambers.[29]

Stemmatic analysis again indicates that the best text of the poem is HM198 part 2, with the next best text being Folger V.a.96: that these are the two copies that were not known to Chambers indicates that the received text needs emendation. HM198 part 2 is distinctive for preserving a number of evidently correct readings including 'I owe', 'will best', 'leaue these lines as cleare', 'Preachers cite to their Auditors', 'A help' and 'the *Grinne*' (lines 8, 9, 17, 19, 22, and 30), thus confirming two of the three amendments proposed by Chambers (cleare, *The Grinne*). HM198 part 2 also has the incorrect reading 'Sendes' for 'Send' (line 14), is weak on punctuation, and erratic on the use of capitals. Although the stemma shows it at one remove from the original, it is likely to have been copied at one or more removes.

On the other hand, Folger V.a.96, Holgate, and Additional 30982 are later manuscripts united by a number of variant readings. Thus Folger V.a.96 reads 'do owe' (line 8), which is contracted to 'dew' in Additional 30982, and altered to 'to owe' in Holgate. Similarly, Folger V.a.96 and Additional 30982 read 'are best' (line 9), with Holgate reading 'best'. The level of agreement becomes clearer with all three manuscripts reading 'keepe these lines as deere', 'Preachers apte', and 'An helpe' (lines 17, 19 and 22). Of the problematic pseudo-play, 'the *Grinne*', all texts are variant: Folger V.a.96 reading '*Gennie*', Holgate 'geinne', and Additional 30982 'Ginne'. The problem, it would seem, is a combination of secretary *r* with secretary *e*, together with the number of minims that can be re-ordered into different letters. Beaumont, at this point, was poking fun at Marston and Sharpham (whom Jonson called 'rogues'),[30] as well as the ways in which plays were commissioned on serial themes.

On the other hand, Folger V.a.96 has a number of variants that agree with HM198 part 2 against Holgate and Additional 30982. Thus, Folger V.a.96 reads 'that stile' (line 13), whereas Holgate and Additional 30982 read 'the stile'; similarly, Folger V.a.96 reads 'his miserie' (line 27), rather than 'this miserie'; 'As his' (line 30), rather than 'As is'; and 'Ionson' (line 44), rather than 'Iohnson'. Folger V.a.96 also introduces a number of variants that are unique to that copy, including 'showers' for 'sharers', 'converse' for 'commerce', and 'makes scuruy' for 'make scuruy' (lines 28, 37, and 38). Additional 30982 similarly introduces many erroneous variants and is wholly unsatisfactory as a witness to the text.[31] The stemma can, therefore, be established as follows:

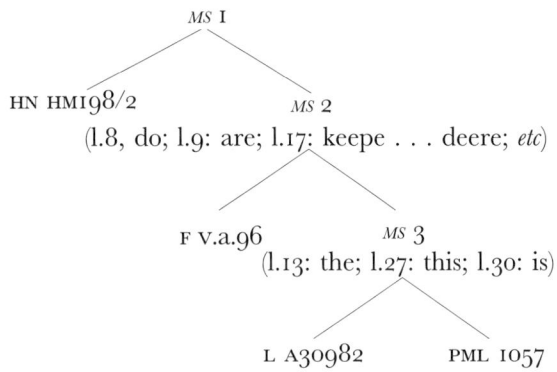

While, the simplicity of the stemma for 'Neither to follow fashion' is slightly misleading, in that there are likely to be as many missing manuscripts as there are ones that are extant or demonstrable, it is notable that the poem had a less extensive circulation than 'The Sun'. This is of interest for a number of reasons. First, given the link between the two poems in the surviving manuscripts, the absence of the first poem in Holgate and the absence of the second in such manuscripts as Grey 7.a.29 and Folger V.a.170 stand out, although it is difficult to know quite what to make of such omissions. Second, given that 'Neither to follow fashion . . .' is a poem that appears to have had a very limited circulation, perhaps because of its attack on the Earl of Salisbury, the reference to Shakespeare serves as an absolute refutation of those who would doubt his identity or existence, as Jonson and Beaumont had no cause to dissimulate in private about their most significant contemporary, or reason to admire his work falsely.

III

Nothing so quickly exposes the instability of a text than when changes can be mapped from one document to the next. As is often remarked, manuscript texts provide particularly obvious examples of this fact, and reflect contexts that are as much personal as they are social to the history of their circulation. Thus, if we wish to understand what the poet (and later bishop) George Morley experienced as 'The Sun', we must turn to Westminster 41: in Morley's case, it is perhaps notable that he proposed the emendation 'deeper' for 'drier heresies' in the margin of his text.[32] Similarly, the most widely circulated version of the poem— and thus what people from the mid-seventeenth century, until the Herford and Simpson edition, read—is that from the Beaumont and Fletcher folio (1647), which was reprinted again in 1679, despite the fact that it was inaccurate and altered by the publisher.

However, in order for these readings to be understood, both for what they purport to represent and for what they mis-understand, we need to recover (in so far as possible) the texts that Beaumont wrote to Jonson. The issue is pragmatic: we can only reconstruct a document in so far as the evidence available allows and logical inference admits: in essence, we do not know exactly what was written down to the last spelling variant or punctuation mark, but it is possible to use the available evidence to establish the history of the antecedent documents and thus a version of the text consistent with that analysis. Without that information, any attempt to distinguish the difference between the extant variants would be historically uninformative.

The stemma have demonstrated that the best text for both the poems is HM198 part 2. This folio manuscript was bound together with another by Henry Huth in the mid-nineteenth century, but before that was a separate document.[33] The manuscript is a collection of 295 poems and two prose characters written on two stocks of paper in several different hands, one of which is responsible for organising the volume. There is considerable internal evidence that HM198 part 2 was not originally prepared in its present order, or as a single entity, although all parts were written at approximately the same time.[34] The three poems by Beaumont (the other is the verse letter to the Countess of Rutland) are to be found at ff. 114–16 between a run of poems by Donne and Jonson, and following sequences of poems by Dudley, Lord North, an anonymous author, and Nicholas Hare. These connections suggest that the manuscript was associated with the Inner Temple. Beaumont's poems are copied by Hand A (see PLATE 1), the principal assistant to the person who organised, paginated, partially wrote, and corrected the volume (Hand B).

The decision to adopt HM198 part 2 as copy-text for both poems brings with it the need for emendation (as, to a greater extent, would any alternative). However, the rationale for making such a choice is not quite as Greg conceived it.[35] In this instance, the best method is to minimise the number of substantive emendations, and use a cross-section of the other witnesses—both to remove the idiosyncracies of the scribe, and to clarify the punctuation of the poems. Any attempt at modernisation is, in fact, unacceptable as such, for it disguises and glosses over the patterns of rhetorical inflexion that constitute the texts as part of a conversation (which is what they purport to be). Yet, owing to the distance of the witnesses from the lost original, it is equally necessary to exercise a degree of editorial discretion in assessing the variations in accidence, with an eye for the deliberate patterning of clauses, and with an ear for the text as an oral performance. As with Jonson, Beaumont evidently used punctuation to inflect the meaning of the text.

The most significant substantive variant of 'The Sun' is the misreading 'sutlest' for 'Sutcliffs' (line 17). The reference is almost certainly to Matthew Sutcliffe, Dean of Exeter (1550?–1629), who wrote antipapal tracts and pamphlets from 1591 onwards.[36] Beaumont is mocking Sutcliffe's puritan temperament, and accusing him of being an interminably dull writer: certainly, neither Beaumont nor Jonson would have had much sympathy for Sutcliffe's virulent anti-catholicism. The importance of the variant, however, goes beyond the scribe's attempt to make sense of the line: the fact that the person does not understand the reference indicates that he is at some remove from Beaumont and, or, Jonson. Elsewhere, 'hard' for 'heard' (line 48) is potentially misleading, and 'of' makes better sense than 'at' (line 65).

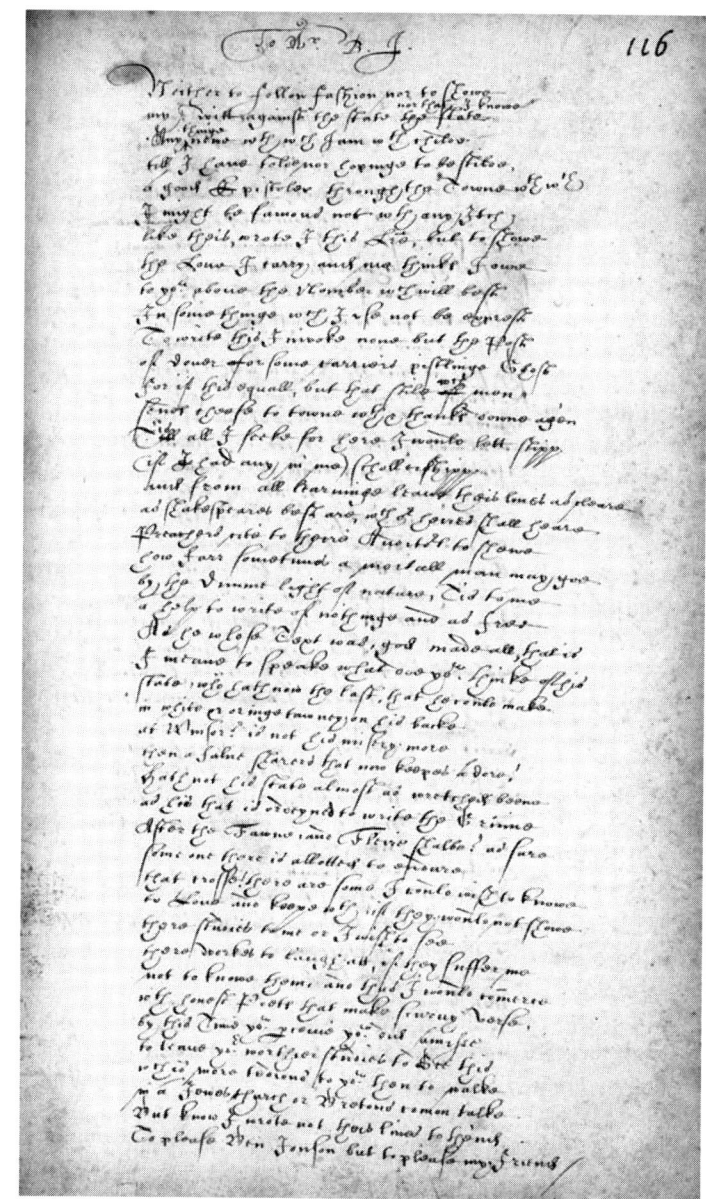

PLATE 1. *First page of Beaumont's verse letter to Jonson* 'Neither to follow fashion nor to showe' *in the second Haslewood-Kingsborough verse miscellany: San Marino, California, Huntington Library, HM 198, Part 2, fol. 116r. (Original page size 308 ×184mm.) Reproduced by permission of the Huntington Library.*

conspicuously maimed, for though the words might be right, the pointing and spelling of the texts leave much to be desired. That approach, in turn, would only perpetuate the negative judgments that have been made about Beaumont's virtues as a poet.

IV

At various times, the authorship of both 'The Sun' and the 'Neither to follow fashion' have been questioned: the first by I. A. Shapiro, and the second by William Ringler. Similarly, there have been claims made about the dates of both poems and, in general, there has been a level of confusion about how to locate the poems and assess their value as witnesses to Beaumont's and Jonson's lives. As Simpson remarked of 'The Sun' in his notes 'The date is not easy to determine', although he then advanced the arguments of Shapiro and Gayley dating the text to 1609–13, before repeating again 'we really have no clear clue'.[39] 'Neither to follow fashion' has similarly eluded satisfactory dating, for while the references to *The Fawne* and *The Fleire* suggest 1606, Chambers decided that the reference to 'the post of Dover' was to Anthony Nixon's *A Straunge Foot-Post*, and suggested a date of *c*.1615.[40] This weak argument led Chambers to overlook the one piece of evidence that would have confirmed a date of 1606.

Before turning to the dating of the poems, the question of attribution must be resolved. Ringler's argument against 'Neither to follow fashion' was based upon a mistake in his notes. His primary criticism was of Chambers who knew only Pierpont Morgan 1057 and Additional 30982, the first manuscript of which attributes the poem to 'FB', and the second 'T. B.' Chambers had simply remarked that 'I see no reason why it should not be Francis Beaumont', against which Ringler noted that Folger V.a.96 and HM198 part 2 were anonymous and cautioned that 'The attribution must remain doubtful'.[41] However, it seems likely that Ringler confused 'The Sun' with 'Neither to follow fashion', for the first is anonymous in Folger V.a.96, whereas the second is clearly attributed to 'Mr Fran: Beaumont'.[42] Further, whilst the text in HM198 part 2 is anonymous, the poem is third in a sequence that begins with the letter to Elizabeth Countess of Rutland ('Maddam, Soe may my verses pleasinge bee'), followed by 'The Sun': it is thus clearly linked to Beaumont in that manuscript by association, whilst the group as a whole is inserted between a run of poems by Donne. The problem with Additional 30982 (the worst text) is simply that Daniel Leare appears to have forgotten to cross the italic F, rendering it as a T. That the three best manuscripts all indicate that Beaumont is the author, and that the error of the fourth is readily explicable, renders Ringler's caution unnecessary.

The doubt cast on the attribution of 'The Sun' by Shapiro simply reflects an unfamiliarity with the evidence. Shapiro knew of the two printed editions, *1640* and *1647*, and one anonymous manuscript (Houghton 966.3). In a perfectly reasonable manner (although a little research would have resolved his question) he commented that it 'would be desirable to investigate whether this poem is correctly ascribed to Beaumont'.[43] To this remark, Simpson responded with some vigour. As well as noting the two printed texts, he added that 'There are seven manuscript copies of the poem', of which, he said, Sloane 1792 identified the author as 'Fr. Beaumont', Additional 30982 as 'ff. B', Egerton 2421 as 'Sr. F. B.', Trinity 877*b* as 'Fr. Beaumont', and Houghton 966.3 as by Donne. He then added 'If the authorship of this well-authenticated poem is to be seriously questioned, there is an end to textual criticism'.[44] In fact, the evidence is slightly better than Simpson knew: Sloane 1792 attributes the poem to 'Fr: Beaumont' and its pair Westminster 41 to 'Fran: Beomont', Additional 30982 to 'ff. B.', Egerton 2421 to 'S^r francis Beamont', Trinity 877*b* to 'Fr. Beaumont', HM198 part 1 to 'Franc: Beamond', St John's S.23 to 'F Beamond', Grey 7.a.29 to 'ffr: Beaumont', Malone 13 to 'ff: Beaumont', and Folger V.a.170 to 'F: B:'. The remaining copies, including Houghton 966.3 (which Simpson never saw), are all anonymous, but in the case of HM198 part 2, the poem is found between the verse letter to the Countess of Rutland and 'Neither to follow fashion'. Apart from Egerton 2421, the manuscript tradition expresses the same level of certainty that Jonson was the recipient. In other words, there is no reason to doubt that 'The Sun' is a verse letter from Beaumont to Jonson, as the evidence for this exists across the entire, rather complicated, history of the poem in manuscript.

Gayley, whose biography of Beaumont was published in 1914, had no doubt that 'The Sun' was genuine, although he did not know of 'Neither to follow fashion'. However, his account of 'The Sun', like the rest of his biography, is written with a touch of purple, portraying 'our Frank' as a carefree, almost magical, spirit. While this approach is very much a product of its time, it continues to matter because Gayley's account has set the terms of all subsequent discussions. His central claim is that the poem must have been written no earlier than 1609–10, a date that Shapiro then moved to 1613. The central point in what follows is that Gayley only knew of one version of the poem, that in the 1647 Beaumont and Fletcher folio, and his argument is predicated on the

final couplet written probably by Moseley, in which Beaumont is pur-
ported to have remarked:

> Ben, *when these* Scenes *are perfect wee'l taste wine,*
> *Ile drink thy Muses health, thou shalt quaff mine.*[45]

For Gayley, such evidence was quite sufficient to date the poem:

> It is written with the careless ease of longstanding intimacy. It is of a
> genial, jocose, and fairly mature epistolary style. It betrays the literary
> assurance of one whose reputation is already established. Beaumont is in
> temporary banishment from London, for lack of funds—therefore, con-
> siderably later than 1606, when he was presumably well off; for in that
> year he had just come into a quarter of his brother, Sir Henry's private
> estate.
>
> If there is any truth at all in the rubric to the Letter, the 'scenes' of which
> Beaumont speaks as not yet 'perfect' were of The Coxcombe . . . written
> about the end of 1609.[46]

Without the 'final' couplet, many of these assertions lack substance.
Far from betraying 'the literary assurance of one whose reputation is
already established', Beaumont defers to Jonson as the master of his
sentences. Further, whilst the genuine text of the poem does suggest
'longstanding intimacy', the earlier we date the possible commence-
ment of Beaumont and Jonson's friendship, the less relevant the
'intimacy' then becomes as a criteria for judging the date of the poem.
More significantly, there is no evidence at all that Beaumont was
profligate of his estate, or that he retired from London 'for lack of
funds'. Beaumont states that he was 'Banish'd vnto my home', not
'Retir'd', which implies that he was sent there by authority. What
generated Gayley's theory, however, was the additions to the title of the
poem in *1647*, for Moseley had added that 'The Sun' was 'written before
he [Beaumont] and Master Fletcher came to London, with two of the
precedent Comedies then not finisht, which deferred their merry meet-
ings at the Mermaid'.[47] Moseley's addition is clearly an oral tradition,
but as Gayley observed, 'We know that the young men had been in
London for years before 1606.'[48]

The most important correction to our knowledge of Beaumont's
early career is the revelation of his difficulties at Cambridge during the
autumn and winter of 1604.[49] Hilton Kelliher's important article has
established that Beaumont was in Cambridge during the latter half of
1604 and the first months of 1605, from mid-November on resident at
the Tolbooth prison on Market Hill.[50] The point, for present purposes,

is not so much Beaumont's skill as a gambler, or the nature of his problems, but his meeting with John Cowell, the Vice Chancellor on 15 March 1605. As Kelliher has commented, 'no record of the final decision survives'.[51] It is reasonable to infer, however, that the judgment does survive in Beaumont's poem, and that he was 'Banish'd vnto my home'. There, his elder brother died three months later, and so the restraint on Beaumont came to an end. At Grace Dieu there were certainly family matters to occupy him, and by mid-June Trinity Term would have ended, so there was little point in his coming to London immediately. Thus, the poem, which refers to the sun as 'our best haymaker', must have been written in late July or August 1605, and anticipates Beaumont's return to London for the first time in more than a year. It is on his return, of course, that he began his theatrical partnership with Fletcher—in other words, the gist of Moseley's oral tradition is correct.

The other poem, 'Neither to follow fashion' can be dated to late May or June 1606. The rationale advanced by Chambers for dating the poem to c.1615 following Anthony Nixon's pamphlet is overtly flimsy in its logic (there is no need to assume that Beaumont must have had a printed text in mind when referring to the post of Dover), and it ignores the other substantive evidence in the poem. As a consequence, Chambers sought to link the reference to the Garter ceremony with either that of Maurice of Nassau who received the honour by proxy in February 1613; or Thomas Erskine, Viscount Fenton, and William, Lord Knollys, in May 1615. The logic for preferring this latter connection was not only that Fenton and Knollys were present, but that Fenton was attended by the entire bedchamber and one hundred of the guard. Among the bedchamber was James, Lord Hay, whose attendants wore tawny liveries on his embassy to France in 1616.[52]

There are two problems with the attempt by Chambers to associate the poem with the installation of Fenton and Knollys. First, the theory is based on a rather desperate attempt to find any link between the poem and the Garter ceremony, even when there is no evidence to support the implied claim that Hay's behaviour was a cause for comment. Second, the date cannot be reconciled with the reference to Marston's *The Fawne* and Sharpham's *The Fleire*, the latter of which was performed in 1606. One of Beaumont's jokes is that someone will be required to write a sequel called *The Grinne*: that comment makes no sense if the sequel has not been written within the previous nine years. There was, however, a very important installation of the Garter in May 1606, in which (as the records indicate) 'the obsolete custom of a procession of a number of attendants before the new knights was revived; and,

My witt for drie bobbs, then I needes must crie:
   I see my daies of ballading are nigh;
I can already riddle, and can singe
   Catches, sell bargaines, and I feare shall bringe
My selfe to speake the hardest wordes I find
   Ouer, as oft as any with one wind
That takes no medicines; but one thought of thee
   Makes me remember all these things to be   70
The witt of our younge men; fellowes that showe
   No part of good, yett vtter all they knowe;
Who, like Trees and the Guard, haue growinge soules.
   Only strong destiny (which all controules),
I hope hath kept a better fate in store
   For me thy friend, then to liue euermore
Banish'd vnto my home; 'twill once againe
   Bringe me to thee, who wilt make smooth and plaine
The way of knowledge for me, and then I
   (Who yet haue no good, but simplicity)   80
Knowe that it will my greatest vertue bee
   T'acknowledge all the rest to come from thee.

Emendations to copy-text.

Sigla: *FI* Folger V.a.96; *F2* Folger V.a.170; *HI* Huntington HM198 part 1; *H2* Huntington HM198 part 2; *SA* South Africa Grey 7.a.29; *T* Trinity Dublin 877*b*.

Expansion of contractions, initial capitals where necessary, indents] *Ed.*

T Title: Francis Beaumont to his his friend Ben Ionson at London] *Ed.* [No title] *FI, T* F: B: to B: I. *F2* Franc: Beamond to Ben: Iohnson *HI* To his Friend B. I: *H2* ffr: Beaumont to B. Iohnson at London *SA*; 'to his friend' also supported by St John's S.23 and Additional 30982 descending from *MS* 10. l.1: Sunn (which] *HI* Sunn w^ch *FI* Sunne, (which *F2* Sunn, w^ch *H2* Sun which *SA* Sunn w:^ch *T* l.3: know,] *SA* know; *FI* know *F2, HI, H2, T* see,] *FI, F2, SA* see *HI, H2, T* absent)] *HI* absent, *FI, SA* distant) *F2* absent *H2, T* l.4: haymaker:] *Ed.* haymaker; *FI* Hay maker. *F2* haymaker, *HI, SA* haymaker *H2* Haymaker *T* this,] *FI, F2* this *HI, H2, SA, T* l.5: stile;] *Ed.* talke, *FI, SA* stile. *F* stile, *HI, T* stile *H2* l.6: lye,] *FI* lie, *F2* ly, *HI* ly *H2* lye *SA* lie *T* wine.] *F2* wyne. *FI* wine, *HI, SA* wine *H2, T* l.7: O,] *Ed.* O *FI, F2, HI, H2, T* Oh: *SA* Clarett] *HI, SA* clarett *FI* clarett *F2, H2* clarret *T* Lees:] *Ed.* lees, *FI, SA* lees: *F2* Lees *HI, H2, T* l.8: Drinke] *FI, F2, T* drinke *HI* drincke *H2* drinke, *SA* l.9: beere;] *Ed.* beere, *FI, HI, SA, T* Beere: *F2* beere *H2*

straine,] *Ed.* straine *FI, H2* strayne; *F2* strayne *HI, SA, T* l.10: Metaphors,]
Ed. Metaphors *FI, H2, SA, T* metaphors, *F2* metaphors *HI* braine;] *Ed.*
braine. *FI* brayne. *F2* brayne *HI* braine *H2, T* brayne, *SA* l.11: mixt,] *FI, F2*
mixt *HI, H2, SA, T* l.12: Almes,] *FI, F2* almes, *HI*(l.18), *SA* Almes *H2, T* stone;]
SA stone *FI, HI, H2, T* Stone. *F2* l.13: 'Tis] *FI* Tis *F2, SA* tis *HI* T'is *H2, T* l.14:
Sacrament.] *FI* sacrament. *F2* Sacrament, *HI* Sacrament *H2, T*
Sacrament; *SA* l.15: fades,] *FI, HI, SA* fades: *F2* fades *H2, T* l.16: Iliades;] *Ed.*
Illiades. *FI* Iliades. *F2* Iliades, *HI* Iliades *H2* Illiads; *SA* Iliads *T* l.17: 'Tis]
FI, SA Tis *F, H2* tis *HI* T'is *T* Sutcliffes] *FI* Sutcliffs *F2* Sutclifs *HI* sutlest *H2*
subtlest *SA* succliffs *T* witt,] *Ed.* witt *FI, F2, HI, H2, SA, T* l.18: lyes,] *FI, SA*
lies, *F2* lyes *HI, T* lies *H2* yet;] *Ed.* yett *FI* yet. *F* yett, *HI* yet *H2, T* yet, *SA*
l.19: Fill'd] *Ed.* ffill'd *FI* Fild *F2* fild *HI, H2* filld *SA* Fil'd *T* moysture,] *HI*
moisture *FI, H2* moysture *F2* moystures *SA* mixture *T* qualme,] *Ed.*
greuious SA grei[struck through] f[normal]uious *HN2* greiuous *HNI*
greeuous *D* greuous *F96* griueous *F170* qualme *FI, F2, HI, H2, SA, T* l.20:
Psalme,] *Ed.* psalme. *FI, F2* psalme *HI, T* Psalme *H2* psalme, *SA* l.21: this:]
F2, HI another, *FI* this *H2* another *SA* this, *T* yet, . . . thinke,] *Ed.* sure . . .
thinke *FI* yet . . . thinke *F2, HI, H2, SA, T* l.22: potion] *FI, F2, SA* Potion *HI, T*
posion *H2* drinke] *FI, F2, HI, SA, T* drincke *H2* l.23: prouidence;] *F2*
Prouidence; *FI* prouidence, *HI, SA, T* Prouidence *H2* alone,] *Ed.* alone *FI,*
F2, H2, SA allone *HI* [omitted] *T* l.24: taken,] *SA* taken *FI, F2* tane *HI* Tane,
H2 [omitted] *T* Ambition,] *Ed* Ambition. *FI* Ambition: *F2* ambition *HI*
Ambition *H2* ambition, *SA* [omitted] *T* l.25: iniuryes,] *SA* iniuries, *FI*
injuries: *F2* iniuryes *HI* Iniuries *H2* [omitted] *T* fights,] *SA* fightes *FI* fights:
F2 frights *HI* fights *H2, T* l.26: knights;] *Ed.* knightes *FI* knights. *F2* knights
HI, H2, T knights, *SA* l.27: mindes] *SA* myndes *FI* Minde *F2* mind, *HI* min-
des, *H2* mynds *T* states,] *FI, SA* state *F* estates *HI* states *H2, T* l.28: obey] *FI,*
F2, HI, SA, T Obay *H2* Magistrates.] *Ed.* Magistrates: *FI* Magistrate. *F2*
Magistrates, *HI, H2* Magistrates; *SA* Magistrates *T* l.29: you;] *FI* you: *F2*
yow, *HI* yo^w. *H2* you, *SA* y^u *T* hate,] *Ed.* hate *FI, F2, HI, H2, SA, T* l.30: state,]
Ed. state *FI, F2, HI, H2, SA, T* l.31: vs;] *FI* vs: *F2* us, *HI* vs *H2, T* vs, *SA* equall;]
FI equall: *F2* equall *HI, H2, SA* equall, *T* l.32: men,] *SA* men *FI, HI, H2, T* men.
F2 here,] *T* here *FI, H2, SA* Heere *F2* heer *HI* witt:] *Ed.* witt *FI, H2, T* witt; *F2*
witt, *HI, SA* l.33: fully;] *FI, F2, T* fully *HI* fully, *H2, SA* l.34: will,] *Ed.* will *FI,*
F2, HI, H2, SA, T l.34: house ieast,] *SA* house=Iest *FI* house jeast *F2* house
ieast *HI* house Iest *H2* house iest *T* l.35: you:] *Ed.* you; *FI* you. *F2* yow, *HI*
yo^u. *H2* you, *SA, T* l.36: trickes;] *FI* tricks; *F2* trick, *HI* trickes *H2* tricks, *SA, T*
hate,] *FI, F2* hate *HI, H2, SA, T* too.] *FI, F2* too *HI, H2, T* too, *SA* l.37: showe,]
FI shew; *F2* show, *HI* showe *H2, SA* show *T* l.38: you] *FI, F2, SA* yow *HI* yo^w.
H2 y^u *T* winke,] *FI, F2, HI* wincke *H2* winke *SA* , *T* blowe;] *FI* blow. *F* blowe
HI, H2 blow, *SA* blow *T* l.39: Mills,] *SA* Mills *FI, F2, H2, T* [omitted] *HI*
grinde,] *SA* grind *FI, T* grinde *F2, H2* [omitted] *HI* l.40: their] *T* the *FI* theyr

F2 [omitted] *H1* there *H2* yᵉ *SA* winde.] *F2* wynde. *F1* [omitted] *H1* winde *H2* winde, *SA* wynd *T* l.41: fellow,] *H1* fellowe *F1* fellow *F2, H2, SA, T* pate] *F1, F2, H1, SA, T* Pate *H2* l.42: vs,] *SA, T* vs *F1, F2, H2* them *H1* l.44: Mee] *F1, F2, H1, T* my *H2* me *SA* thinks.] *Ed.* thinkes *F1, H1, SA* thinks *F2, H2, T* That] *Ed.* that *F1, F2, H2, SA, T* the *H1* l.45: you:] *F2* thee; *F1* yow, *H1* yoᵘ *H2* thee, *SA* you, *T* is] *F1, F2, H1, SA, T* Is *H2* l.46: Tennis,] *F1, H1, SA* tennis, *F2* Tennis *H2, T* l.47: Gamsters.] *Ed.* gamsters; *F1* gamsters. *F2* Gamsters, *H1, SA* Gamsters *H2* gamesters *T* What] *F2* what *F1, H1, H2, SA, T* scene?] *Ed.* seene *F1, F2, H1, H2, SA, T* l.48: heard] *F1, F2, H1, SA, T* hard *H2* l.49: nimble,] *F1, F2* fyry *H1* nimble *H2* milde, *SA* nymble *T* flame,] *Ed.* fame *F1* frame *F2* flame *H1, H2, T* fame *SA* l.51: meant] *F1, F2, H1, SA, T* ment *H2* l.51: ieast,] *SA* Iest *F1* jeast *F2* ieast *H1* iest *H2* Iest *T* l.53: life:] *F2* life; *F1, SA* life, *H1,* life *H2* lyfe, *T* then,] *Ed.* then *F1, F2, H2, SA, T* [omitted] *H1* l.54: iustifie] *T* iustiefie *F1* justify *F2* iustefy *H1* Iustifie *H2* Iustifye *SA* l.57: gone,] *Ed.* gone *F1, F2, H1, H2, SA, T* l.58: ayre] *F1, F2, H1, SA, T* heire *H2* l.60: downeright] *SA* downe right *F1, H1, H2* right *F2* downe=right *T* Cockeneys.] *F2* Cockneyes *F1* Cockneys, *H1* Cockeneys *H2* Cocknies, *SA* Cockneys *T* l.61: this,] *F1, F2, SA, T* this *H1, H2* l.63: crie:] *Ed.* cry *F1, H1, SA, T* crie *F2, H2* l.64: of] *F1, F2, H1, SA, T* at *H2* ballading] *F2, T* ballating *F1* ballatting *H1* ballatinge *H2* Ballading *SA* l.65: can] *F2, H1, SA, T* cann *F1* Cann *H2* l.68: wind] *Ed. (F1* revision) minde *F1* (first version) *F2, SA* wind, *H1* wind. *H2* wynd *T* l.69: medicines;] *Ed.* medcines: *F1* medicines. *F2* medcines, *H1, SA* medicines, *H2, T* l.70: these] *F1, SA, T* this *F2* theyse *H1* theis *H2* l.71: men;] *F1, T* [omitted] *F2* men, *H1, SA* men? *H2* showe] *H1* knowe *F1* [omitted] *F2* showe, *H2* know *SA* show *T* l.72: good,] *F1, SA* [omitted] *F2* good *H1, H2, T* l.72: knowe;] *Ed.* knowe. *F1* [omitted] *F2* knowe *H1* knowe, *H2* know, *SA* know *T* l.73: Guard,] *Ed.* guard, *F1, SA* [omitted] *F2* Guard *H1, T* guard *H2* soules.] *Ed.* Soules *F1, H1* [omitted] *F2* soules *H2, T* soules; *SA* l.74: Destiny] *F1, SA, T* [omitted] *F2* desteny *H1* destiny *H2* (which . . . controules),] *Ed.* wᶜʰ . . . controules *F1, H2, SA* [omitted] *F2* (wᶜʰ . . . controuls) *H1* wᶜʰ . . . Controlls *T* l.77: home;] *F1, F2* home, *H1, H2, SA, T* 'twill] *F1* twill *F2, H1, H2, SA* t'will *T* l.80: (Who . . . simplicity)] *Ed.* [omitted] *F1* Who . . . Simplicity, *F2* (who . . . simpliciety) *H1* who . . . simplicity *H2* [Variant line] *SA* Who . . . simplicity *T*.

To Mʳ: Ben: Ionson.

> Neither to follow fashion, nor to showe
> My witt against the state, nor that I knowe
> Any thinge newe (with which I am with childe
> Till I haue tolde), nor hopinge to be stilde
> A good Epistler through the towne (with which
> I might be famous), nor with any itch

Like these, wrote I this Letter; but to showe
The Loue I carry, and me thinkes I owe
To you aboue the number, which will best,
In somethinge which I vse not, be exprest.   10
To write this, I invoke none but the Post
Of *Douer*, or some carriers pistlinge ghost;
For if this equall but that stile which men
Send cheese to towne with, and thankes downe agen,
'Tis all I seeke for: heere, I would lett slipp
(If I had any in me) schollershipp,
And from all learninge leaue these lines as cleare
As *Shakespeares* best are, which our heires shall heare.
Preachers cite to theire Auditors to shewe
How farr sometimes a mortall man may goe   20
By the dimme light of Nature. 'Tis to me
An help to write of nothing; and as free
As he whose Text was, *God made all*; that is,
I meane to speake: what doe you think of his
State, who hath now the last, that he could make
In white and oringe-tawney on his backe
At Windsor? is not his misery more
Then a falne sharers that now keepes a dore?
Hath not his state almost as wretched beene
As his that is ordeyned to write the *Grinne*   30
After the *Fawne*, and *Fleire*, shalbe? as sure
Some one there is allotted to endure
That crosse! There are some I could wish to knowe,
To Loue and keepe with, if they would not showe
Their studies to me; or I wish to see
Their workes to laugh att, if they suffer me
Not to knowe them: and thus I would commerce
With honest Poetes that make scuruy verse.
By this time, you perceiue you did amisse
To leaue your worthier studies to see this,   40
Which is more tedious to you, then to walke
In a *Iewes* church, or *Bretons* Common talke:
But know I wrote not these lines to th'end
To please *Ben: Ionson*, but to please my friend.

Emendations to copy-text.

Sigla: *H* Huntington HM 198 part 2; *F* Folger V.a.96; *P* Pierpont Morgan
MA 1057.

Initial capitals where necessary] *F, Ed.* Expanded contractions] *Ed.*

Title] *F* To M^r. B. J. *H, P* l.1: fashion,] *P* fashon, *F* fashion *H* l.3: newe (with] *Ed.* newe, with *F* newe wth *H* now, with *P* l.4: tolde),] *Ed.* told, *F* tolde *H* tould, *P* stilde] *P* stild *F* stilde, *H* l.5: Epistler] *F, P* Epistleler *H* towne (with] *Ed.* towne, with *F, P* Towne, with *H* l.6: famous), *Ed.* famous, *F, P* famous *H* itch] *F* Itch *H* ytch *P* l.7: these,] *F, P* theis, *H* Letter;] *Ed.* Letter, *F* L^re *H* Letter *P* l.8: carry,] *F* carry *H* carrie *P* l.9: number,] *P* number *F* Nomber *H* best,] *Ed* best *F, H, P* l.10: exprest.] *f, p* exprest *h* l.11: this,] *F* this *H, P* l.12: *Douer,*] *F* douer *H* Douer. *P* ghost;] *Ed.* ghost *F* Ghost *H* ghost, *P* l.13: equall] *F, P* equall, *H* l.14: Send] *F* sendes *H* send *P* with,] *F, P* with *H* agen,] *P* agen *F, H* l.15: for:] *P* for *F, H* heere,] *F* here *H* heere *P* l.16: schollershipp,] *Ed.* schollershipp *F, H* schollershippe, *P* l.17: these] *F, P* theis *H* l.18: *Shakespeares*] *F* shakespeares *H* Shakespeares *P* heare.] *Ed.* heare *F, H, P* l.19: Auditors] *F* Auditores *H* auditors *P* l.21: Nature.] *F* nature, *H, P* 'Tis] *F* Tis *H* tis *P* l.22: An] *F* A *H* an *P* nothing;] *P* Nothing, *F* nothinge *H* l.23: *God made all;*] *Ed.* God made all *F* god made all, *H* god made all *P* is,] *Ed.* is. *F, P* is *H* l.24: speake:] *P* speake, *F* speake *H* l.25: oringe-tawney] *Ed.* Orendge=tawney *F* oringe tawney *H* Orrenge tawny *H* l.27: Windsor] *F, P* Winsor *H* l.30: *Grinne*] *Ed.* Gennie *F* Grinne *H* geinne *P* l.31: *Fawne,*] *F* Fawne, *H* fawne, *P* *Fleire,*] *Ed. FLEERE F* Fleire *H* fleare *P* l.33: There] *F* there *H, P* knowe,] *Ed.* knowe *F, H, P* l.35: Their] *F* there *H* their *P* me;] *P* mee, *F* me *H* l.36: Their] *Ed.* Theire *F* there *H* their *P* l.37: them:] *F, P* them, *H* l.38: verse.] *F* verse, *H* verse *P* l.39: time,] *Ed.* tyme *F* Time *H* time *P* you] *F, P* y^ow. *H* l.40: see this,] *P* see this *F* See this *H* l.41: you,] *F, P* y^ow. *H* l.42: *Iewes . . . Bretons*] *Ed.* Iewes . . . Britons *F* Iewes . . . Bretons *H* Iews . . . Bretons *P* Common] *F, P* comon *H* talke:] *Ed.* talke, *F* talke *H, P* l.43: these] *F, P* theis *H* l.44: *Ben: Ionson,*] *Ed.* Ben: Ionson *F* Ben Ionson *H* Ben: Iohnson *P.*

NOTES

I would like to thank the Open University for their support during the preparation of this article.

1 For instance, R. C. Evans, *Ben Jonson and the Poetics of Patronage* (Lewisburg, 1989).

2 For instance, J. B. Leishman, 'You Meaner Beauties of the Night. A Study in Transmission and Transmogrification', *The Library*, 4th Ser. 26 (1945), 99–123; E. Wolf II, '"If shadows be a picture's excellence": An Experiment in Critical Bibliography', *Publications of the Modern Language Association*, 63 (1948), 831–57; T.-L. Pebworth, 'Sir Henry Wotton's "Dazel'd Thus, with Height of Place" and the Appropriation of Political Poetry in the Early Seventeenth Century', *Papers of the Bibliographical Society of America*, 71 (1977), 151–69; H. Love, 'The Ranking of Variants in the Analysis of Moderately Contaminated Manuscript Traditions', *Studies in Bibliography*, 37 (1984), 39–57.

3 [W. H. Cooke (ed.)], *Students admitted to The Inner Temple. 1547–1660* (London, 1877), p. 156.

4 Cooke, *Inner Temple*, p. 159. On Rosenbach MS 240/1, p. 82, North notes that the poem 'Doe not reiect those titles of your due' was 'made at 17 as some others' [*i.e.* 1598]. He did not publish *A forest of varieties* until 1645 (Wing N1283).

5 J. Carey, *The Ovidian Love Elegy in England* (Oxford: MS D.Phil, c.374; 1960), pp. 232–42. Hare is the author of 'Variety' and a number of elegies to be found in Huntington MS 198 part 2: for further details, see M. B. Bland, *The Manuscripts of Ben Jonson and his Contemporaries* (forthcoming 2005), chap. 4.

6 H. A. C. Sturgess (comp.), *Register of Admissions to the Honourable Society of the Middle Temple*, 2 vols (London, 1949), I, 64–77.

7 Cooke, *Inner Temple*, pp. 4, 34, 44, 99, 148, & 150.

8 W. R. Prest, *The Inns of Court 1590–1640* (London, 1972), pp. 27–40, 52 & 245.

9 B. Jonson, *Workes* (STC 14751–52; 1616), sig. G2^r; *Ben Jonson*, ed. C. H. Herford and P. and E. Simpson, 11 vols (Oxford, 1925–52), III, 421.

10 H. Kelliher, 'Francis Beaumont and Nathan Field: New Records of their Early Years', *English Manuscript Studies*, 8 (2000), 1–42.

11 Love proposes using STC or Wing locations symbols for sigla, and the manuscript number with (where appropriate) the first letter(s) of the word(s) identifying the collection (eg. 'A' for 'Additional'), or the alphanumeric shelfmark (e.g. Folger V.a.96): see Harold Love, 'Systematising Sigla', *English Manuscript Studies*, 11 (2002), 217–30.

12 P. Beal, *Index of English Literary Manuscripts 1450–1625*, 2 vols (London and New York, 1980), I, 75–76 (BmF 100–16); W. Shakespeare, *Poems* (STC 22344; 1640), sigs L4^r–5^r; F. Beaumont and J. Fletcher, *Comedies and Tragedies* (Wing B1581; 1647), sigs 3X3^v–4^r.

13 This is the manuscript that Simpson called Dobell: Herford & Simpson, XI, 377. I am grateful to the South African Library, Cape Town, for providing copies from the relevant pages of the manuscript, which is the only one I have not examined in person.

14 L. M. Jones, *A Critical Edition of a 17th Century Poetical Miscellany (HM 172)* (M. A.: University of Calgary, Alberta, 1980), pp. lviii–lxvii: Huntington Library, shelfmark: PR 1209.J66 1980.

15 Thus, 'person' for 'man' (line 34), 'like to Mills' for 'like Mills' (line 39), 'milde, and yet so full' for 'nimble and so full' (line 49: this is a mix of a minim problem with confusion between bl and ld), 'then where there' for 'then when there' (line 53), 'forced do I' for 'forced I' (line 63), and 'that do know' for 'that know' (line 71).

16 Thus, 'cleare' for 'quite' (line 16, but here line 10); 'twould' for ''Twill' (line 12, but here line 18); 'fitts our mind, to our estates' (line 27); 'heer in' for 'here, is' (line 32); 'men' for 'man' (line 35); 'hate ly' for 'ly, hate' (line 37); 'for heer is none' for 'Here are none' (line 38); 'them' for 'vs' (line 42); 'the little' for 'that little' (line 44); 'fyry' for 'nimble' (line 49); 'one' for 'man' (line 50); 'when throwne up and doune' for 'when there hath beene throwne' (line 53); 'weeks' for 'days' (line 55); 'quitted' for 'cancel'd' (line 57); 'that' for 'which' (line 58); 'fast . . . without wind' for 'oft . . . with one wind' (line 68).

17 These are, 'the full', 'kills ambition', 'that which', a version of 'we do', and 'In selling' (lines 6, 24, 27, 33, and 43).

18 Thus, 'where ere it lyes', 'He doth consider', 'greatest man', 'perhaps', 'that little wit', 'euery man', and 'next two' (lines 18, 33, 34, 42, 44, 50, and 59).

19 Thus, 'to allow', 'Who yet' (lines 62, 80).

20 For a summary of the theoretical issues involved, see H. Love, 'The Ranking of Variants of Moderately Contaminated Manuscript Traditions', *Studies in Bibliography*, 37 (1984), 39–57.

21 Bodleian English Poetry e.97 also has a number of unique readings, such as 'As Land' for 'Of land' and 'I can vnread a riddle' for 'already riddle' (lines 32, 65).

22 W. Cartwright, *Comedies, Tragicomedies, with other Poems* (Wing C709; 1651), sig. [a]5[r].

23 Thus, 'fitts our minds, to our estates', 'for heer is none', 'soe fyry', 'when throwne up and doune', 'three weeks after', and 'quitted' (lines 27, 37, 49, 53, 55).

24 Cf. T-L. Pebworth, 'Sir Henry Wotton's "Dazel'd thus, with height of place" and the appropriation of political poetry in the earlier seventeenth century', *Papers of the Bibliographical Society of America*, 71 (1977), 151–69.

25 The software involved is PAUP beta 4.0. I would like to thank Peter Robinson for his considerable assistance and guidance in preparing the files.

26 See also Love, 'The Ranking of Variants', 44–46 & 57.

27 See also, R. W. Hanna III, 'The Application of Thought to Textual Criticism in All Modes—With apologies to A. E. Housman', *Studies in Bibliography*, 53 (2002, for 2000), 167–79.

28 E. K. Chambers, *William Shakespeare*, 2 vols (Oxford, 1930), II, 222–25.

29 Herford & Simpson, XI, 377–79.

30 Herford & Simpson, I, 133.

31 Thus, 'dew', 'deare', 'teare', 'as he whoe was', 'all to (speake) I meane', 'the ffawne, & feare', and 'the worthyer . . . to vse this' (lines 8, 17, 18, 24, 31, and 40).

32 For Morley, who later became Bishop of Winchester, see *DNB*. He was one of Aubrey's most important sources for his notes about Jonson.

33 C. M. Armitage, 'Donne's Poems in Huntington Manuscript 198: New Light on "The Funerall" ', *Studies in Philology*, 63 (1966), 697–707.

34 For a full discussion, see Bland, *The Manuscripts of Ben Jonson and his Contemporaries*, ch. 4, part III.

35 W. W. Greg, 'The Rationale of Copy-Text', *Collected Papers* (Oxford, 1966), 374–91.

36 *DNB*, XIX, 175–77; STC 18445–67, 18469–73. Fourteen volumes of Sutcliffe's man-uscripts are now in Emmanuel College, Cambridge. The identification was first made by Fleay, who argued that the reference helped date the poem to *c*.1606 (*Biographical Chronicle of English Drama*, I, 170). This was dismissed by Gayley and by Shapiro, 'The "Mermaid Club" ', *Modern Language Review*, 45 (1950), 14. For further comment on the dating see below.

37 A full record of variants will be published when the edition is prepared, but is avail-able on request.

38 Beal, *Index*, BmF 151; M. Eccles, 'Francis Beaumont's *Grammar Lecture*', *Review of English Studies*, 16 (1940), 402–16.

39 Herford & Simpson, XI, 377.

40 Re-issued as *The Foot-Post of Dover* in 1616 (STC 18591–91a). Chambers, *Shakespeare*, II, 223.

41 Chambers, *Shakespeare*, II, 225; W. A. Ringler, 'The 1640 and 1653 *Poems: By Francis Beaumont, Gent.* and the Canon of Beaumont's Nondramatic Verse', *Studies in Bibliography*, 40 (1987), 120–40 especially 123.

42 Folger Shakespeare Library MS V.a.96, f.71v.

43 Shapiro, 'Mermaid Club', 14.

44 P. Simpson, 'Francis Beaumont's Verse-letter to Ben Jonson: "The Sun, which doth the greatest comfort bring" ', *Modern Language Review*, 46 (1951), 435–6.

45 Beaumont & Fletcher, *Comedies and Tragedies*, sig. 3X4[r].

46 C. M. Gayley, *Francis Beaumont: Dramatist. A Portrait* (London, 1914), p. 99.

47 Beaumont and Fletcher, *Comedies and Tragedies*, sig. 3X3[v].

48 Gayley, *Francis Beaumont*, p. 97.

49 Kelliher, 'Francis Beaumont and Nathan Field', 1–42.

50 Kelliher, 'Francis Beaumont and Nathan Field', 10–11.

51 Kelliher, 'Francis Beaumont and Nathan Field', 13.

52 Chambers, *Shakespeare*, II, 223.

53 G. F. Beltz, *Memorials of the Order of the Garter* (London, 1841), p. cvi.

54 *Calendar of State Papers Venetian 1603–06*, 4 May 1606 (24 April), item 517, p. 344.

55 *ibid.*, 31 May 1606, item 527, p. 354.

56 York City Archives, York House Book, 33, f. 25r. I am grateful to Dr. Eileen White for drawing my attention to the Brooke correspondence here.

57 For a full discussion of the manuscript sources, see G. Heaton, *Performing Gifts: The manuscript circulation of Elizabethan and early Stuart court entertainments* (unpublished Ph.D. thesis: Cambridge, 2003), pp. 97–130.

58 *CSPD*, 1603–10, item 44, p. 318.

59 L. Hotson, 'Shakespeare and Mine Host of the Mermaid', *Atlantic Monthly*, 151 (1933), 708–14. Hotson's account of the document is very overblown.

60 Shapiro, 'The Mermaid Club', 6.

61 Shapiro, 'The Mermaid Club', 6–7.

62 T. Coryate, *Thomas Coriate; Traveller for the English Wits* (STC 5811; 1616).

63 Heaton, *Performing Gifts*, p. 118.

64 Shapiro, 'The Mermaid Club', 14; G. M. Gayley, *Francis Beaumont*, pp. 97–98.

65 Shapiro, 'The Mermaid Club', 14; *DNB*. The first stone of Chelsea College was laid on 8 May 1609, and the charter of incorporation dates from 8 May 1610.

66 Shapiro, 'The Mermaid Club', 15.

67 Shapiro, 'The Mermaid Club', 15–16.

68 Simpson and Shapiro, "The Mermaid Club': An answer and rejoinder', *Modern Language Review*, 46 (1951), 58–63.

69 Simpson and Shapiro, 'Answer and rejoinder', 58; Bodleian MS Aubrey 8, f. 91. For Stuart, see M. Butler, Sir Francis Stewart: Jonson's Overlooked Patron', *Ben Jonson Journal*, 2 (1995), 101–27.

70 Simpson and Shapiro, 'Answer and rejoinder', 59.

71 Simpson and Shapiro, 'Answer and rejoinder', 60.

72 Simpson and Shapiro, 'Answer and rejoinder', 60–63.

73 For a map see *STC*, III, insert between 246 and 247, co-ordinates 8–9 longitude and 10 latitude.

74 *DNB*, III, 733.

Manuscript Evidence and the Author of 'Aske me no more': William Strode, not Thomas Carew

Margaret Forey

I

It has always been generally assumed that 'Aske me no more'—one of the most enchanting and most popular of Caroline lyrics—is the work of Thomas Carew. Few discussions of Carew's poetry fail to mention it; Rhodes Dunlap, whose edition has been the standard work for half a century, called the poem 'one of Carew's best known in his own day and now';[1] more recently Mary Hobbs in her study of manuscript miscellanies described it confidently as being known to be Carew's 'on good evidence'.[2] Yet, as Scott Nixon has recently shown,[3] the poem has no known connection with Carew except its inclusion, together with other spurious pieces, in the 'bad' section tacked on to the first printed edition of his work, the 1640 edition of *Poems by Thomas Carew Esquire* which an entrepreneurial publisher rushed into print shortly after the poet's death.

Nor can any clue to its authorship be found in other early printed versions. *Poems by Wil. Shakespeare, Gent*, published in London in the same year as *Poems by Thomas Carew Esquire*, is a collection mainly of Shakespeare's sonnets and of songs from the plays, but these are followed by a section headed 'An Addition of some Excellent Poems, to those precedent, of renowned *Shakespeare* . . . By other Gentlemen'. The final poem, in this section and in the book, is 'Aske me no more'. No author's name is given. The same is true of its publication in Oxford in 1659 in John Wilson's *Cheerful Ayres or Ballads*, where it appears with a musical setting. The previous year it had appeared in *Wit Restor'd* as the second in a series of answer-poems,[4] the first providing the questions which 'Aske me no more' purports to answer; all are anonymous. It is found also, assigned to Pembroke, in the collection of poems published in 1660 under the names of Pembroke and Ruddier;[5] this miscellany—

for despite the title, that is largely what it is—cannot be trusted, for it includes a number of poems by other writers (for instance, three by William Strode are attributed to Pembroke and one to Ruddier, while a fifth lacks any attribution).

Manuscript versions of 'Aske me no more' are numerous (Beal's *Index* lists no fewer than 41[6]), but these do nothing to strengthen Carew's claim, for apart from one late and implausible ascription to Wotton[7] added in paler, apparently different, ink, none gives any attribution, either to Carew or to anyone else. Moreover, Nixon makes the point that the absence of this poem from all major manuscript collections of Carew's verse, including one apparently compiled under the poet's direction, can be regarded as evidence against his authorship.[8]

Nevertheless, Dunlap included this lyric without question in the Carew canon, the many textual variations found in manuscripts being interpreted as 'what looks like an early draft', 'extensive reworkings' or (a particularly cavalier claim) 'the cancelled sixth stanza'.[9] Nixon, rejecting this theory, reaches instead the conclusions that the manuscript variants derive both from the process of transmission and from deliberate reworking by copyists, and also that the poem 'was, and should still be treated as, a lyric of uncertain authorship'.[10] He allows himself only one hypothesis: what he calls the 'intriguing possibility' that 'Aske me no more' was actually the work of William Strode.[11] It is the argument of this article that this hypothesis is correct, and can be demonstrated to be so from the manuscript evidence.

Of the forty-one manuscript texts listed by Beal, nearly half are or may be from the 1630s (some from early in that decade); none is earlier. Most of the remainder belong to the 1640s, a few to the second half of the century. Three are connected with the musician William Lawes, three with another musician, John Wilson, while a seventh contains a setting by an unknown composer. There are three manuscripts showing Cambridge associations and eleven which appear to be related to Oxford. Four of the Oxford manuscripts have Christ Church connections; and one of the four—Corpus College MS 325 (Beal's Δ 1: cited hereafter as *325*)—is out of all these manuscripts the only one to be devoted almost entirely to the work of one poet.

When the Corpus manuscripts were lodged temporarily in the Bodleian Library some years ago, *325* was recognised by Margaret Crum as being in the hand of the Christ Church poet William Strode, and as consisting largely of a collection of his own English and Latin poems with numerous revisions, particularly to the former. She was also able to demonstrate that a later owner, William Fulman, was acquainted with a second Strode holograph in which the poems were arranged according to genre, probably with a view to publication.[12] In *325* Fulman listed the titles of several poems not in *325* that he found in what he called 'Strodes other Copie' (Beal's Δ 2), copied some other poems in, and attached to each poem in his own manuscript the number of the page on which it appeared in the 'other Copie'. Very occasionally he added a different reading, apparently also from the other manuscript. Investigation of Crum's findings shows that the two volumes must have been of similar size, for it can be seen that poems occupied about the same amount of space in each. Thus, although the whereabouts of Strode's second manuscript—if indeed it still exists—is unknown, a good deal is known about its contents and make-up.

In my own subsequent work on Strode,[13] I was able to carry these investigations further and show that Strode's English poems in *325* fall into two groups.[14] Group One (fols 52–99v) consists of poems that Strode composed in the 1620s. These he copied into the manuscript in a secretary hand (though the last few poems in the group show this entering a transitional phase) and in dark brown ink, also during the 1620s; they are entered consecutively without gaps, though not in the order of composition. Most of these poems circulated widely in the university and elsewhere, and it is not uncommon for Strode's authorship to be known to those who copied them. The second and smaller group, written in the italic hand that he used from about 1630 and in a lighter brown ink, begins on fol. 99v and continues until 126v, although there are also some poems from this group on previously blank pages earlier in the book and at the end. Poems from Group Two hardly circulated at all, and usually when they do appear in other manuscripts Strode's authorship seems not to have been known.

At some point in the 1630s or later, Strode began to revise the poems he had entered in *325*, in several cases extensively. Except for corrections made at the time of copying or at any rate in the ink used for transcribing Group One, the revisions can be seen to have been done in two stages: first in the light brown ink used for transcribing the Group Two poems, and finally in black ink. The revised versions were unknown to those among whom his poems circulated (except for the copyist of BL Add. MS 30982, discussed in the next section), but the 'other Copie' apparently post-dated the last revision. The final entry in the 'other Copie' was also the latest of Strode's datable poems, an elegy composed after July 1641, but this could have been added some time after the rest of the manuscript was completed. But whatever plans Strode had in mind for this copy, his death early in 1645 prevented his carrying them out.

On fol. 100v of *325*, among the other poems of Group Two, Strode copied out 'Aske me no more' (PLATE 1), followed on the next page by an abusive parody entitled 'Answere or Mock-song'. On the page before it (*i.e.* fol. 100), he entered 'A Moderating Answere to Both' which uses the format of the other poems, but is a response from the lady to whom the other two are addressed. All three poems contain alterations. When editing Strode in the 1960s I described the changes in 'Aske me no more' as the correction of slips made in copying (p. 154), and ascribed to him only the second and third components of this trio. 'Aske me no more' was 'known' to be by Carew, and I accepted this as given; besides there was, it seemed, clear evidence in the manuscript that whoever the author might be, it could not be Strode. Fulman, finding 'Aske me no more' published in Pembroke and Ruddier's *Poems*, had added a note beside the poem in *325*: 'Penbr.p.92. But in Strode's other Copie ascr. to Shakespeare'. Since Strode apparently believed the poem to be by Shakespeare, for an editor of Strode the actual authorship of the poem was largely immaterial. As Fulman noted that 'Aske me no more' appeared on page 144 in the 'other Copie' (the other two poems were allotted 145 and 146), I assumed that Strode wanted 'Aske me no more' published beside his own work so that the two following poems might be properly understood.

Able recently to return to the editing of Strode after an extensive gap, I noticed something the importance of which I had previously overlooked. In his transcription of 'Aske me no more' Strode has changed the text in two places, but there is a significant difference between the two alterations. In line three he wrote 'For in your [this word struck through] pure Love heaven did prepare': this is indeed what I had called it, the correction of a slip made in copying. The alteration had been made immediately, for the word 'pure' had been substituted on the same line, immediately after the erasure, before he continued with 'Love'. In line thirteen, however, which originally read 'Aske me [no] more where Jove bestowes', 'Jove' has been struck through in black ink, and the same ink has been used to insert 'Time' above the line. The change was therefore made during Strode's second bout of reworking. There is no reason to suppose that Strode was correcting what he regarded as an erroneous version of another man's poem, for the reading he substituted is not found in any of the extant manuscripts, nor does it appear in printed texts. Furthermore, while Strode tinkered endlessly with his own poems, adding marginal revisions even in printed texts whose publication he had authorised,[15] there is no indication that he tampered with other men's work. The handful of poems by his friend Corbett which appear in *325* show no signs of emendation;[16] and in the

from the page before. Two of these ('A Superscription' and 'On a Butcher') required between them twelve lines for text and two, more likely three, for titles, as well as some space between the poems; the third, 'Upon Will: Bridle' (text 68 lines, title five lines), could therefore be expected to finish at the bottom of page 21 or more probably some way into page 22. So it did, for the next poem is assigned the number 22. This, with 26 lines and three more for the title, would occupy at least a page; but 'An Answere made to Maudlins Rimes' started on p. 23. Whether it started at the top of the page or further down is unimportant; it is plainly impossible for 'On the Loss of C. Church Proctorship' to have been inserted before it, the only position that would have justified its appearance in the manuscript at all.

Using the same method, similar conclusions can be reached about two more of Strode's originals. After the ignominious failure of the Cadiz expedition he wrote a satire on the courtiers who had taken a leading part in it, which he entitled 'An Answeare to an Old Soldier of the Queenes'. There are two poems with this title: the earlier, which was not satirical, has no bearing on Strode's poem except inasmuch as it initiated a distinctive and easily imitated format which he and others made use of. The second 'Old Soldier', mocking Mansfeld's disastrous campaign of 1624,[19] portrayed a ragged, ill-equipped scarecrow useless in warfare; 'An Answeare' describes the 'New Soldier' who set out for Cadiz as a fashionable dandy, but equally incompetent. In the 'other Copie' it would have required a minimum of two and a half pages (depending on the treatment of the refrain, which in *325* is given in full only in the first and last stanzas). Starting calculations from the beginning of the section ('Songs and Sonnets') in which 'An Answeare' appeared, it can be demonstrated that the 34 lines of the 'Old Soldier' were also not included.

Strode later, by request from 'a well-wisher to that side', wrote a reply to an anti-puritan satire which he refers to as 'the song against the New-Inglanders'. This is identifiable as a ballad called 'The Summons to newe England':[20] both poems have the same structure, contain refrains making constant use of the word 'pure' (generally rhymed with 'sure'), conclude with an Envoy and refer to the Exeter preacher John Warham, who with his supporters had sailed for New England from Plymouth in 1630. Although 'An answer to the song against the New-Inglanders' was preceded in the 'other Copie' by two lost poems, the second of these began on p. 150 and 'An answer' two pages later; 'The Summons to newe England' would have required at least four.

Only in one instance is evidence from page-numbers less than conclusive. Strode's 'An Opposite to Melancholy' is a response to Fletcher's (or Middleton's) 'Hence all you vain delights'; the two are paired in several manuscripts[21] and also in *Wit Restor'd* (1658), on page 66 of which 'An Opposite' is headed 'The answer, by Dr. Stroad'. The connection is also shown by general similarities in format; by Strode's substitution of such features as 'An arme for joy flung out of joynt' and 'an eye still dancing' for Fletcher's folded arms, downcast eyes, and other signs of melancholy; and above all by his opening instruction 'Returne my joyes'. But the shortness of Fletcher's poem makes its absence from the 'other Copie' impossible to prove conclusively on the grounds of space. However, when revising *325* Strode added a couplet at the head of 'An Opposite' which was clearly designed to dissociate it from its original and allow it to stand alone; he had thus no reason to include Fletcher's poem in the 'other Copie'.[22]

The difference between the treatment of, on the one hand, 'Aske me no more' and its companion pieces and, on the other, the poems Strode wrote as answers to other men's verses is clear. Poems by other people to which he had written a reply were not included in the 'other Copie'. There can be little doubt that he included all three 'Aske me' poems because he was himself the author of them all.

But what then of Fulman's statement that, in the 'other Copie', 'Aske me no more' was 'ascr. to Shakespeare', the red herring that for so long has led scholars away from recognising its true authorship? Fulman was a careful observer and conscientious recorder; his note cannot merely be ignored. Of course, he does not state that the ascription is in Strode's hand; since he himself saw the volume after the publication of 'Penbr.' in 1660, at least fifteen years had elapsed since Strode's death during which a later owner could have inserted the ascription.[23] Nevertheless, Fulman's implication would seem to be that Strode had written it. The truth surely, as Scott Nixon and I have independently surmised, lies in a mistake on Fulman's part that has a certain irony about it. Read in full, his comment is 'Penbr.p.92. But in Strode's other Copie ascr. to Shakespeare'. What Fulman jotted down first was that he had found the poem in print; he gave the reference as a matter of interest. It is likely that, though Fulman did not realise it, Strode had done precisely the same: turning over a copy of *Poems of Wil. Shakespeare, Gent,* he had found a poem of his own printed anonymously at the end, and noted this fact beside his own transcript of that poem. If the 'other Copie' were some day to be found, Strode's annotation beside this poem would, I believe, say not 'By Shakespeare' but '*Poems of Wil. Shakespeare, Gent*'; though as the pages of that edition were unnumbered, he could not add a page number as Fulman himself did. Since the editor of *Poems of Wil. Shakespeare, Gent* was well aware that the pieces he added at the end were 'by other Gentlemen', Fulman himself cannot have been familiar with the *Poems*, otherwise he could not have made the mistake he did. As it was, he read the note as implying Shakespeare's authorship, and so initiated a wild-goose chase for later scholars.

II

The realisation that Strode is the author of this poem provides some clues to its dating. In *325* it appears among the poems entered in italic, Group Two, which implies that it was probably composed between *c.*1630 and 1637:[24] indeed, had it been written earlier, when Strode was making his work generally accessible, it is unlikely that so popular a piece would not have been labelled as his by any of its transcribers, even those in Oxford. That the three 'Aske me' poems were the first of the Group Two entries in the holograph does not necessarily mean that they were written early in the 1630s, but there are other indications that this was the case.

A probable *terminus a quo* for composition of these poems is limited to 1630–33 by their appearance in BL Add. MS 30982 (Beal's Δ 10: cited hereafter as *30982*), a manuscript of particular interest for Strode studies. Its original ownership is attested by inscriptions on several pages: 'Daniel Leare his book' (fol. 1); 'Mr Daniel Leare eius liber' on the end page (fol. 164); and most interestingly of all, 'Daniell Leare his booke. witnesse William Strode' (fol. 1v). Leare, who was an undergraduate at Strode's college, Christ Church, between 1630 and May 1633,[25] has been identified by Mary Hobbs as William Strode's second cousin, who haled from the same part of Devon as the poet himself;[26] furthermore, Strode was the tutor who paid his Caution Money (a deposit on an undergraduate's behalf against unpaid bills).[27] Close relations between the two are also attested, not only by the fact that Leare had an exceptional number (over eighty) of Strode's known poems in his own miscellany, but also by evidence that some of these were copied directly from 325 itself.[28] Moreover *30982* has several poems not known to other copyists (indeed, Leare's is the only manuscript other than the holograph to contain not only 'Aske me no more' but also both its related poems).[29] Since, as Hobbs comments, internal evidence shows most of Leare's manuscript to have been copied in 1631–32, the obvious assumption would be that any Strode poem in his miscellany was entered before Leare left Oxford for London in the spring of 1633, and that the 'Aske me' trio can be dated accordingly.[30]

The position which these three poems occupy in Leare's book is interesting also. For some reason Leare made entries in his book from both ends. Thirty-two of Strode's poems are among entries made in the first half of the book in the normal way; but starting at the reverse end (fol. 157) with the book upside down Leare also entered a large number of poems in the opposite direction. This second sequence ends with an unbroken run of thirty poems by Strode, the last of which finishes on fol. 119v rev. None of these poems is found in Group Two in *325*; all can be assumed to have been written by the time Leare arrived in Oxford (the latest that can be dated was inspired by a death in 1629).[31] But on fol. 119 rev.—still with the book upside-down, and therefore later—a different hand has entered 'Aske me no more' (see PLATE 2); the same hand follows this with its companion poems on fols. 118v rev. and 118 rev.[32] The few remaining entries, occupying pages left blank in the middle of the volume between the two sequences, are later both in content and in handwriting; the 'Aske me' trio, was therefore the last of the Caroline entries. Not only does this provide further evidence that poems which appear in *325* in Group Two are later than those of Group One; it also suggests that the 'Aske me' poems may not have been written till towards the end of Leare's Oxford career.

There is a tantalising probability that the entries from fol. 119 rev. to fol. 118 rev. are actually in Strode's hand, although written more hastily than their counterparts in *325*, which were entered with something of a flourish. Inevitably such a judgement must be largely subjective, but it may be worth recording that when I first encountered *30982*, at a time when I had been using the holograph daily for months, I thought I recognised Strode's handwriting on these three pages and made a note to that effect; forty years later—by which time my previous impression had been forgotten—my reaction was the same, and only afterwards did I find my original note. Spelling and letter formation in the two copies of these poems are not always identical, but forms used in *30982* can be matched elsewhere in the holograph. Interestingly, verses three and four of 'Aske me no more' are reversed in *30982*, producing the verse-order most common in other manuscripts. In *30982* all verses begin 'Aske me no more' although in *325* the final verse starts 'Nor ask me more'; other manuscripts appear evenly split between the two forms. Apart from this, while the two texts of this poem are not wholly identical the differences are few and trivial, and can easily be attributed to carelessness, or to Strode's having second (or third, or fourth) thoughts, as he was so apt to do.

The text of the 'Mock-song' in *30982* increases the likelihood that Strode's handwriting appears here in this manuscript, for not only does

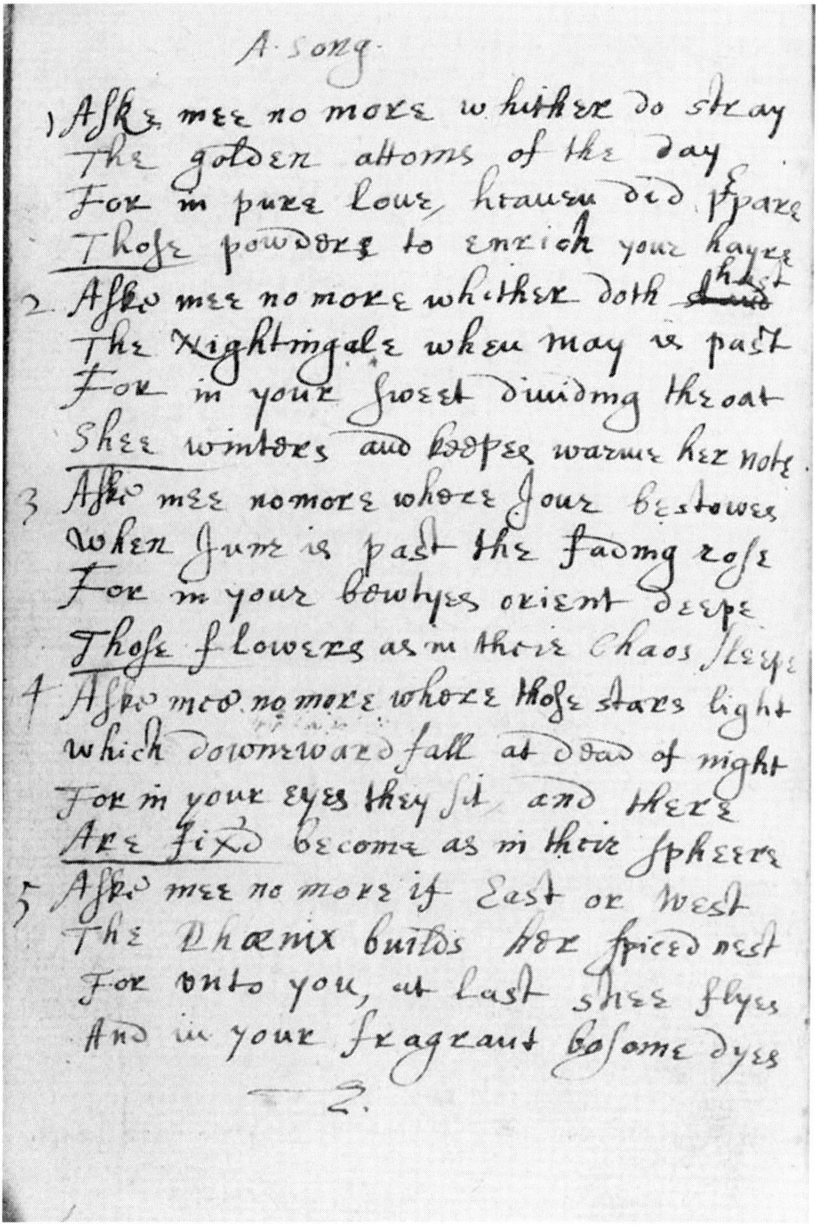

A · song ·

1 Aske mee no more whither do stray
The golden attoms of the day
For in pure love heaven did spare
Those powders to enrich your hayre

2 Aske mee no more whither doth hast
The Nightingale when may is past
For in your sweet dividing throat
Shee winters and keepes warme her note.

3 Aske mee nomore whose Jour bestowes
When June is past the fading rose
For in your bowtyes orient deepe
Those flowers as in their Chaos sleepe

4 Aske mee no more whose those stars light
which downeward fall at dead of night
For in your eyes they sit and there
Are fixd become as in their spheere

5 Aske mee no more if East or West
The Phoenix builds her spiced nest
For unto you, at last shee flyes
And in your fragrant bosome dyes

⸺ Z.

PLATE 2. *The copy of 'Aske me no more' in Daniel Leare's verse miscellany: London, British Library, Additional MS 30982, fol. 119r. (Original page size 145 × 90mm.) Reproduced by permission of the Board of the British Library.*

it provide examples of the indecisive tinkering just mentioned: it also contains readings and alterations that link it specifically to the holograph. In line eight 'comes with' has been crossed out and 'is in' written above; in similar fashion 'feathers' has been altered to 'Thistles' in line sixteen. The holograph contains both these original readings and both these alterations, in the light brown ink used by Strode to copy the poem. In lines eleven and twelve the reading of *30982* is that of the holograph before the stage of black revision; in line seventeen it reads 'wherein whose', whereas the holograph originally had 'within whose', later changed to 'within what'. In other respects both copies are identical. The text of the 'Moderating Answere' in *30982* is identical to that of the holograph before alteration, except that in line ten a nonsensical reading has been produced by the accidental rendering of 'as' as 'and', and a patent error in the holograph has not been reproduced. The texts of all three poems in both *325* and *30982*, with their alterations, are given below in the appendix.

In conclusion, it appears that the 'Aske me' trio initiated the new phase in Strode's poetic career that began in the 1630s, when—perhaps because career successes removed him further from the company of the young[33]—he no longer showed his poems to the youthful enthusiasts busily compiling their miscellanies. His young cousin seems to have been an exception. That these three poems were the last entries to be made in *30982* while it was in Leare's possession suggests that they were copied in shortly before his departure from the university in May 1633: perhaps Strode wrote out his latest work as a parting gesture.

III

It is unlikely that Leare's manuscript played much part in the subsequent popularity of 'Aske me no more'. That the 'Mock-song' had little and the 'Moderating Answere' no further circulation suggests that they were unknown to most copyists of their companion piece. Moreover, although Leare seldom bothered to attach a name or initials to his transcriptions of Strode's poems, plainly he was often aware of their authorship and in this case must have been: the lack of any ascription even in manuscripts of Oxford provenance hardly suggests that they derive from *30982*. The contrast is marked between the fate of 'Aske me no more' and that of Strode's even more popular poem, 'I saw fair Cloris walk alone': the latter, which appears in more than eighty manuscripts (Beal, StW 747–834), has Strode's name or initials appended in a dozen of these, while a further eleven show some awareness, though not always accurately understood, of who inspired it. Knowledge of author and subject are detailed in some instances, hazy in others, and absent in most, suggesting a process of transmission following the course one would expect. 'Aske me no more', on the other hand, appears to have jumped straight to the last of these three stages.

Such wide yet anonymous popularity may well have resulted from its transformation into a song. Nixon argues convincingly that the compiler of the 1640 edition of Carew was familiar with the text as set by William Lawes,[34] but, using stanza order as a basis, he adds that this version had only limited currency. Verse order is not, however, the most reliable indicator for a poem structured like 'Aske me no more'; anyone transcribing from memory might easily rearrange the verses, as indeed Strode himself deliberately or accidentally did, if my identification of the hand found in *30982* is correct. Lawes could have encountered the poem in 1636 when writing settings for the songs in *The Floating Island*, a play written by Strode for performance during the royal visit to Oxford that summer. The likelihood is that Lawes was present in Oxford to confer with the author and coach the singers, for the three-day visit was intended by Laud, the organiser, to be an impressive affair. Strode—a music-lover, as several of his poems show—would probably have relished acquaintance with the foremost musician of the Caroline court; at any rate it is not far-fetched to assume that he might have shown Lawes other poems of his on this occasion. But whether or not the composer encountered 'Aske me no more' in this way, Lawes was sufficiently charmed by the piece to write a musical setting for that also. In musical form it might well have spread beyond Oxford fast and widely, without authorship of the words being known or even thought of much interest. Yet ten manuscripts exist which show Oxford connections,[35] at least one of which predated Lawes' connection with Strode: in BL Sloane MS 1446 (dated 1633 by Beal) a number of Strode's poems appear, ascribed to 'W.S.', but 'Aske me no more' is anonymous. If Lawes helped to make the poem more widely known, Strode's apparently new reluctance to publicise his poetry beyond a very limited circle must have played its part in keeping his authorship unknown.

IV

Discovery of the true authorship of 'Aske me no more' also establishes the text. Throughout this article I have referred to the poem by an abbreviated version of its opening line, for what is generally known as

the first line must now be called the thirteenth.[36] Later editions have
followed *Poems of Thomas Carew* by starting 'Aske me no more where Jove
bestows', even though the manuscripts, with only three exceptions,[37]
follow Strode's original by beginning 'Aske me no more whither do
stray'. The next three stanzas are found in all possible orders; the fifth,
however, appears to have been generally recognised as providing a
conclusion. An exception is provided by Bodleian MS Don. d. 58, where
the poem is weakened by the addition of an inferior sixth stanza which
cannot be regarded as authorial. Bodleian MS Eng. poet. f. 27 likewise
contains additional matter in the form of two extra stanzas inserted after
the first (Bodleian MS Ashmole 47 contains one of these); again, these can
be presumed to be imitations by another writer. Not only does the holograph contain no hint that extra stanzas ever existed: the 'Answere or
Mock-song', which matches the first poem stanza by stanza, has only
five.

Although Nixon (p. 104) states that 'there is [no evidence] whatsoever
to suggest that any of the variant forms are due to authorial revision', in
view of the slight differences between the texts of *325* and *30982*, and
Strode's ingrained tendency to fiddle endlessly with his poems, it is by
no means impossible that some of the variant readings widespread in
other manuscripts are also authorial in origin. This could explain why,
although no manuscript transmission can be demonstrated to account
for it, such a large number of manuscripts omit 'Ar' in line twelve, thus
making 'fixed' into two syllables; likewise in line eighteen 'spicy' appears
in place of 'spiced' on a number of occasions. But such trivial alterations
could easily have arisen independently. It is particularly tempting to
think genuine the reading 'Causes' in line sixteen, which is not only that
found in editions of Carew, but also the reading of the great majority of
manuscripts. 'Chaos' was, however, known to the scribe of Bodleian MS
Ashmole 47 and likely to lie behind the reading 'cahus' in MS Ashmole
38. It appears also in *30982*, and was therefore Strode's choice both in
the early 1630s and when compiling the 'other Copie' perhaps ten years
later. While it would not be entirely out of character for Strode to have
altered his text from 'Chaos' to 'Causes' and later reversed this decision,
to argue for the authenticity of 'Causes' on such hypothetical grounds
would be risky.[38]

What is undeniable is that both the Jove/Time alteration and the
substitution of 'Chaos' for 'Causes' are likely to be regretted by readers
familiar with the long-established version. In the replacement of
'Causes' by 'Chaos' one may today regret a loss of euphony (though to
what extent 'C*au*ses' and '*O*rient' shared a vowel sound in the seventeenth century I am not aware). The loss of the long *o* in Jove, picked

up again in the rhymes of the couplet, is particularly unfortunate; replacement of the softer *J* by the staccato *T* is likewise to be deplored. Nevertheless, this alteration is comprehensible when one looks at Strode's revisions of his work as a whole. After taking Orders he seems to have found some of his early work inappropriate for a clergyman; although the sexual material that later disturbed Dobell[39] was not altered, in several poems a theological flavour was introduced, generally to their detriment. A similar attitude seems to have prevailed here. Although Cupid remained allowable in other of Strode's love poems, to allow power over Nature and Time to the ruler of the Olympians evidently struck him as going too far.

In other respects the text of *325* appears more polished. The atoms of the day are more appropriately given a plural verb, and the activities of the phoenix a subjunctive one. Stars that descend to the lady's eyes when they set are preferable to stars that merely sit there (though this distinction may not have been a real one to Strode); in particular, the variant opening of the final stanza shapes and concludes the poem better than a mere fifth repetition of 'Aske me'.

But both for good and for ill, the version of the poem found in *325* must be accepted as the latest known intention of its author, just as surely as that author must at last be recognised as William Strode.

THE TEXTS

Strode's final texts in *325* of 'Aske me no more' and its companion pieces appear below. Readings of the holograph before alteration are given in the apparatus, indicated as *325 b.a.* except for those which are patently slips made in copying; these are given as *325 b.corr.* Variants found in *30982* (including those which may be attributable merely to spelling) are also included; where alterations appear in this manuscript, the original reading is given as *30982 b.a.* Alterations in both manuscripts are in ink of the same colour as the original texts except where otherwise indicated. Verses 3 and 4 of 'Aske me no more' are reversed in *30982*.

Song

Aske me noe more whether doe stray
The Golden Atomes of the Day;
For in pure Love heavn did prepare
Those powders to enrich your hayre.

5   Aske me no more whether doth hast
           The Nightingale when May is past;
           For in your sweete dividing throate
           She winters and keepes warme her Note.

           Aske me no more where those stars light
10   Which downeward fall at dead of Night;
           For in your Eies they sett, and there
           Ar fixed become as in their Sphere.

           Aske me no more where Time bestowes
           When June is past, the fading Rose;
15   For in your beauties Orient deepe
           Those flowers as in their Chaos sleepe.

           Nor aske me more if East or West
           The Phœnix build her spiced Nest;
           For unto you at last she flies,
20   And in your fragrant bosome dies.

Song *Title supplied*] A song *30982*   1 whether] whither *30982*   3 pure] your *325 b.corr.*   5 whether] whither *30982*   hast] *an erased word which can be partially read as* 'sh[?] . . . d' *30982 b.a.*   11 sett] sit *30982*   13 no *30982: om.* 325   Time *added interlineally in black ink*] Jove *325 b.a. (erased in black ink)*, *30982*   17 Nor aske me more] Aske mee no more *30982* 18 build] builds *30982*

Answere or Mock-song

           Ile tell you true, whereon doth light
           The dusky Shade of banishd Night,
           For in iust vengeance heavns allow
           It still should frowne upon your brow.

5   Ile tell you true where men may seeke
           The Sound which once the Owle did shreeke;
           For in your false dividing throate
           It lies, and death is in its Note.

           Ile tell you true whether doth pass
10   The smiling looke out of the Glass;
           It leapes into your face, for there
           The falsest Shadow doth appeare.

           Ile tell you true whether ar blown
           The Ayry wheeles of thistle-downe:
15   They fly into your minde whose care
           Is to be light as Thistles are.

Ile tell you true within what Nest
The Stranger Cuckoes Eggs doe rest;
It is your bosome, which can keepe
20   Nor Him nor Him, where one should sleepe.

Answere or Mock-song] The answeare *30982*   8 is in] comes with *325 b.a., 30982 b.a.*   11 leapes *formed by partially overwriting original in black ink*] leapd *325 b.a., 30982*   12 The falsest *formed by partially overwriting original in black ink*] A falser *325 b.a., 30982*   16 be] be be *325 b.corr.*   Thistles] feathers *325 b.a., 30982 b.a.*   17 within what] within whose *325 b.a.:* wherein whose *30982*

A Moderating Answere to Both

Ile tell you of another Sun
That setts as Rising it begun;
It is myself, who keepe one sphere,
And were the Same if Men so were.

5   What need I tell that Life and Death
May pass in Sentence from one Breath?
So issue from myne Equall heart
Both Love and Scorne on Mens Desart.

Ile tell you in what heavnly Hell
10   An Angell and a Feind doe dwell:
It is mine Eie, whose Glassy booke
Sends back the gazers diverse looke.

Ile tell you in a diverse scale
One Weight can up and downeward hale:
15   You call mee Thistle, you a Rose;
I neither am, yet Both of those.

Ile tell you where both Frost and Fire
In Peace of common League conspire:
My frozen Brest the Flint is like,
20   Yet yeilds a Sparke if well you strike.

Concl.

Then you that love and you that loath,
With one Aspecte I answere both:
For round about me gloes a Fire
Can melt and harden cross desire.

4 were   the *30982*: were to the *325*   8 on] of *325 b.a., 30982*   10 An] And *30982*

In spite of the readings of both MSS I suspect that line 11 should read 'glassy brooke', which makes much better sense. Since the previous line in *30982* obviously contains a careless error, it is feasible that a slip in *325* could have been copied into the other manuscript without being noticed and corrected.

NOTES

1 *The Poems of Thomas Carew*, ed. R. Dunlap (Oxford, 1949), p. 263.

2 Mary Hobbs, 'Early English Verse Miscellanies', *English Manuscript Studies*, 1 (1989), p. 185.

3 ' "Aske me no more" and the Manuscript Verse Miscellany', *English Literary Renaissance*, 29, pt. 1 (Winter 1999), 97–130.

4 The first poem, on p. 113, is entitled 'A Question' (beginning 'I aske thee whence those ashes were'); this is followed by 'Aske me no more' on p. 114, headed 'The Reply'. Then come, under the titles 'The Mock-Song' and 'The Moderatrix', William Strode's 'Answere or Mock-song' and 'A Moderating Answere to Both'; the series concludes with a misogynistic piece, 'The affirmative answer' (beginning 'Oh no, heavens saw mens fancys stray').

5 *Poems . . . by . . . William Earl of Pembroke [and] . . . Sr Benjamin Ruddier* (London, 1660), p. 92.

6 P. Beal, *Index of English Literary Manuscripts*, II, i (1987), pp. 89–91; referred to hereafter as Beal. Forty-three items are recorded for this poem, but CwT 729 (in London, British Library, Harley MS 6918) and CwT 763 (in New Haven, Yale University, Osborn Collection, b 197) contain only a parody of 'Aske me no more' with an identical opening line.

7 In Oxford, Bodleian Library, MS Tanner 465, compiled in the mid or late seventeenth century by William (later Archbishop) Sancroft. The ascription, according to Beal (p. 90), is in different ink. Certainly the ink normally used in this volume is dark, whereas 'by Sr H. Wotton' has been added to the original title, 'An Ode', in noticeably paler ink. But the underlining of the whole of this enlarged title is also in paler ink. Since the rest of the manuscript shows that the scribe made a practice of underlining the whole of his titles, on this particular occasion either he failed to do so until adding to the title later, or he originally drew (for some reason in paler ink) a line much too long for his original title, or else the whole title and its underlining were written at the same time using two forms of ink.

Exactly the same situation occurs in one other entry in this manuscript, curiously enough also related to Wotton. On fol. 43 'Ye meaner beauties of the night' has the title 'A Song' in the same dark ink used for the poem, but 'by Sr H. Wotton' and a line under the whole have been added in ink of the paler shade. At present I can suggest no explanation for this feature. There is no evidence anywhere in the manuscript of the ink's becoming gradually paler as the pen ran dry.

Although she was a notable beauty, that 'Aske me no more' was actually written with Elizabeth of Bohemia in mind cannot be credited, for she was in exile on the continent from 1620 till after the Restoration (Wotton, a courtier of long standing, had known her before); as will be shown, 'Aske me no more' can be dated to the early 1630s. The ascription in Bodleian MS Tanner 465 may have been added by someone acquainted with BL Add. MS 70639. This manuscript, which appears in

Beal according to its former location as Trumbull Add. MS 51 in Berkshire Record Office (CwT 738), is dated by him *c.*1630. It consists of two sections: the first is a journal of proceedings in Parliament from January to March 1629, following which comes a handful of poems in a different hand. This second section contains 'Aske me no more' under the title 'verses on ye Queen of Bohemia', but of the date of transcription nothing can be said except that it was later than March 1629. The name 'Arthur Langford' appears in the manuscript with the date May 1629; later it was in the possession of the Trumbull family of Easthampstead Park.

8 *loc.cit.* p. 100.

9 *op.cit.* p. lxiii.

10 *loc. cit.* p. 99.

11 *ibid.*, p. 101.

12 M. Crum, 'William Fulman and an Autograph Manuscript of the Poet Strode', *Bodleian Library Record*, 4, No.6 (December 1953), pp. 324–35. While in the Bodleian the manuscript was known as MS CCC. 325.

13 'A Critical Edition of the Poetical Works of William Strode, excluding *The Floating Island*', unpublished Oxford B.Litt. thesis, 1966, currently being revised for publication.

14 A few English poems by authors other than Strode appear in various places in the manuscript. Among the Latin poems at the beginning of the book are two English poems on the birth of Prince Charles, followed by Latin translations at the end of which Strode has written 'Latin'd by WS'. Strode has ascribed the first of the English poems to 'R.Ox' (his friend Richard Corbett, Bishop of Oxford) and labelled the second 'For Dr. Leonard Hutton' (Corbett's father-in-law, and Strode's colleague at Christ Church); as his Latin versions appear above the names of Corbett and Hutton in the university's congratulatory volume on the birth, it may be assumed that both English poems were written by Corbett and turned into publishable form by Strode, the better Latinist. These are followed by two further English poems attributed to Corbett, also with Strode's translations. After entries in Latin conclude on fol. 48r, eleven blank pages are followed by three more poems (fols 49v–50v), attributed by Strode to 'R. Norv.' (Corbett became Bishop of Norwich in 1632).

Neither are two English poems at the end of the volume by Strode. Between blank pages that follow the consecutive transcription of his own poems, Strode has copied out Henry Rainold's 'Why lovely boy', followed by Henry King's reply, 'Black maid complain not'; neither poem is assigned a title or author. King's poem contains two mistakes corrected at the time of transcription, one by rewriting the word more clearly, the other by striking out a patently wrong word and adding the correct reading above, with a caret. The use of a caret in *325* appears always to indicate a correction made at the time of copying. Fulman has, as usual, added the *325* page number (134), but nothing else.

15 Forey, p. 354.

16 Nixon (p. 102) states that in *325* Strode 'transcribes and answers' poems by Richard Corbett and Peter Apsley. This is not quite correct; Strode translated but did not reply to poems by Corbett (see note 14). Nor is any poem by Apsley found in *325*: there is, however, a poem on the burning of a lock of hair at the end of which Strode has written 'p*er* [or just possibly 'p*ro*', as given in M. Crum, *First-line Index of English Poetry 1500–1800 in Manuscripts of the Bodleian Library Oxford* (2 vols, Oxford, 1969), II, 1093: W1560] P. Apsley', indicating that he is the subject.

17 This poem, beginning 'Why how now C.Church Lads? What, all a Mort', appears in Bodleian MSS Douce f. 5, fol. 6, and Eng. Poet e.14, fol. 59, and in BL Sloane MS 542, fol. 40v.

18 The secretary hand used for the Group One poems was slightly smaller, and usually produced a minimum of 26 lines per page. The 'other Copie' is likely to have been in the italic hand which Strode used in later life.

19 Published in *Merry Drollery*, Part I (London, 1661), pp. 22–23. See also C. Firth, 'The Reign of Charles I', *Transactions of the Royal Historical Society*, 3rd Ser., 6 (1912), p. 21, where several parodies, including Strode's, are quoted.

20 'The Summons to newe-Ingland' (beginning 'Lett all that putrifidean secte') is found in Bodleian MSS Tanner 306, fol. 286, and Ashmole 38, fol. 225, and also in *Merry Drollery* Part II (1661), p. 203.

21 e.g. Bodleian MSS Malone 21, fol. 80; Rawl. poet. 142, fol. 42v; Rawl. D. 1092, fol. 273v. The last-named makes the mistake of attributing both poems to Strode. In fact the 'Fletcher' poem was in existence before 1616, since it appears as a song in *The Nice Valour*, a play traditionally attributed to John Fletcher, but more recently to Thomas Middleton: see *The Dramatic Works in the Beaumont and Fletcher Canon*, ed. F. Bowers, VII (Cambridge, 1989), 427–9.

22 I exclude from the category of imitations Strode's 'Song of Death and the Resurrection', although this also is based on a format created by another poet (the unknown author of the *Sic Vita* poem 'Like as the Damaske Rose you see'). This was widely imitated, and it is not possible to say which or how many of the poems in this mode Strode was familiar with. However, his poem is not dependent on models for its point. Instead he creates a twist unusual in this genre by reversing the theme of the poem halfway through: the first verse speaks of the brevity of a falling star or a wave breaking upon a rock, leading to the usual conclusion 'Ev'n such is man'; the second uses the same images to demonstrate that 'Ev'n soe man's life, pawnd in the grave, Waites for a rising it must have'. It is thus of interest in relation to 'Aske me no more' only as another example—though this time within the confines of a single poem—of Strode's writing an answer-poem to his own work.

23 The likelihood is that the 'other Copie', a saleable commodity, was disposed of after the poet's death, which was followed shortly afterwards by that of his wife. It is unlikely that the guardian of their young daughter, her maternal uncle, would have seen any reason to keep his brother-in-law's papers, some of which certainly ended up in the possession of one of Strode's colleagues. It is likely that bound items were eventually sold through the great Oxford bookseller Richard Davis. Fulman himself both bought and borrowed books from Davis, to whom he may owe his ownership of *325* and his apparently temporary acquaintance with the 'other Copie'. (Forey, *op. cit.* pp. lxxv–lxxvi).

24 Forey, p. lxii.

25 Admissions Register, MS DP i.a.1, fols.179–180; Caution Book 1625–41, MS xiii.b.1, p. 23; both at Christ Church, Oxford.

26 Mary Hobbs, *Early Seventeenth Century Verse Miscellany Manuscripts* (Aldershot, 1992), pp. 121–22.

27 Caution Book 1625–41, MS xiii.b.1, p. 22, at Christ Church, Oxford.

28 Forey, p. lxxxi. This applies only to some of the Strode poems in *30982*; others were probably or in some cases almost certainly obtained by Leare from other sources.

29 The curious fact, already mentioned, that 'A Moderating Answere' in *325* is followed, not preceded, by the other two poems suggests the possibility that it was an afterthought, not composed at the same time as the other two. After copying the last of the Group One poems into the holograph (ending on fol. 99v) Strode seems to have put the manuscript aside, returning later to enter a short poem composed before May 1629 (Forey, pp. 308–10) on the same page in a rather cramped and stiff

version of his italic hand. On the following pages the italic hand has become fluent and relaxed, suggesting a time-lag. It seems possible that when for the second time he resumed copying into his book he left a page blank before embarking on his more recent poems, which enabled him later to insert 'A Moderating Answere' next to its companion pieces. Later composition of 'A Moderating Answere' might also explain why this poem is found in no manuscripts other than *325* and *30982* (though published in *Wit Restor'd* in 1658) while the 'Mock-song' is slightly better known. This appears not only in *Wit Restor'd*, but also following its original in Bodleian MS Engl. poet. f. 25, fol. 63, and Washington, Folger Shakespeare Library, MS V.a.160, pp. 14–15; in BL MS Harley 6918, fol. 41, it is attached to a parody of 'Aske me no more' which, having the same opening line as Strode's original, has been mistakenly listed by Beal with copies of that poem. The Bodleian manuscript is dated *c.*1633–4 by Beal (the other two manuscripts are later).

30 This *terminus a quo* accords with its appearance in BL MS Sloane 1446; Philadelphia, Rosenbach Library, MS 239/27; and Folger MS V a 160, all dated by Beal 1633–4.

31 'An Epitaph on Sir Henry Lees 3 children', written after July 1629 and before Sir Henry's death two years later (Forey, p. 288).

32 Entries in a different hand had also occurred earlier in the manuscript: while Leare's solid, curly hand fills most of the book, Beal notes (I, ii, 355) that fols. 80–86 and 134–119 rev. are written in a 'variant neat hand', and that several other contemporary hands appear on fols 44, 87–96v and 119–117 rev.; he calls these 'possibly for the most part variants of the same predominant hand', a judgement with which I would concur.

33 He was made proctor in 1629, but this temporary post is less likely to have busied him as much as his appointment as Public Orator in the same year.

34 BL Add. MS 31432, f. 11, *c.*1638–45 (Beal CwT 747, location omitted); London, Lambeth Palace, MS 1041, mid-seventeenth-century; and New York Public Library, Music Division, Drexel MS 4257, No.3, 1630s–1650s (Beal CwT 757–758).

35 Although one of these, Bodleian MS Don.c 57, contains a third setting of the poem as a song (not, as stated in Beal, another copy of Lawes' setting), this manuscript belongs to the 1640s, by which time the poem had already become well known.

36 Likewise the poem should properly now be referred to as 'Aske me noe more', although I have retained the usual spelling in this article.

37 BL Add. MSS 23229 and 31432, and Folger MS V a 169.

38 It is attractive to hypothesise that the alteration was asked for or even made by Lawes, on the grounds that both the wide *a* of 'chaos' and the doubled *s* (too easily heard as 'chaos leap') would not be easy to sing: both difficulties could be eliminated by substituting 'Causes', which retains the idea of the flowers sinking back into the constituent parts from which they derived. It would be comprehensible that in his definitive version Strode would nevertheless prefer to retain the reading he had originally intended. However, I am informed that such an attitude to a singer's text is unlikely at this period.

39 *The Poetical Works of William Strode*, ed. Bertram Dobell (London, 1907), p. 259. Dobell's comments refer only to passages in *The Floating Island*, which suggests that he had read some of the poems without full comprehension.

The Date and Script of Hobbes's Latin Optical Manuscript

Timothy Raylor

One of Ferdinand Tönnies's many contributions to Hobbes studies was the identification and attribution to Hobbes of the anonymous Latin treatise on optics in London, British Library, Harley MS 6796, fols 193–266.[1] Tönnies noted that the document was the first draft of the work that would become *De homine*, and suggested that it was started as early as 1637, immediately after the appearance of Descartes's *Dioptrique*, to which it responds.[2] The arguments of Max Kohler and Frithiof Brandt that the Latin Optical Manuscript was written in the mid-1640s have been thoroughly discredited by Richard Tuck and Noel Malcolm.[3] Dr Malcolm has shown that some parts of it were substantially the same as parts of the (lost) letter Hobbes sent to Descartes on 5[/15] November.[4] And he has further suggested that palaeographical evidence supports a dating 1637–1640. I wish to begin by reviewing his argument.

Dr Malcolm makes his case by pointing out that, in addition to the Latin Optical Manuscript, Harley MS 6796 contains several manuscript treatises in the hand of the same amanuensis.[5] The documents in question are:

fols 155–61	[Jean de Beaugrand], 'De la manière de trouuer les tangentes des lignes courbés par l'algebre et des imperfections de celle du S. des C'.
fols 175–77	[Jean Le Maire], 'Méthode pour la musique almerique'.[6]
fols 178–92	'Recueil du calcul qui sert à la géométrie', taken from Descartes's *Géométrie*. Endorsed by Sir Charles: 'Mr de Cartes his tract sent me by Mersennus March 1. 1640' (fol. 178r).
fols 193–266	[Hobbes], Latin Optical Manuscript. Autograph corrections and additions by Hobbes[7] (*Beal HbT 42)[8] (see PLATE 1)

201

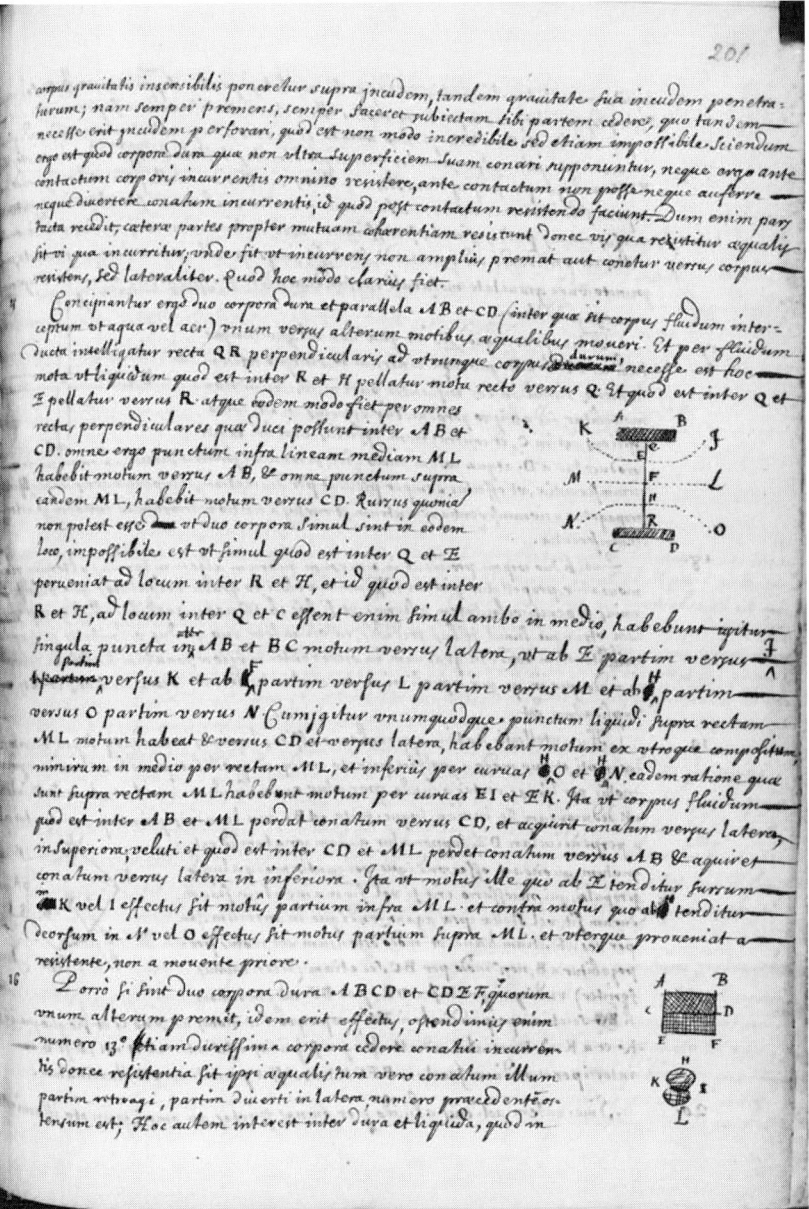

corpus grauitatis insensibilis poneretur supra incudem, tandem grauitate sua incudem penetra-
ret; nam semper premens, semper faceret subiectam tibi partem cedere, quo tandem
necesse erit incudem perforari, quod est non modo incredibile sed etiam impossibile. Sciendum
ergo est quod corpora dum quae non ultra superficiem suam conari supponuntur, neque ergo ante
contactum corporis incurrentis omnino resistere, ante contactum non posse neque auferre
neque ducere conatum incurrentis id quod post contactum resistendo faciunt. Dum enim pars
tacta recedit, caeterae partes propter mutuam adhaerentiam resistunt donec vis qua resistitur aequaliter
sit vi qua incurritur, unde fit vt incurrens non amplius premat aut conetur versus corpus
resistens, sed lateraliter. Quod hoc modo clarius fiet.

Concipiantur ergo duo corpora dura et parallela AB et CD (inter quae sit corpus fluidum inter-
ceptum vt aqua vel aer) vnum versus alterum motibus aequalibus moueri. Et per fluidum
ducta intelligatur recta QR perpendicularis ad vtrunque corpus durum; necesse est hoc
mota vt liquidum quod est inter R et H pellatur motu recto versus Q. Et quod est inter Q et
Z pellatur versus R atque eodem modo fiet per omnes
rectas perpendiculares quae duci possunt inter AB et
CD. omne ergo punctum infra lineam mediam ML
habebit motum versus AB, & omne punctum supra
eandem ML, habebit motum versus CD. Rursus quum
non potest esse vt duo corpora simul sint in eodem
loco, impossibile est vt simul quod est inter Q et Z
perueniat ad locum inter R et H, et id quod est inter

R et H, ad locum inter Q et C essent enim simul ambo in medio, habebunt igitur
singula puncta in AB et BC motum versus latera, vt ab Z partim versus H
partim versus K et ab C partim versus L partim versus M et ab partim
versus O partim versus N Cum igitur vnumquodque punctum liquidi supra rectam
ML motum habeat & versus CD et versus latera, habebant motum ex vtroque compositum,
nimirum in medio per rectam ML, et inferius per curuas O et N eadem ratione quae
sunt supra rectam ML habebunt motum per curuas EI et ZK. Ita vt corpus fluidum
quod est inter AB et ML perdat conatum versus CD, et acquirit conatum versus latera,
insuperiora, veluti et quod est inter CD et ML perdet conatum versus AB & acquiret
conatum versus latera in inferiora. Ita vt motus ille qui ab Z tenditur sursum
in K vel I effectus sit motus partium infra ML et contra motus quo ab tenditur
deorsum in N vel O effectus sit motus partium supra ML et vterque proueniat a
resistente, non a mouente priore.

Porro si sint duo corpora dura ABCD et CDZ F quorum
vnum alterum premit, idem erit effectus, ostendimus enim
numero 13° etiam durissima corpora cedere conatui incurrentis donec resistentia fit ipsi aequalis tum vero conatum illum
partim retroagi, partim diuerti in latera numero praecedente or-
tensum est; Hoc autem interest inter dura et liquida, quod in

fols 267–90   [Florimond de Beaune], 'Notes brièves sur la methode de M^r. D[es] C[artes]'. Endorsed by Sir Charles: 'Fermat'; this deleted by John Pell, and the correct author's name inserted.

Dr Malcolm goes on to note that these documents share a number of common features, the prime one being that (with the exception of the Latin Optical Manuscript they are all copies of works deriving from Mersenne in Paris. He then argues that the amanuensis responsible for these transcriptions must have worked for Sir Charles Cavendish for a brief period in 1640, and does so on the basis that the transcript of the 'Recueil du calcul' was 'very likely' taken from a manuscript copy requested of Mersenne by Sir Kenelm Digby on 14[/24] February 1640.[9] This conjecture, together with his observation that the work of this scribe is not found in other manuscripts of Sir Charles Cavendish, and his assertion that this document and those of de Beaugrand, de Beaune, and Hobbes, feature diagrams drawn by Hobbes, allows him to infer that they must have been copied before the end of 1640, when Hobbes left for Paris.

This seems all very sound. But, as Dr Malcolm notes, there are some problems with it. First, the attempt to associate the copy of the Cartesian 'Recueil' in Harley MS 6796 with that sent to Digby does not accord well with the latter's claim, in a letter of 5[/15] March 1640, that he had returned the document to Mersenne two weeks earlier—unless by this he meant that he had done so via Sir Charles.[10] But this would not square with Sir Charles's note that the tract was 'sent me by Mersennus March 1. 1640'. Dr Malcolm's evidence also raises the more perplexing question of why Sir Charles Cavendish should have employed an amanuensis to work exclusively (with the exception of the Latin Optical Manuscript of Hobbes) on documents written by Frenchmen.

The more plausible explanation for the common features of these manuscripts is a simpler one: rather than being copies made for Sir Charles Cavendish, these are the very documents sent to him by Mersenne, having been copied by an amanuensis in Paris. This suggestion squares with the character of the hand itself: a very pure italic, unmarked by native English features. The presence in several of these documents of diagrams in the hand of Hobbes must therefore imply that they were sent to Sir Charles *after* Hobbes's arrival in Paris in late 1640. There is no contradiction between this suggestion and the date of Sir Charles's endorsement of the 'Receuil' ('sent me by Mersennus March 1. 1640') if we read the latter as old style (*i.e.* 1640[/41]), as we surely should, since Sir Charles was in England at the time. We might then be able to account for Sir Charles's possession of the 'Notes brièves' of Florimond de Beaune on Descartes's *Géométrie* as a consequence of Hobbes's writing to Sir Charles on 8 February 1641 about his recent meeting of de Beaune through Mersenne.[11] Sir Charles's misidentification of the author of the 'Notes' as Fermat does not, however, support this claim.

We find further evidence for dating these documents to the period immediately following Hobbes's arrival in Paris if we turn to the Hobbes Papers at Chatsworth House, Derbyshire, among which several works by the same amanuensis are found.[12] Two of the Chatsworth Hobbes manuscripts are undoubtedly in the same hand as the documents in Harley MS 6796:

Hobbes MS B. 4.   'Opus d. de Fermat'. (Beal HbT 52)
Hobbes MS B. 6.   Jean de Beaugrand, 'Geostatice . . . 1636'. (Beal *HbT 54) (see PLATE 2)

And several others are, according to the Historical Manuscripts Commission report of 1977, also in this hand:[13] *viz.*

Hobbes MS A. 3.   *De cive*. Presentation copy on vellum. Title page dated Paris, 1641.[14] Epistle Dedicatory signed by Hobbes. (Beal *HbT 18) (see PLATE 3)
Hobbes MS A. 4.   A 'chapter XIX', intended for *De corpore*. (Beal HbT 15)
Hobbes MS A. 5.   Fragment of *De homine*, comprising chapter 3 and part of chapter 2. (Beal HbT 17) (see PLATE 4)
Hobbes MS A. 7.   Untitled compilation of geometrical axioms. (Beal *HbT 46)

The reader who compares what have until now been the most readily accessible reproductions of this hand—the facsimile of le Maire's tract on almeric music in the Mersenne *Correspondance* and the sample page of Hobbes's dedicatory epistle to *De cive* printed in facsimile by Warrender—may well wonder about this assertion, for those examples appear to have little in common other than their pure italic form. But there is a difference in stylistic register between these two documents: the musical tract is written in a cursive, or running script, the dedication to *De cive* in a set hand. If one looks elsewhere in *De cive* one finds pages on which the pace of work evidently speeds up and the script becomes increasingly cursive in appearance (as, for example, on p. 62: see PLATE 3). And if one looks elsewhere in the documents in Harley MS 6796, one finds passages written with slightly more formality (as, for

quod hoc potissimum tempore facere instui, quo tu
vicissim illius opem artis ac ministerium studes ad-
ciscere, vt classis illa quam instructam habes singu-
lari perte prouidentia frabricata ad regni tute-
lam & hostium terrorem secundo cursu per vtrum-
que mare prouehatur. Mihi vero vt hoc Me-
chanicorum nostrorum operum specimen ac pro-
dromum *Eminentiæ Tuæ* dicarem, inui-
tamento fuit non solum doctrinæ illius quam præ-
dicaui vtilitas & præstantia, sed etiam singula-
ris & omni prædicatione major humanitas tua,
quâ cum cæteros omnes bonarum studiosos artium
tum me priuatim complexus es, non adhibendo
solum ad interiora maritimis de rebus colloquia,
sed hortando vt pro virili parte rem illam labo-
re meo ac vigilijs adjuuarem. quod quidem man-
dato tuo, *Cardinalis Eminentissime*,
Lubens suscepi, ac cum hujus obsequij mei tum
erga *Eminentiam Tuam* voluntatis
testem atque obsidem hanc lucubratiunculam
esse volui, quæ si breuis cuiquam videbitur, ve-
lim is apud se cogitet non exigua illa censeri
quæ primùm reperta & nullius hactenus com-
mentationibus illustrata sint, cujusmodi sunt quæ
hoc opere continentur de proportione grauium
pro varijs à Terræ centro interuallis disputata
& à nobis ita demonstratione conclusa nihil
vt assumeretur aliud quam quod ab *Euclide*
& *Archimede* demonstratum fuerat. Tum
verè istud à *Cardano* pronuntiatum memi-

PLATE 2. *A page in de Beaugrand's* Geostatice: *Chatsworth House, Derbyshire,
Hobbes MS B. 6, p. 8. (Original page size 325 × 231mm.) Reproduced by permission of His Grace the Duke of Devonshire.*

instance, on fol. 201r of the Latin Optical Manuscript: see PLATE 1). Comparison of PLATES 1 and 3 on the one hand (especially the letters *P*, *D*, *d*, and the set form of *p*) and of PLATES 1 and 2 on the other (especially *C*, *E*, *P*, *h*, and the running, open-stemmed form of *p*) leaves one with little doubt that these documents are all products of the same hand.

Chatsworth Hobbes MSS A. 4 and A. 5 (chapter 'XIX' of *De corpore* and the fragment of *De homine*) are written in a highly formal, 'set' script (see PLATE 4), but are undoubtedly the work of the same writer. Although this more formal and fuller-bodied script does not at first sight exactly match the other manuscripts we have examined here, its distinctive letter forms nevertheless connect it with the other Chatsworth and Harleian manuscripts (compare, for instance, *D*, *Q*, and the 'set' form of *g* with that in PLATE 2, and the set form of *p* with that in PLATE 3). These Chatsworth and Harleian documents are therefore all the work of the same scribe, with the draft of the Latin Optical Manuscript (Harley MS 6796) representing relatively informal work and the fair copies of the chapters intended for *De corpore* and *De homine* his more formal work (Chatsworth Hobbes MSS A. 4, A. 5).

An additional connection between the Chatsworth documents and those in BL Harley MS 6796 is that the Latin Optical Manuscript (Harley MS 6796, fols 193–290) appears to have been written on the same stock of paper as Chatsworth Hobbes, MS B. 4: the two share a watermark (39 × 29 mm) comprising a crown surmounting a rectangular frame containing the letters 'IF'. The watermark on Hobbes MS B. 6 displays the same design, but contains the letters 'MA' (or, perhaps, 'AM').

The evidence afforded by Harley MS 6796 and the Hobbes Papers at Chatsworth suggests that the transcription of the Latin Optical Manuscript was made after, rather than just before, Hobbes's arrival in Paris. We cannot say exactly how long after, but the evidence points to a period soon after his arrival: Mersenne sent Sir Charles the copy of the 'Receuil' on 1 March 1641; and the vellum *De cive* is dated 1641. The evidence therefore seems to suggest that Hobbes was still working on his Latin Optical Manuscript at a point later than that proposed by Noel Malcolm and Richard Tuck.[15]

NOTES

I am most grateful to his Grace the Duke of Devonshire and the Trustees of the Chatsworth Settlement for permitting me to consult the Hobbes manuscripts at Chatsworth and to reproduce images from them here. I thank Peter Day for his continued assistance on matters relating to the Chatsworth collections and Dr Noel Malcolm for his comments on a draft of this essay.

1 Tönnies printed an excerpt from the treatise in Appendix II of his edition of *The Elements of Law* (London, 1889), pp. 211–26. The full text, though without the diagrams, has been printed by Franco Alessio, 'Thomas Hobbes: Tractatus Opticus', *Rivista critica di storia della filosofia*, 18 (1963), 147–228.

2 *Elements*, ed. Tönnies, pp. xii–xiii.

3 Richard Tuck, 'Hobbes and Descartes', in *Perspectives on Thomas Hobbes* , ed. G. A. J. Rogers and Alan Ryan (Oxford, 1988), pp. 11–41 (18–27); Thomas Hobbes, *Correspondence*, ed. Noel Malcolm, 2 vols (Oxford, 1994), I, lii–lv. I follow Noel Malcolm in referring to it as the Latin Optical Manuscript, as opposed to the title given to it by Tönnies, 'Tractatus Opticus', in order to avoid confusion with Hobbes's essay of that title published by Mersenne.

4 Hobbes, *Correspondence*, I, lii–lv.

5 Hobbes, *Correspondence*, I, liv.

6 Reproduced in facsimile in Marin Mersenne, *Correspondance*, ed. Cornélis de Waard, Armand Beaulieu, René Pintard, and Bernard Rochot, 17 vols. (Paris, 1933–88), IX, 565–9.

7 Printed in Alessio, 'Hobbes: Tractatus Opticus'.

8 Peter Beal, *Index of English Literary Manuscripts*, Volume II: *1625–1700*, Part 1: *Behn-King* (London & New York, 1987).

9 Hobbes, *Correspondence*, I, liv–lv; Mersenne, *Correspondance*, IX, 122.

10 Mersenne, *Correspondance*, IX, 203.

11 Hobbes, *Correspondence*, I, 85.

12 Noel Malcolm offers the authoritative account of these documents, demonstrating that many are in fact written by or connected with Hobbes's friend and intellectual associate, Robert Payne, in 'Robert Payne, the Hobbes Manuscripts, and the "Short Tract"', in *Aspects of Hobbes* (Oxford, 2002), pp. 80–145 (80–85, 139–44).

13 Historical Manuscripts Commission, *Report on the Manuscripts and Papers of Thomas Hobbes . . . in the Devonshire Collections*, No. 77/22 (London, 1977).

14 The title-page and dedicatory epistle are reproduced in facsimile in *De cive: the Latin version*, ed. Howard Warrender (Oxford, 1983), frontispiece and Plate II.

15 Hobbes, *Correspondence*, I, lii–lv; Tuck, 'Hobbes and Descartes', pp. 18–27.

Hobbes, the Latin Optical Manuscript, and the Parisian Scribe

Noel Malcolm

I am very grateful to Timothy Raylor for making me reconsider the question of the dating of Hobbes's Latin Optical Manuscript.[1] The central claim he has advanced—that this manuscript, like several others bound with it in BL Harley MS 6796 and a number of manuscripts among the Hobbes papers at Chatsworth, was written by an amanuensis in Paris—strikes me as entirely convincing. And the evidence on which I previously relied to argue that the Latin Optical Manuscript was written in England before Hobbes's departure for France in November 1640—namely, the fact that the diagrams in that manuscript are drawn and lettered by Hobbes himself—indicates, as Professor Raylor points out, that this manuscript must have been written after Hobbes's arrival in Paris. However, while Professor Raylor has thereby provided a *terminus a quo* for the date of the transcription of this copy of Hobbes's treatise, the *terminus ad quem* has now become very unclear. Hobbes was, after all, based in Paris until the end of 1651; if all that can be established about the Latin Optical Manuscript is that it was copied out at some time during his stay there, then the question of its dating must remain essentially unsolved. The main aim of what follows is to narrow the chronological field. First, however, in order to acquire as full a picture as possible of this scribe's activities, it is worth considering the other manuscripts specified by Professor Raylor (which, thanks to his research, I have been impelled to look at again), as well as a few other items in the same scribal hand which he has not mentioned.

In addition to the manuscripts gathered together in Harley MS 6796, there are, as Professor Raylor correctly observes, several other items in the same hand among the Hobbes manuscripts at Chatsworth. The same scribe was undoubtedly reponsible for Hobbes MSS B.4 (Fermat), B.6 (de Beaugrand), A.3 (*De cive*), A.4 (*De corpore*, ch. XIX) and A.5 (*De homine*, fragment). The Historical Manuscripts Commission report is mistaken, however, in describing MS A.7 (the geometrical compilation) as in the same hand: some of the letter-forms are different (such as minuscule *p*, where the stem is splayed out to the left), and the overall effect on the page is quite unlike that produced by the copyist of the other documents (who, for simplicity's sake, will be referred to hereafter as 'the Parisian scribe'). On the other hand, there is one other item at Chatsworth by the Parisian scribe, not noticed by the HMC report because it has not been classified among the Hobbes manuscripts: it is the short treatise on phlebotomy by Samuel Sorbière, 'Discours contre la fréquente saignée', catalogued as a Hardwick MS, drawer 145, item 21. In addition, three other items by the Parisian scribe can be noted. The first is a copy of one section of an astronomical work by the mathematician François Viète (Vieta), preserved in a volume of John Pell's papers in the British Library (Add. MS 4417, fols 26–37r: see PLATE 1). The second is a manuscript in the Bibliothèque de Sainte-Geneviève, Paris (MS 1060), a compilation containing treatises on geometry, trigonometry and fortification, and instructions on the use of mathematical instruments and the compass. And the third is the fair-copy manuscript of Hobbes's *Leviathan* in the British Library (Egerton MS 1910: see PLATE 2).

Most of these items are datable, with varying degrees of accuracy. The only one for which no evidence is available for dating purposes is the copy of the treatise by Jean de Beaugrand at Chatsworth (Hobbes MS B.6). This manuscript is a very accurate copy of the entire printed text of de Beaugrand's *Geostatice*, a short work published in 1636; it begins by reproducing the printed titlepage, replicating even the glaring misprint in the title.[2] There are a few annotations in another hand; the identification of this hand with Hobbes's, made in the HMC catalogue, is unconvincing. Nevertheless, given the fact that this manuscript has come down to us in a group of manuscripts owned by Hobbes, its overall Hobbesian provenance need not be doubted. Hobbes had been introduced to Jean de Beaugrand by Mersenne during his European tour of 1634–36, and can therefore be expected to have taken a special interest in his works.[3] Conceivably, this manuscript copy might have been made before Hobbes's return to England from Paris in October 1636. That seems unlikely, though, for two reasons: first, because it would surely have been simpler to buy a copy of the printed work, if it had just gone on sale and was easily available, and secondly because of the evidence of the watermark, which will be considered below. It is more reasonable to suppose that Hobbes commissioned this transcription of the work at some time in the early 1640s, when he was on what might be called a learning curve, familiarizing himself with recent work by members of Mersenne's scientific circle. De Beaugrand might well

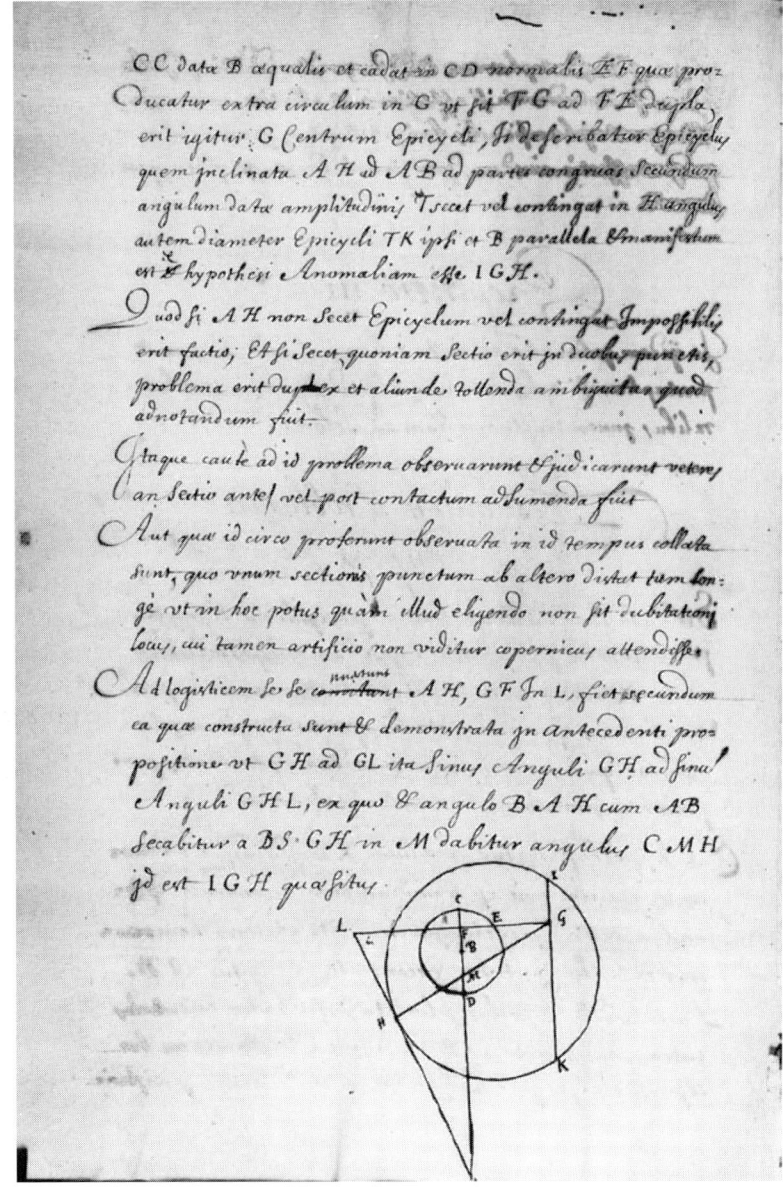

CC data B aequalis et cadat in CD ~~normalis~~ EF quae pro-
ducatur extra circulum in G ut fit FG ad FE ~~regula~~
erit igitur G Centrum Epicycli, Si describatur Epicyclus
quem inclinata AH ad AB ad ~~partes congruas~~ Secundum
angulum datae amplitudinis T secet vel ~~contingat in~~ H ~~angulo~~
autem diameter Epicycli TK ipsi et B parallela &manifestum
erit ex hypothesi Anomaliam esse IGH.

Quod si AH non Secet Epicyclum vel ~~contingat Impossibil~~i
erit factio; Et si Secet, quoniam Sectio erit in duobus ~~punctis~~
problema erit du~~plex~~ et aliunde tollenda ambiguitas ~~quod~~
adnotandum fuit.

Itaque cause ad id problema observarunt &judicarunt ~~veteres~~
an Sectio ante, vel ~~post~~ contactum adsumenda fuit

Aut qua id circo proferunt observata in id tempus collata
sunt, quo vnum sectionis punctum ab altero distat tam lon-
ge vt in hoc potius quam illud eligendo non fit dubitationi
locus, cui tamen artificio non viditur copernicus attendisse.

Ad logisticem Se Se ~~constituunt~~ AH, GF in L, fiet secundum
ea quae constructa sunt & demonstrata in Antecedenti pro-
positione vt GH ad GL ita Sinus Anguli GH ad sinal
Anguli GHL, ex quo & angulo BAH cum AB
Secabitur a BS GH in M dabitur angulus CMH
id est IGH quaesitus.

PLATE 1. *A page in the copy of part of Vieta's* Harmonicon coeleste *in the hand of the Parisian scribe, with diagram in Hobbes's hand: London, British Library, Additional MS 4417, fol. 31v. (Original page size 310 × 203mm.) Reproduced by permission of the Board of the British Library.*

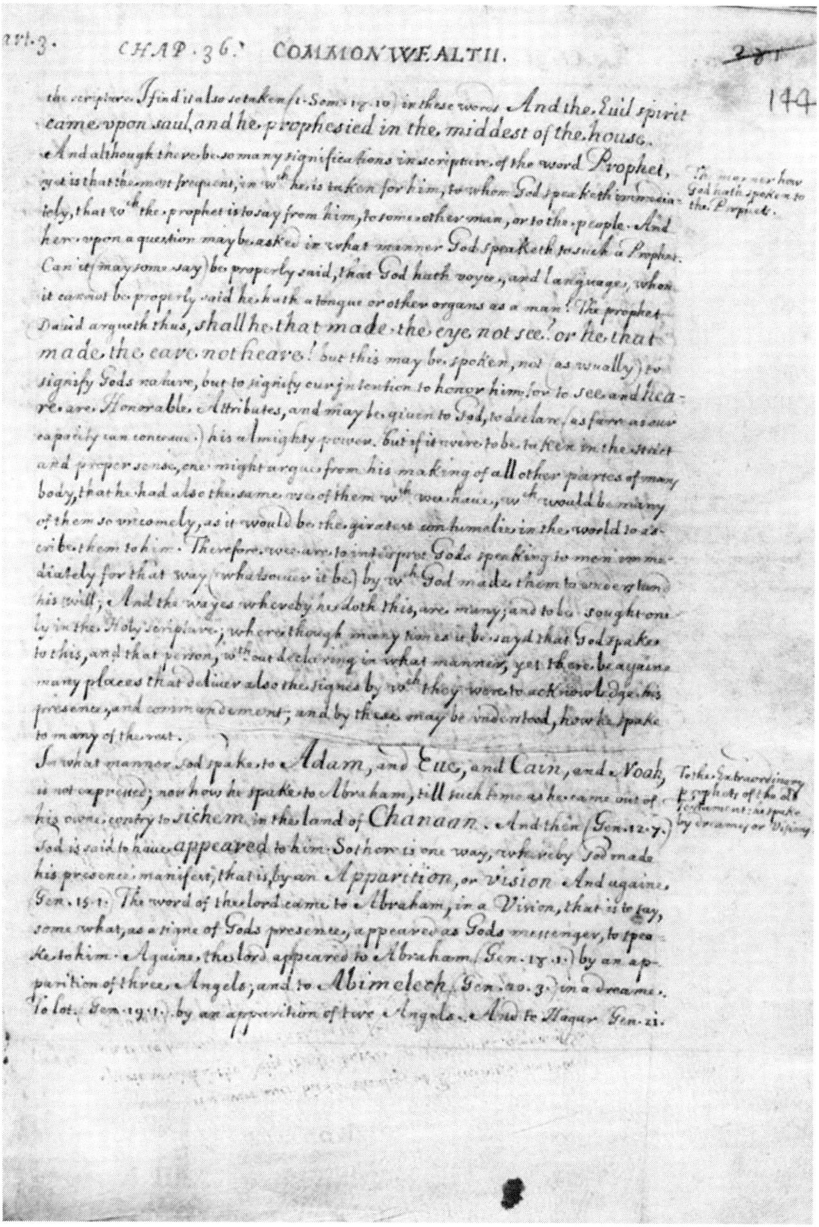

Part.3. CHAP.36. COMMONWEALTH. ~~281~~ 144

the scripture. I find it also so taken (1 Sam. 18.10) in these words And the Euil spirit came vpon saul, and he prophesied in the middest of the house.

And although there be so many significations in scripture, of the word Prophet, yet is that the most frequent, in wch he is taken for him, to whom God speaketh immediately, that wch the prophet is to say from him, to some other man, or to the people. And here vpon a question may be asked in what manner God speaketh to such a Prophet. Can it (may some say) be properly said, that God hath voyce, and language, when it cannot be properly said he hath a tongue or other organs as a man? The prophet David argueth thus, shall he that made the eye not see? or he that made the eare not heare? but this may be spoken, not (as usually) to signify Gods nature, but to signify our intention to honor him, for to see and heare are Honorable Attributes, and may be giuen to God, to declare (as farre as our capacity can conceiue) his almighty power. but if it were to be taken in the strict and proper sense, one might argue from his making of all other partes of mans body, that he had also the same vse of them wch we haue, wch would be many of them so vncomely, as it would be the greatest contumelie in the world to ascribe them to him. Therefore we are to interpret Gods speaking to men immediately for that way (whatsoeuer it be) by wch God makes them to vnderstand his will; And the wayes whereby he doth this, are many; and to be sought onely in the Holy scripture; where though many times it be sayd that God spake to this, and that person, wthout declaring in what manner, yet there be againe many places that deliuer also the signes by wch they were to acknowledge his presence, and commandement; and by these may be vnderstood, how he spake to many of the rest. — *In what manner God hath spoken to the Prophets.*

In what manner God spake to Adam, and Eue, and Cain, and Noah, is not expressed; nor how he spake to Abraham, till such time as he came out of his owne contry to Sichem in the land of Chanaan. And then (Gen.12.7.) God is said to haue appeared to him. So there is one way, whereby God made his presence manifest, that is, by an Apparition, or vision. And againe, Gen.15.1. The word of the lord came to Abraham in a Vision, that is to say, some what, as a signe of Gods presence, appeared as Gods messenger, to speake to him. Againe the lord appeared to Abraham (Gen.18.1.) by an apparition of three Angels; and to Abimelech (Gen.20.3.) in a dreame. To lot (Gen.19.1.) by an apparition of two Angels. And to Hagar Gen.21. — *To the Extraordinary prophets of the old testament he spake by dreames, or Visions.*

PLATE 2. *A page in the copy (on vellum) of Hobbes's* Leviathan *in the hand of the Parisian scribe. (Original page size 240 × 178mm.) Reproduced by permission of the Board of the British Library.*

have been one of the first authors whose work he approached in this way, given that he had known him personally; sadly, the French mathematician died in December 1640, just a few weeks after Hobbes's arrival in Paris.[4]

In the case of the astronomical treatise by Vieta a *terminus a quo* can be established, as the key feature of this manuscript (hitherto unnoticed) is that its diagrams too were drawn and lettered by Hobbes. It was thus written some time after his arrival in Paris in November/December 1640. A *terminus ad quem* is supplied by a letter from John Pell to Samuel Hartlib of 12 October 1642, in which Pell referred to this manuscript: 'I have in mine owne hands an imperfect Astronomicall manuscript of 6 sheetes of paper, entitled Hypotheses francelinidis said to be a piece of a greater worke of Vieta's called by him Harmonicum caeleste, which may perhaps be found complete in France whence mine came.'[5] As it is so close in nature to the other items in Harley MS 6796 which contain diagrams by Hobbes, and since it probably passed, like them, through the hands of both Sir Charles Cavendish and John Pell, it will be considered in more detail together with those items below.

Of the other manuscripts mentioned above, the first in chronological order is the presentation copy of *De cive* (Chatsworth Hobbes MS A.3). The dedicatory epistle of this work is dated (in the printed version, though not in the manuscript, where the epistle appears without a date) 1 November 1641. The manuscript may therefore have been written either a little before that date (Hobbes was known to be composing the work as early as August 1641) or a little after: its pictorial title-page is dated simply '1641'.[6]

The next, probably, is the work by Fermat (Chatsworth Hobbes MS B.4)—though the dating of this item is much more uncertain. This manuscript is an incomplete and untitled copy of a short treatise on spherical tangents, 'De contactibus sphaericis', which remained unpublished until 1679.[7] The main body of Fermat's treatise consisted of fifteen problems and their solution; in this manuscript only the first eight problems are presented, even though the introductory section (given here) clearly refers to fifteen. The only clue as to the dating of this manuscript is the fact that Mersenne evidently had a copy of the treatise by late 1643 or early 1644: he listed its fifteen problems in his mathematical compilation *Universae geometriae synopsis* (pp. 384–85), which was apparently ready for the press by February 1644 at the latest.[8] The date of composition of Fermat's treatise is not known; Michael Mahoney suggests 1643, but notes that it may well be earlier.[9] Given Hobbes's closeness to Mersenne at this time, it seems reasonable to assume that he had this copy made from the manuscript in Mersenne's possession, in or around 1643.

The manuscript compilation in the Bibliothèque de Sainte-Geneviève is more easily datable. It contains a printed folio broadsheet, entitled *Trois tables de la grandeur des parties d'une fortification royale*, dedicated 'A Monsieur le duc de Buckingham Vostre tres humble & tres-obeissant seruiteur Roberval', and dated 'A Paris, 1645 Pour l'Autheur'. These tables refer to material in one of the manuscript treatises, 'Traicté des Fortifications regulieres et irregulieres' (fols 61–132: specifically, they refer to the plan attached to fol. 63v, and the text on fols 64–66). The entire manuscript is in the most elegant and formal version of the Parisian scribe's hand; this, together with the nature of its contents, suggests that it was specially prepared, under Roberval's supervision, for the young Duke of Buckingham's studies. It is known that Hobbes gave some tuition in geometry to the Duke during the latter's stay in Paris (which ended in May 1646).[10] As Hobbes is known to have been particularly close to Roberval at this time, it seems likely that it was thanks to him that the Duke was passed on to Roberval for further tuition—especially in the science of fortification, where Roberval had expertise which Hobbes lacked.[11]

The next item, chronologically, is the chapter of a draft of Hobbes's *De corpore*, entitled 'Philosophia prima Capvt 19', dealing with geometrical figures such as parabolas, hyperbolas and ellipses (Chatsworth Hobbes MS A.4). This is again a very fair copy; it was evidently prepared on its own, not as part of a longer transcription (it has original foliation numbers, starting with '1'), and it bears some manuscript corrections by Hobbes. Presumably it was made in order to be submitted to other geometers for their opinions; indeed, it is quite possible that this manuscript was sent to Hobbes's friend the mathematician Robert Payne, and that it ended up among the Hobbes papers at Chatsworth only because many of the manuscripts found in Payne's study after his death were passed by his executor to Hobbes.[12] If so, we may conclude that Payne's opinion was unfavourable, as the chapter was not eventually included in the printed text of this work. The dating of the various drafts, notes and precursor texts to *De corpore* is a complex matter; one of the fullest treatments of it, by Arrigo Pacchi, presents persuasive reasons for dating this manuscript to 1648–49.[13]

The fragment of *De homine* (Chatsworth Hobbes MS A.5) must also come from the last few years of Hobbes's stay in Paris. The material it contains, chapter 3 and part of chapter 2, is a modified Latin version of material originally written in English in 1645–46 (the 'Minute or First Draught of the Optiques', BL Harley MS 3360, where the corresponding

sections are in part 2, chapters 1 and 2). When Hobbes published
De corpore in 1655, he stated in the dedicatory epistle that *De homine* was
still in preparation, but he also added that the first eight chapters of
that work had been prepared six years before (*i.e.* in 1649), and that he
had even had the plates of the accompanying figures engraved at that
time.[14] This dating is confirmed by a letter from Hobbes to Sorbière of
4/14 June 1649, in which he explained: 'I am getting the figures which
I use in my demonstrations engraved on brass plates every day, so that
everything will be ready for the press as soon as I stop writing.'[15] A page
of diagrams printed from one such plate, designed to accompany chapter 3, is included with this manuscript: it appears exactly as in the eventual printed edition of *De homine*, except that the engraver here has
entitled it only 'AD CAP', leaving the chapter-number to be cut later.
This manuscript can thus be dated with some confidence to 1649.

The fair-copy manuscript of *Leviathan* (BL Egerton MS 1910) is an
exact counterpart to the fair-copy manuscript of *De cive*: both are on
vellum, and both imitate the format of printed works, with pictorial
titlepages, running-heads and (occasionally) catchwords. The text of
Leviathan was substantially written in 1649–50; Hobbes was receiving
sheets from the printers for proof-reading in April 1651; he added a
dedicatory epistle, which was printed over the date 15/25 April 1651;
and the work was on sale in England by early May 1651.[16] This copy
was probably made in late 1650 or early 1651 from the authorial manuscript retained by Hobbes, after he had sent off his copy to the printers
in London, but before he had made those final changes that were added
in proof. (There are numerous minor textual divergences between this
manuscript and the printed version; and the dedicatory epistle is lacking in the manuscript.) What distinguishes this manuscript from all the
other items by the Parisian scribe is that it is in English. One might
therefore assume that the scribe must have had a reasonable knowledge
of this language, especially if he was working from Hobbes's crabbed
handwriting. Just how good the scribe's linguistic skills were is, however,
a puzzling question. Some of his errors suggest considerable unfamiliarity with the language: 'goesh' for 'goeth' (fol. 8v), 'lengsh' for 'length'
(fol. 14r), 'nade' for 'made' (fol. 35v), 'te' for 'the' (fol. 127r), and so on.
Several of his spellings also bear the impress of French forms, such as
'montaynes', corrected by Hobbes to 'mountaynes' (fol. 35v), or
'entend' for 'intend' (fol. 88r). And he also has a tendency to present
Biblical names in more or less Gallicized forms: 'Josue' for Joshua (fol.
37v), 'Moyses' for Moses (fol. 67v), and so on.

The final item in this group (Chatsworth MS Hardwick, drawer 145,
item 21) is also datable with some accuracy: the treatise on phlebotomy

was sent by Sorbière to Hobbes in early 1657, and Hobbes wrote to thank him for it on 10/20 February of that year.[17]

The dates of these items range, therefore, from 1641 to 1657. All of them are connected, directly or indirectly, with Hobbes; but if the writer was a professional scribe he would presumably have had a much wider clientele, and the Hobbesian connections of these pieces may reflect nothing more than the fact that it is research into Hobbes's life and writings that has generated this particular selection of evidence. (Alternatively, if the writer was not a professional scribe, he may have been a Minim friar at Mersenne's convent.) Although there is a significant chronological spread here, there is no obvious pattern of development in the nature of the writing, except, perhaps, for a slight shakiness in the final item; as Professor Raylor has pointed out, there are variations in some of the letter-forms, but these reflect different degrees of formality, not different periods of work. They are also sometimes intermingled: the most striking 'formal' element is a minuscule *g* which imitates the standard printed form, with a hooked loop and an upper right-hand stalk, but in documents where this is present, such as Chatsworth Hobbes MS A.4 and BL Egerton MS 1910, it is often also accompanied by the more normal cursive *g*.

These items use paper with a variety of watermarks. Only two of them, the pieces by de Beaugrand (Chatsworth Hobbes MS B.6) and Fermat (Chatsworth Hobbes MS B.4) have watermarks that appear in the Latin Optical treatise in BL Harley MS 6796. In each case the mark is an oblong containing two letters, surmounted by a crown with a central fleur-de-lys; the countermark is a bunch of grapes (arranged geometrically in a lozenge pattern, five grapes across, with a stalk attached). Similar designs of mark and countermark are given as Nos. 2237 and 2239 in Heawood's collection.[18] In the de Beaugrand treatise the letters in the oblong are 'AM' (*e.g.* pp. 3–4); in the Fermat work the letters are 'IF' (*e.g.* pp. 1–2). The Latin Optical Manuscript has both versions: 'AM' is present especially in some of the earlier pages (*e.g.* fols 202, 203), and 'IF' predominates thereafter (*e.g.* fols 207, 210). This may suggest—though the evidence is far from conclusive—that the scribe was working through two batches of paper, and that the order of writing was de Beaugrand—Hobbes—Fermat. Such a suggestion is at least consistent with the arguments presented above about the dating of the de Beaugrand and Fermat items, which supposed that the former was copied quite soon after Hobbes's arrival in Paris at the end of 1640, and the latter in approximately 1643.

Of the items by the Parisian scribe bound with the Latin Optical Manuscript in Harley MS 6796, just one shares the same watermark: the

'Notes briefves' by Florimond de Beaune, which has the 'IF' version of the mark (together with the 'grapes' countermark). As we shall see, there is one other way in which this item specially resembles the Latin Optical Manuscript. Frustratingly, this de Beaune transcript is also hard to date with accuracy. However, several of the other items bound with it in the Harley manuscript can be dated with reasonable certainty to the period 1640–41; and important evidence has survived of the history of the later transmission of some of these manuscripts, which strongly suggests that they had been sent to England by, probably, the summer of 1642, or, at the very latest, April 1643. These items (together with the treatise by Vieta) form, I believe, a distinct group, which is why my discussion of them has been held over until this point.

II

The collection of pieces in the hand of the Parisian scribe in Harley MS 6796 comes to six items altogether. To the five items listed by Professor Raylor—by de Beaugrand, Le Maire, Descartes (strictly speaking, this text is a digest of Descartes by Godefroid van Haestrecht), Hobbes and de Beaune—one more should be added: the short mathematical text, on both sides of fol. 162, beginning 'Ce que vous dites avoir arresté M^r. de Roberval . . .'. This text is in the same scribal hand, though the heading it bears on fol. 162r, 'Extraict d'vne autre lettre', is in a different hand—a large, irregular and rather coarse script, which is definitely not that of Mersenne, Hobbes, Cavendish or Pell. The text itself can be identified as an extract from a letter sent by Descartes to Mersenne (on 15 November 1638), discussing the type of curved line known as the 'folium', 'galand' or 'noeud de ruban'.[19] Among the papers of John Pell I have found a similar text in the Parisian scribe's hand: an extract from another, earlier, letter sent by Descartes to Mersenne (on 27 July 1638), containing a discussion of the curve known as the 'roulette'.[20] It seems reasonable to suppose that these two manuscripts form a pair, with the superscription 'Extraict d'vne autre lettre' indicating that it was sent as a follow-up to the excerpt from the earlier letter. That previous extract was presumably the text which Mersenne sent to Theodore Haak, for Pell, on 12 May 1640, with the explanation: 'I enclose a demonstration which Mr Pell wanted to see, and which you will please show him, namely, that the cycloid line of the "roulette" contains a space three times larger than the roulette itself.'[21] Pell had requested the demonstration in his letter to Mersenne of 29 March 1640, having been asked by Mersenne in an earlier letter (1 March 1640) if he could construct his own proof for this proposition.[22]

We thus have six items contained in Harley MS 6796, plus the first extract from a Descartes letter (in Add. MS 4416). One other item, the section of Vieta's treatise (in Add. MS 4417), can be treated as belonging to this group, bringing the total to eight. Of these, we have seen that one (the first extract from a Descartes letter) can be dated to May 1640, and another (the second extract) can be presumed to have been sent shortly thereafter. A third, the digest of Descartes, is dated by Sir Charles Cavendish's annotation 'sent me by Mersennus March 1. 1640'. As Professor Raylor has pointed out, this should probably be read as 1640/1. It is conceivable that Cavendish was copying the date from a (now lost) letter from Mersenne himself, in which case the year would have been dated from 1 January; but a small scrap of paper included in this treatise has notes on the text by Cavendish on one side of the paper, and, on the other, a draft of the beginning of a letter to Mersenne, dated 'Jan: 16. 1640'—which, as written by Cavendish himself, would certainly have meant 1640/1.[23]

A fourth item, the text on musical notation by Le Maire, can also be dated fairly accurately. Mersenne discussed Le Maire's treatise in another letter to Haak, written on 20 March 1640, referring to 'the notation of his music,' and promising to send him a copy: 'I shall send it to you, with the request that you neither publish it nor teach it to anyone, because I have promised him that I shall keep it secret until he decides to make it known.'[24] The fact that—contrary to his usual practice—Mersenne was not generally circulating the text must add to the likelihood that the copy sent to Haak some time after 20 March 1640 can indeed be identified with the copy in the Harley manuscript.

A fifth item, the text by de Beaugrand criticizing Descartes's method of finding the tangents of different types of curve, was probably sent to England in 1640 or 1641. The date of composition of this text is not known precisely; Cornélis de Waard has suggested that it was written at some time between September 1638 and August 1640, while the editors of Mersenne's *Correspondance* propose a date in the spring of 1640.[25] There are two mentions of manuscripts in Mersenne's letters that may refer to this text; in each case, however, there is an aspect of the evidence that does not quite fit. The first is in a letter written on or about 12 May 1640, when Mersenne informed Haak: 'I have one or two excellent treatises on geometry, of the most refined sort, but because they would take rather a long time to describe, I shall ask M. Vegilin to take the trouble to transcribe them, in order to send them to you; then you can let Mr Pell read them too.'[26] The 'M. Vegilin' here was

Philip Ernst Vegelin van Claerbergen, a young Dutchman of German origin who was giving occasional clerical assistance to Mersenne at this time; however, Vegelin's hand cannot be identified with that of the Parisian scribe, for both visual and chronological reasons.[27] The editors of the Mersenne *Correspondance* have suggested that one of these treatises was a text on tangents by Fermat, which Mersenne had received from the author in the previous month, and that the other was 'very probably'—despite the incompatibility with Vegelin's hand—the de Beaugrand text in the Harley manuscript (which discusses the same topic).[28] To reconcile the Mersenne letter with the manuscript, we would have to assume that, in the event, Mersenne chose a different scribe.

The second reference comes in a letter from Mersenne to John Pell, written on 1 May 1641. In that letter Mersenne first mentioned a treatise by Fermat (the 'De locis planis', a reconstruction of two of the lost books of Apollonius) which he was sending to Pell via Theodore Haak, and then added: 'and here is a copy of a work by another very learned friend of mine, who thinks he justly censures those things in M. Descartes's book which you will see in that treatise.'[29] That description fits very accurately the contents of de Beaugrand's treatise; but, on the other hand, Mersenne's use of the present tense here implies—probably, though not necessarily—that the author is still alive (whereas de Beaugrand died in December 1640). Pell himself, writing to Sir Charles Cavendish on 9 August 1641, reported the arrival of these treatises: 'I have received from Mersennus a supplement of Apollonius & a censure on des Cartes.'[30] Also among Pell's papers there is what seems to be a different draft of the same letter to Cavendish, in which the treatises are described as follows: 'Pere Mersenne hath sent me in Manuscript 2 bookes of Apollonius restored by a judge in one of their Parliaments And a censure of some Geometricall passages of de Cartes but I have not yet reade y^m & doubt not but ere this he hath sent you a Copy of ye same & 't is likely in a fairer hand.'[31] That last remark is striking, in view of the fact that the Parisian scribe's hand was nothing if not fair. Unfortunately the manuscript by Fermat does not survive, and so cannot be used as a 'control' here. But Pell's comment does suggest that, if the text was the one by de Beaugrand, what he received must have been a somewhat scruffy transcript, while the copy made by the Parisian scribe was sent by Mersenne to Cavendish. Given that Pell and Cavendish were in regular contact, that Pell had evidently not heard anything about this work from Cavendish up to this moment, and that Mersenne was aware of the closeness of the links between them (so that sending a copy to Cavendish a long time after sending one to Pell would have been both pointless and rather contrrary to protocol), we may assume that Cavendish's copy was sent at roughly the same time. Possibly it was one of the items airily referred to by Cavendish in his letter to Pell of 24 July 1641: 'I haue latelie receiued some propositions out of France. some demonstrated & some not, but I will not diuert you from the business you haue in hand.'[32]

There are thus two possible datings of the de Beaugrand item in the Harley manuscript: May 1640 and May–July 1641. If my original supposition was correct, that the lettering of the diagrams in the Harley manuscript copy of this text was by Hobbes, then the first of these could be eliminated, as Hobbes reached Paris only at the end of 1640. However, a closer inspection of the diagrams in these manuscripts now inclines me to think that the lettering is in Hobbes's hand in only three cases: his own Latin Optical Manuscript, the treatise by de Beaune, and the section of a treatise by Vieta. In the de Beaugrand text and the digest of Descartes the lettering in the diagrams is certainly different from the scribal hand of the texts themselves, and is also remarkably similar to Hobbes's hand; but there are one or two letters that are differently constructed, and the letters in these texts are notably larger than Hobbes's usual size of majuscule.[33] The person who lettered the diagrams in these two texts appears to have written also the marginal annotations on fols 185r and 185v of the Descartes text: this writing, which is more obviously different from Hobbes's, may perhaps be the same coarse hand as that of the heading 'Extraict d'vne autre lettre', mentioned above, on one of the extracts from Descartes's letters. The possibility that the de Beaugrand text was written in either 1640 or 1641 thus remains open.

A sixth item, the copy of the treatise by de Beaune, must by the same token be dated after Hobbes's arrival in Paris. Professor Raylor's suggestion that Hobbes had taken a particular interest in de Beaune's work after meeting him in January or early February 1641, and that this copy of the treatise was a fruit of that special interest, is also very plausible. The text of the 'Notes briefves' had, however, been in circulation for some time (Descartes had received a copy from de Beaune before 20 February 1639).[34] So the copy from which Hobbes had this transcription made may have come not from de Beaune himself, but from Mersenne—as is suggested, too, by the fact that the scribe used for this purpose by Hobbes was one Mersenne also employed.

As with the Latin Optical Manuscript, there is no direct evidence, either in the text itself or in related correspondence, to show when this de Beaune manuscript was sent to England. But it is clear that Hobbes was in quite frequent correspondence with Sir Charles Cavendish during 1641; this is evident not only from the contents of the one surviving letter from that correspondence (in which Hobbes thanks Cavendish for two letters, refers to his own previous 'letters from hence', and refers to various scientific enquiries he is conducting on Cavendish's behalf), but also from a note on Hobbes made by Samuel Hartlib some time in the second half of 1641, recording (probably) information he had obtained from John Pell: 'Writes often to Sir Charles Candish. Is now in Fraunce publishing in Latin his Politica. Hee hase also in readines other parts of Learning. Hobs.'[35] It seems reasonable to assume, therefore, that this de Beaune text was sent to Cavendish with one of the letters in this correspondence—a correspondence which may well have continued into 1642, but would probably have been disrupted by the outbreak of the Civil War in the summer of that year. (This dating, together with the fact that Sir Charles was the original recipient of the de Beaune manuscript, is confirmed by further evidence from the Pell-Cavendish correspondence, which I present below.)

Similar considerations apply to the manuscript of Vieta (PLATE 1) which contains diagrams drawn and lettered by Hobbes. This manuscript presents an extract from the second book of Vieta's astronomical treatise, the 'Harmonicon coeleste'—a treatise which had not been published at the time of Vieta's death in 1603, and has indeed remained unpublished to this day. The history of the transmission of this text is rather obscure. Vieta's papers first passed to his pupil Jacques Alleaume, and were later dispersed after Alleaume's death in 1627. Two manuscripts of the 'Harmonicon coeleste' were then acquired by the scholar and bibliophile Pierre Dupuy. One of them, a corrected draft in Vieta's hand, he gave to his brother Jacques. The other, a fair copy, was passed by Pierre Dupuy to Mersenne, who lent it in turn to someone who refused to give it back: eventually, after that person's death, it was returned (in 1647) to the Dupuy brothers, from whom it later passed, by bequest, to the astronomer Ismaël Boulliau. This fair-copy manuscript is now in the Biblioteca Nazionale Centrale, Florence.[36] Given the connections between Mersenne and several of the manuscripts by the Parisian scribe in Harley MS 6796, it is tempting to conclude that Mersenne had had at least some parts of the fair-copy manuscript transcribed while it was in his possession, and that the copy in Add. MS 4417 was made by the Parisian scribe, at Hobbes's behest, from materials thus retained by Mersenne. But, given the various uncertainties surrounding the distribution of manuscripts of this text, the conclusion is tentative, at best.

The diagrams in this copy are in a black ink clearly different from the ink used by the Parisian scribe for the text itself; and a comparison between the lettering of these diagrams and that of the diagrams in the Latin Optical Manuscript shows that, as mentioned above, the diagrams in the Vieta manuscript were also added by Hobbes.[37] The Vieta manuscript also contains occasional corrections to the text, made in the same black ink as the diagrams: where letters or words are added, the handwriting is that of Hobbes himself.[38] This manuscript now rests among the papers of John Pell, and was, as we have seen, in his possession by 12 October 1642. (Given the way in which Pell referred to it in his letter of that date, showing no sign of regarding it as a novel acquisition, this *terminus ad quem* could reasonably be pushed back by some months at least.) Pell appears to have thought of it as his own property (he referred to it first as 'in mine owne hands', then as 'mine'); the simplest explanation would therefore be that it had been sent to him as a gift by Hobbes, either directly or via Sir Charles Cavendish. Pell had come under Cavendish's patronage in the first half of 1640, and no doubt had opportunities to become personally acquainted (through Cavendish) with Hobbes at that time.[39] But, on the other hand, there is no other evidence of direct contacts between Hobbes and Pell during this period; and paying a scribe to produce a fair copy—of a short text which Hobbes could easily have copied himself—does seem more appropriate to the preparation of a gift for a patron. So it is perhaps more likely that this manuscript was first sent by Hobbes to Cavendish, and then passed by him to Pell.

Thus, of the eight items in the same scribal hand in Harley MS 6796, Add. MS 4416 and Add. MS 4417, three (or possibly four) were sent by Mersenne to Haak (for, in some cases, Pell) in 1640; two (or possibly one) were sent by Mersenne to Cavendish in 1641; and one, the text by de Beaune, was probably sent by Hobbes to Cavendish, in 1641 or perhaps in the first half of 1642. The two other items, Hobbes's Latin Optical Manuscript and the section of a treatise by Vieta, are similar in character to the treatise by de Beaune: in all three cases, the lettering of the diagrams is in Hobbes's hand. And of those three items, two—the de Beaune treatise, and the Latin Optical Manuscript—share the same watermarks. Every aspect of the evidence thus suggests that the Hobbes treatise had a closely similar history to the piece by de Beaune—that it was sent from Paris to England, for Sir Charles Cavendish (who had, indeed, played a key role in developing Hobbes's interests in optics, and was by far the most scientifically-minded of his patrons). What unites all these manuscripts is the fact that they seem to have come originally into the hands of either Cavendish or Pell; two ended up among Pell's manuscripts, the other six in a collection of Cavendish's papers. Some of the intervening history of their transmission can in fact be constructed from evidence in the Pell-Cavendish correspondence—evidence which bears directly on the story of the de Beaune manuscript.

III

As we have seen, some of the manuscripts now gathered in Harley MS 6796 must have been passed on originally from Theodore Haak to John Pell, while others had probably been sent directly to Sir Charles Cavendish. One manuscript in the latter category, the item by de Beaune, also has numerous annotations in Pell's hand. At the head of the manuscript Pell wrote: 'Notae in 4° Anno 1649 Lugduni Batavorum Latine, sub hoc titulo [*line deleted*] Florimundi de Beaune (In Curia Blaesensi Consiliaris Regii) in Geometriam Renati des Cartes Notae Breves' ('*Notae*, published in Latin at Leiden in 1649, in quarto, under this title: *In geometriam Renati des Cartes notae breves*, by Florimond de Beaune, *conseiller* of the royal court at Blois').[40] Some of Pell's annotations were corrections of errors in the manuscript (either faults of transcription, or errors in the calculations themselves), while others involved comparison with the printed Latin text; evidently, this manuscript was in Pell's possession at some time after the publication of the Latin edition in 1649, and was returned to Cavendish thereafter.

The surviving correspondence between Pell and Cavendish includes what is clearly a reference to the return of this manuscript. On [19 February/] 1 March 1650 Cavendish (who was in Antwerp) wrote to Pell (who was in Breda): 'manie thankes for your letter, & bookes; you haue set such a marcke in your letter on the manuscript, that makes me not esteem Monsr: de Baune so excellent an Analyst as I did, for I doute diuers of those places you haue corrected are not the fault of the Transcriber but mistakes of the Author.'[41] Later in the same letter Cavendish referred to the return of other manuscripts: 'I expected Monsr: Fermats manuscripts when you returned the rest, & doe still when you shall returne those yet in your handes, for I hope you haue some of his.'[42] This shows that Pell was in the process of sending back a number of manuscripts to Cavendish, some of which had been out of Cavendish's possession for so long that he was not sure which they might be. The origin of this transfer of manuscripts can be traced in the correspondence to a request made by Cavendish on [25 September/] 5 October 1649, when he asked Pell to return to him a treatise on algebra by Chauveau, a book by a Jesuit, '& allso anie treatises which came from england to you which I had left with you'.[43]

In response to this, Pell wrote on 3/13 October 1649: 'The next weeke I intend to send back Chauveau wth the Catalog of your bookes & papers.'[44] Unfortunately the 'Catalog', which may well have included a reference to Hobbes's Latin Optical Manuscript, does not appear to have survived; out of the entire run of 47 letters sent by Pell to Cavendish between 1644 and 1651, the only ones missing from the numbered sequence of Pell's drafts are the three which followed his letter of 3/13 October 1649. However, the next surviving letter, dated 7/17 May 1650, shows that he had made some progress in performing his task: 'I have now in my hands no manuscripts of yours but in folio & 5 printed bookes in quarto.'[45] Perhaps some of the transcripts now in Harley MS 6796, which are all on folio-sized paper, were still in Pell's possession; but we can assume that they were eventually sent to Cavendish, since they ended up not among the Pell manuscripts but (together with the de Beaune treatise) in a collection of Cavendish's papers.[46] One other transcript from this group had demonstrably been in Pell's hands: the de Beaugrand text, which has some underlinings in a red ink similar to that used by Pell for his corrections to de Beaune. Among Pell's own papers there is a copy of this entire text, in his own hand: the same names and phrases are underlined there too, also in red ink.[47]

The Pell-Cavendish correspondence also helps to explain what had happened to these manuscripts before Pell started to send them back in 1649–50. John Pell had moved from London to Amsterdam at the end of 1643, and was appointed Professor of Mathematics at the Amsterdam Athenaeum in the spring of 1644.[48] In August of that year he wrote to Cavendish:

> I came over hither in December last, not bringing any of my bookes or papers with me . . . Nor did I imagine that, before I gat out of this towne againe, I should be persuaded to clime the Cathedra and . . . reade publikely 5 dayes in a weeke, an houre every day in Latine. Which had I forseene, I thinke yt all the bookes and papers that I had, both yours and mine, should have come along with me, to enable me to doe those things the more easily. And yet I have no great minde to goe fetch them, nor to send for them. So long as they are there unstirred, they seeme to be safe.[49]

More than a year later, Pell's papers were still in his family home in London: he described himself as 'banished from all y^t is deare to me my bookes & papers my wife & children, not seeing when it will be otherwise'.[50] Even a pay increase of 50 per cent in early 1646 was not sufficient to cover the costs of moving his family and belongings from London: 'This city hath lately multiplied me by 3/2,' he wrote in

February; 'had they done it by 3, I should have presently sent for all that I have.'[51] But in the summer of 1646 Pell was recruited by the newly founded 'Collegium Auriacum' at Breda, an academy or 'École illustre' set up by the Prince of Orange; and at some time during the next two or three years he was able, at long last, to transport his books and papers (as well as his long-suffering family) to the Netherlands. According to Ferdinand Sassen, the governors of the academy paid him, in addition to his salary of 1,000 guilders, the sum of 500 guilders to cover the cost of shipping his books from England.[52] The surviving records of the academy, however, merely state that he was awarded (in April 1651) a payment of 600 guilders 'for travel and other expenses incurred by him for his transportation to Breda': books are not specified, but the huge cost (compared with similar awards to other professors at the academy) indicates that this was indeed a payment for transporting goods and people from England.[53] From Pell's letters to Cavendish it is clear that his wife and children had joined him in Breda by March 1648, and that he was re-reading some of his own mathematical papers (written '9 yeares agoe') by April 1649.[54]

From this evidence, it is reasonable to conclude that the manuscripts sent by Pell to Cavendish in 1650 had been in Pell's possession at the time of his departure from London in December 1643. This provides a *terminus ad quem*, certainly for the de Beaune text, and probably for the other items in the same scribal hand in the Harley manuscript. Further evidence from the Pell-Cavendish correspondence allows us to shift this *terminus* a little further back, to the spring of 1643.

In August 1644 Cavendish wrote to Pell, asking him to give his opinion about a dispute between Pierre Gassendi and Anton Maria Schyrle von Rheita (an astronomer and Capuchin friar).[55] On several nights in late December 1642 and early January 1643 Rheita had observed what he believed to be new satellites of the planets Jupiter, Saturn and Mars; he had described them in a letter, written on 6 January, to Erycius Puteanus (Errijck van de Put), copies of which were widely circulated in manuscript. Gassendi read the letter and penned a brief refutation; the two were published together in Paris in April 1643, and republished (with further additions) in Louvain later that year.[56] On 7/17 September 1644 Pell drafted his reply to Cavendish's query as follows:

I perceive you have seene Gassendus his judgement of y[e] new Joviales. [I received y[e] friers Epistle from *deleted*] S[r] William Boswell sent me y[e] friers Epistle, [I received it y[e] day y[t] you went out of London *deleted*] the next morning after I received it I brought it to your Lodging, where I learned you were gone out of [*words deleted*] London y[e] day before. I returned [a

pretty large judgement of it *altered* to to Sr William a large letter] shewing many grounds of suspicion y^t it was a meere fable & there was no
such matter . . . A coppy of my letter was sent to a frend in France who
thereupon sent me Gassendus his censure.[57]

The significance of this evidence is that it gives us an approximate date
for the last personal contacts between Pell and Cavendish—indeed,
probably the last date at which Cavendish was in London, before his
eventual return there in late 1651. The details given here by Pell suggest
that this episode took place before the publication of Gassendi's refutation in April 1643: Sir William Boswell, a man of keen scientific interests and wide-ranging intellectual contacts, would surely not have sent
Pell a mere manuscript copy of Rheita's original letter if the printed version, with Gassendi's objections, had already been available at the
time.[58] We may therefore conclude that Sir Charles Cavendish was in
London at some time between January and April 1643. This fact is itself
somewhat surprising. The Civil War was raging; Cavendish's brother,
the Earl of Newcastle, was the chief Royalist commander in the north-
east of England; and on 2 February 1643 Newcastle was impeached in
the House of Commons and expressly excluded, as one of the most
dangerous enemies of the state, from any future amnesty.[59] Pell's comments refer to Sir Charles Cavendish's 'Lodgings' in London; no doubt
it would have been too risky for him to stay in his brother's large town
house in Clerkenwell, and indeed he may have been travelling *incognito*.
The reasons for such a visit to London can only be guessed at; but they
may well have included a desire to rescue items of value (especially personal papers, books and manuscripts) from his brother's house before
the entire contents of the building were seized by the Parliamentary
authorities. This, perhaps, was the occasion on which so many of
Cavendish's 'bookes & papers' were passed to John Pell for safe-
keeping. If so, the *terminus ad quem* for these manuscripts—not just for
their transcription, but for their presence in England—can definitely be
assigned to the early months of 1643. Less definitely, but still very plausibly, we may also suppose that, given the disruptions of the Civil War
(during which, for the most part, Sir Charles Cavendish seems to have
accompanied his brother) these were papers Sir Charles had received in
London or in Wellingor (his Lincolnshire seat) before the outbreak of
the conflict in August 1642.

To sum up: the arguments presented here suggest that the Latin
Optical Manuscript was copied in the period between December 1640
and April 1643 (or, more likely, August 1642). They do not, however,
amount to conclusive proof. Sir Charles Cavendish was himself in Paris,

in direct contact with Hobbes, between 1645 and 1648, and it might therefore be argued that the manuscript came into his possession only then. However, it is noteworthy that the stock of paper used by the scribe when copying out this work was the same as that used for the de Beaune treatise, which was definitely sent to England between those earlier dates. All the evidence suggests that a scribe used by Mersenne before Hobbes's arrival in Paris was then passed on by him to Hobbes—perhaps, initially, to copy items in Mersenne's possession, such as the little book by de Beaugrand; that Hobbes then commissioned this scribe to make fair copies of other materials for transmission to his patron in England; that these materials included the Latin Optical Manuscript; and that Hobbes continued to use the same scribe's services until the end of his stay in Paris, even entrusting to him—despite the language-barrier—the task of producing the most prestigious item Hobbes ever commissioned, the presentation copy of his greatest work.

NOTES

1 T. Raylor, 'The Date and Script of Hobbes's Latin Optical Manuscript' (above, pp. 201–9).

2 In the subtitle, '*seu de vario pondere gravium secundum varia a terrae centro intervalla*', the word '*centro*' was omitted. It is supplied in manuscript in the British Library copy of the book (pressmark 530.m.2 (2)), and as an interlineation in the Chatsworth manuscript.

3 In his letter to Mersenne of 20/30 March 1641 Hobbes referred to a conversation he had had 'seven years ago . . . in your house, in the presence of M. de Beaugrand': T. Hobbes, *Correspondence*, ed. N. Malcolm, 2 vols (Oxford, 1994), I, 108.

4 Hobbes left London *c.*20 November (*ibid.*, I, 114–15); De Beaugrand died *c.*22 December (M. Mersenne, *Correspondance*, ed. C de Waard *et al.*, 17 vols (Paris, 1933–88), X, 519).

5 BL Add. MS 4280, fol. 206r.

6 See Mersenne, *Correspondance*, X, 728 (Hübner and Haak to Mersenne, 29 August 1641); T. Hobbes, *De cive: the Latin version*, ed. H. Warrender (Oxford, 1983), frontispiece (the pictorial title-page).

7 It appeared in the compilation of Pierre Fermat's works edited by his son, *Varia opera mathematica*, ed. S. Fermat (Toulouse, 1679), pp. 70–88, and is reproduced from there in Fermat, *Oeuvres*, ed. P. Tannery and C. Henry, 5 vols (Paris, 1891–1922), I, 52–69. The contents of the Chatsworth manuscript have not apparently been identified before; it was unknown to Tannery and Henry, and is not mentioned in the discussion of this treatise in M. S. Mahoney, *The Mathematical Career of Pierre de Fermat, 1601–1665*, 2nd edn (Princeton, NJ, 1994), pp. 419–20. Also unmentioned there is the copy of the complete text of the treatise, in the hand of John Pell, in BL Add. MS 4415, fols 255v–9. This copy, probably made from one loaned to Pell by Sir Charles Cavendish, unfortunately does not furnish any evidence that would assist in the dating either of the treatise itself, or of the Chatsworth manuscript.

8 This book was prepared in tandem with Mersenne's other compilation, *Cogitata physico-mathematica*, which was also published in Paris in 1644. Both works were

apparently covered by Mersenne's application to the Corrector General of his order in August 1643; by the 'Privilège du Roi' of 2 October 1643; and by the statement of approval by the two Minim theologians who had scrutinized the work, issued on 27 February 1644 (for all these, see *Cogitata physico-mathematica*, sig. a3v). John Pell had a copy of *Universae geometriae synopsis* in Amsterdam by 14/24 August 1644, when he wrote to Sir Charles Cavendish: 'Mersennus hath put forth 2 Tomes in large quarto . . . they came out of ye presse about 4 months agoe' (BL Add. MS 4280, fol. 106v).

9   Mahoney, *Mathematical Career of Fermat*, p. 420.

10 Aubrey recorded that 'Mr Hobbes told me, that G. Duke of Buckingham at Paris when he was about xx yeares old, desired him to read Geometry to him; his Grace had great naturall partes and quicknesse of wit; Mr Hobbes read, and his Grace did not apprehend, wch Mr Hobbes wondered at: at last, Mr Hobbes observed that his Grace was at mastrupation (his hand in his Codpiece.) That is a very improper age, for that reason for learning' (Oxford, Bodleian Library, MS Aubrey 10, fol. 11v; printed with some inaccuracies in *Aubrey on Education: A Hitherto Unpublished Manuscript by the Author of* Brief Lives, ed. J. E. Stephens (London, 1972), p. 160). Hobbes had misremembered the Duke's age: he was born in January 1628. For the date of his departure from Paris (11/21 May 1646) see Historical Manuscripts Commission, *Report on the Manuscripts of the Earl of Denbigh*, part V (London, 1911: modern ref. No. 68), p. 79.

11 Sir Charles Cavendish reported to Pell from Paris on 1/11 May 1645: 'M^r: Hobbes commends M^r: Roberual extreamelie' (BL Add. MS 4278, fol. 205r). On Roberval's expertise in fortification see P. Costabel, 'Gilles Personne de Roberval (1602–1675)', in *Cahiers d'histoire et de philosophie des sciences*, N.S., No. 14 (1986), pp. 21–31, esp. p. 28, n. 3. On his relationship with Hobbes during this period see N. Malcolm, *Aspects of Hobbes* (Oxford, 2002), pp. 156–99.

12 See Malcolm, *Aspects of Hobbes*, pp. 80–85, 102–3.

13 A. Pacchi, *Convenzione e ipotesi nella formazione della filosofia naturale di Thomas Hobbes* (Florence, 1965), pp. 24–29.

14 Hobbes, *Opera philosophica quae latine scripsit omnia*, ed. W. Molesworth, 5 vols (London, 1839–45), I, 'Epistola dedicatoria' (unpaginated), final paragraph.

15 Hobbes, *Correspondence*, I, 177.

16 See N. Malcolm, 'A Summary Biography of Hobbes', in *The Cambridge Companion to Hobbes*, ed. T. Sorell (Cambridge, 1996), pp. 13–44 (p. 31). Robert Payne reported that *Leviathan* was on sale in Oxford on 6 [/16] May 1651 (BL Harley MS 6942, No. 132).

17 Hobbes, *Correspondence*, I, 447–8.

18 E. Heawood, *Watermarks Mainly in the 17th and 18th Centuries* (Hilversum, 1950): 2237 is from an English manuscript dated 1641, 2239 from an English manuscript dated 1652. Most paper used in England at this time was imported from France.

19 Descartes, *Oeuvres*, ed. C. Adam and P. Tannery, revd edn, 11 vols (Paris, 1974), II, 425–7; Mersenne, *Correspondance*, VIII, 189–91.

20 BL Add. MS 4416, fols 10–18; Descartes, *Oeuvres*, II, 254–66; Mersenne, *Correspondance*, VII, 404–14.

21 Mersenne, *Correspondance*, IX, 306: 'je mets icy une demonstration que Mr Pell a desiré, et laquelle vous luy monstrerez, s'il vous plaist, à sçavoir que la ligne cycloide de la roulette contient un espace triple de la roulette.' This is the conclusion reached by Descartes (*Oeuvres*, II, 262).

22 Mersenne, *Correspondance*, IX, 170–1, 231.

23 BL Harley MS 6796, fol. 188. The notes on fol. 188v and the beginning of the letter on fol. 188r are in Cavendish's hand, but in different inks, and were presumably not contemporaneous. For examples of letters written by Cavendish in which the year is dated from 25 March, not 1 January, see BL Add. MS 4278, fols 170–1 (to Pell, 8 January '1641'), 173–4 (to Pell, 5 February '1641').

24 Mersenne, *Correspondance*, XI, 407–8: 'les charactères de sa Musique'; 'Je vous les mettray en vous priant de ne les publier ni enseigner à personne, par ce que je lui ay promis le secret jusqu'à ce qu'il le vueille esclore.'

25 C. de Waard, 'Un Écrit de Beaugrand sur la méthode des tangentes de Fermat à propos de celle de Descartes', *Bulletin des sciences mathématiques*, 2nd Ser., 17 (1918), 157–77, esp. 165–7; Mersenne, *Correspondance*, VIII, 90 n.

26 *Ibid.*, IX, 306 ('J'ay un ou deux excellens traitez de Geometrie la plus raffinée, mais parce qu'ils sont un peu longs à descrire, je prieray M. V(egilin) de prendre la peine de les transcrire pour vous les envoyer; et puis vous en ferez part à Mr Pell').

27 For details of Vegelin's biography see C. de Waard, 'Philips Ernst Vegelin', in *Nieuw nederlandsch biografisch woordenboek*, 10 vols (Leiden, 1911–37), VII, cols 1224–5, and N. Malcolm, 'Six Unknown Letters from Mersenne to Vegelin', *The Seventeenth Century*, 16 (2001), 95–122. Although his hand shares some features with the Parisian scribe's, it is clearly not the same, even in its most formal register (*e.g.* his letter to Constantijn Huygens of 10 January 1642, Amsterdam University Library, MS Bn 29 (1), or the passports written out by him in 1651, in Rijksarchief in de Provincie Friesland, Leeuwarden, Stadhouderlijke Archief MS 353). In any case, Vegelin left Paris for The Hague by September 1641 at the latest, and remained in the Netherlands thereafter.

28 Mersenne, *Correspondance*, IX, 310.

29 *Ibid.*, X, p. 610 ('en et doctissimi alterius ex amicis, qui credit se meritô ea reprehendere in libro Dni de Cartes, quae in eâ dissertatione videbis').

30 BL Add. MS 4278, fol. 165v.

31 *Ibid.*, fol. 175r. The reasons for thinking that this draft was also intended for Cavendish are that it repeats the same information as the other draft; that its intended recipient was also receiving letters from Mersenne; and that that person, as Pell's comment here shows, would have had a higher status in Mersenne's eyes. The only other member of Pell's circle of acquaintances who was in regular contact with Mersenne was Haak; but it is known that Mersenne had sent the Fermat manuscript to Haak in the first place.

32 *Ibid.*, fol. 163r.

33 The differently constructed letters are majuscule *E* (Hobbes uses both a curved letter, and one simply constructed out of straight lines; the writer of the diagram-lettering in the de Beaugrand and Descartes texts uses the straight-lined form much more rarely, and adds little serifs to each horizontal when he does so), majuscule *I* (where Hobbes has an *I* different from his *J*, using a neat vertical line with small cross-bars at head and foot, while the other writer has a sloping and curve-footed *J* written as a single line, without the right-hand half of the cross-bar), and majuscule *D* (where the other writer's curve, unlike Hobbes's, continues well past the top of the vertical stroke and curls round behind it).

34 Descartes, *Oeuvres*, II, 510–19 (Descartes to de Beaune, 20 February 1639).

35 Hobbes, *Correspondence*, I, 80–85 (Letter 31, Hobbes to Cavendish, [29 January/] 8 February 1641); Hartlib Papers (CD-Rom edition), 30/4/76B (Ephemerides, 1641). The Hobbes letter is also contained in BL Harley MS 6796 (fols 291–5).

36 On the complex manuscript history of this work see G. Targioni-Tozzetti, *Notizie degli aggrandimenti delle scienze fisiche accaduti in Toscana nel corso di anni LX. del secolo XVII*, 3 vols (Florence, 1780), I, 499–501; G. Bigourdan, 'Sur un ouvrage de F. Viète, supposé perdu: l'*Harmonicon coeleste*', *Comptes rendus hebdomadaires des séances de l'Académie des Sciences*, 162 (1916), 237–40; G. Vacca, 'L'*Harmonicon coeleste* de François Viète', *Comptes rendus hebdomadaires des séances de l'Académie des Sciences*, 162 (1916), 676–9 (with a further note by Bigourdan appended to it, pp. 679–80); Mersenne, *Correspondance*, I, 619–20, and XI, 312–14. The manuscript in the Bibliothèque Nationale, Paris, f.l. 7274, is identified by Bigourdan as the other manuscript owned by the Dupuys. The manuscript associated with Mersenne is Florence, Biblioteca Nazionale Centrale, MS Biblioteca Magliabechiana, classe xi, cod. 37. Bigourdan and Vacca also refer to another manuscript in Florence, MS Biblioteca Magliabechiana, classe xi, cod. 36, which is in Vieta's hand, and may perhaps be more plausibly identified with the other Dupuy-owned manuscript. H. L. L. Busard has identified another manuscript in the Bibliothèque Nationale (f.l. n.a. 1644, fols 67–79) as a fragment of this treatise, also in Vieta's hand: see 'Über einige Papiere aus Viètes Nachlass in der Pariser Bibliothèque Nationale', *Centaurus*, 10 (1964), 65–126 (p. 68). The editors of Mersenne's *Correspondance* mention (XI, 314) another manuscript, derived probably from a copy given by Vieta to Marino Ghetaldi, now in the Biblioteca Nazionale Vittorio Emanuele, Rome. Another manuscript was owned by Guglielmo Libri (see P. A. Maccioni Ruju and M. Mostert, *The Life and Times of Guglielmo Libri (1802–1869)* (Hilversum, 1995), p. 127); its present location is not known.

37 The forms of the majuscules match very closely: this is especially striking in the case of *A*, *B*, *G*, *I*, *M* and *Q*. Cf., for example, the diagrams in BL Add. MS 4417, fols 27r and 28v with those in BL Harley MS 6796, fols 226r and 227r.

38 BL Add. MS 4417, fols 26v ('perigeunt' corrected to 'perigaeas'; 'et' added), 27v ('signum' added) and 30r ('vt' added).

39 The first dated record of contacts between Pell and Cavendish (indicating that Pell had been giving Cavendish tuition in mathematics) is from 6 May 1640: BL Add. MS 4431, fol. 270v.

40 BL Harley MS 6796, fol. 267r.

41 BL Add. MS 4278, fol. 295r; the expression 'I doute' here means 'I suspect'.

42 *Ibid.*, fol. 295r.

43 *Ibid.*, fol. 291r.

44 BL Add. MS 4280, fol. 134v.

45 *Ibid.*, fol. 135r.

46 Some of them, as we have seen, had originally passed from Haak to Pell, and need not have been considered as belonging to Cavendish. The most likely explanation is that Pell had in turn passed them on to Cavendish in England, and had later come to regard them as part of the stock of Cavendish's manuscripts.

47 BL Add. MS 4407, fols 38–39. The same bound volume of Pell's papers also includes his copy (in his own hand) of the treatise by Chauveau (fols 31–37), and a short text about tangents which Pell annotated 'Sr Charles Cavendish hath a coppy' (fol. 112r). The original copy of the Chauveau treatise, which Pell returned to Cavendish, is in BL Harley MS 6083, fols 350–79.

48 His appointment was made on 27 April 1644: see *Gedenkboek van het Athenaeum en de Universiteit van Amsterdam 1632–1932*, ed. H. Brugmans, J. H. Scholte and P. Kleintjes (Amsterdam, 1932), p. 651.

49 BL Add. MS 4280, fol. 105 (7 August 1644).

50 *Ibid.*, fol. 115v (15/25 November 1645).

51 *Ibid.*, fol. 117r (9/19 February 1646).

52 F. L. R. Sassen, 'Levensberichten van de hoogleraren der Illustre School te Breda', *Jaarboek van de geschied- en oudheidkundige kring van stad en land van Breda "De Oranjeboom"*, 19 (1966), 123–57 (p. 137).

53 Algemeen Rijksarchief, The Hague, 1.08.11 (Nassause Domeinraad, 1581–1811), document 7989, fol. 188r: 'ouer reys en andere oncosten by hem gehadt op syn Transport naer Breda' (17 April 1651). Several other professors received similar (but smaller) payments (fols 182–7); this was clearly a long-delayed reimbursement, relating in some cases to their original move to Breda in 1646.

54 BL Add. MS 4280, fols 132r ('Since my wife & family came hither': 1/11 March 1648), and 133v (4/14 April 1649).

55 BL Add. MS 4278, fol. 107r: 'I desire your opinion of the late discourse of newe stars, I see Gassendes doutes of it' (8/18 August 1644).

56 See A. Reita [*sic*], *Novem stellae circa Iovem, circa Saturnum sex, circa Martem non-nullae, A P. Antonio Reita detectae & satellitibus adiudicatae* (Louvain, 1643), esp. pp. 3–8 (Rheita, letter to Puteanus), 12–59 (Gassendi, 'Iudicium').

57 BL Add. MS 4280, fol. 107r.

58 Confirmation of this point can be found in a list compiled by Pell of books he owned, with, in the case of works he had received as gifts, the names of the donors: this contains the entry 'Novem stellae circa Jovem visae & de eisdem Petri Gassendi Judicium. Parisijs 1643. Mr Hart[*page torn*]' (BL Add. MS 4394, fol. 113r). He thus received a copy of the Paris edition not from Boswell but from Hartlib, and it must seem unlikely that Hartlib, who was in close contact with him, would have given him a copy if he had possessed one already.

59 G. Trease, *Portrait of a Cavalier: William Cavendish, First Duke of Newcastle* (London, 1979), p. 104.

The Textual Transmission of Marvell's 'A Letter to Doctor Ingelo': The Longleat Manuscript

Edward Holberton

In February 1654 Andrew Marvell sent his Latin poem 'A Letter to Doctor Ingelo' to Nathaniel Ingelo, a fellow of Eton College, whom Marvell met shortly before Ingelo accompanied Bulstrode Whitelocke on his 1653–54 embassy to Sweden in the dual capacity of chaplain and leader of Whitelocke's music.[1] Marvell had been staying at Eton tutoring Cromwell's ward William Dutton, where he met a circle of scholarly and musical friends including Ingelo and the composer Benjamin Rogers, who is mentioned in the poem. Ingelo took some of Rogers' compositions to Sweden and played them to Queen Christina when an opportunity presented itself, and apparently she enjoyed them.[2] Marvell wrote 'A Letter to Doctor Ingelo' hoping for a similar opportunity: his panegyric on Christina is clearly designed for her ear.

After the diplomatic disaster of Oliver St John's and Walter Strickland's embassy to the United Provinces, it was vital for the Republic's prestige that its embassy to Sweden was received with as much respect as had been shown to ambassadors of the Crown.[3] Whitelocke was instructed to negotiate a treaty based upon diplomatic recognition, a defensive alliance and commercial agreements.[4] Secretly, he was to broach the possibility of sending a fleet to open the Sound, which the Dutch and Danish had closed to English shipping.[5] The Protectorate was established on 16 December 1653, and Christina was pleased at the change.[6] She made many shows of favour towards Whitelocke, but he became increasingly frustrated by the delaying tactics of Christina and the Swedish commissioners, who preferred to wait for the conclusion of Anglo-Dutch peace negotiations and then, after Christina announced her plan to abdicate, for her successor's coronation, although Whitelocke's threats to return to England eventually pressured Christina to sign an outline treaty on 28 April 1654.[7] Whitelocke recorded the progress of his embassy in a journal, in which he wrote memorials of his interviews and transcribed correspondence and documents relating to the negotiations. This journal exists in several manuscript versions.[8] Longleat MS 124a is the first, 'on-the-spot' version of the journal, which has yielded the manuscript copy of 'A Letter to Doctor Ingelo' transcribed below.[9] This was later expanded into a didactic account of the embassy (London, British Library, Additional MSS 37346 and 37347): 'The History of Whitelockes Ambassy from England to Sweden with Notes theruppon And touching the Governement Publique Councells & Persons in those and in other Countries with some Resemblances To the Commonwealth of Israel'.[10] In this autograph manuscript, Whitelocke's conversations with Christina and other court officials become rhetorical dialogues in English that prompt lengthy meditations on government and morality. Another set of manuscripts in two folio volumes, BL Add. MSS 4991A and 4991B, are slightly misleadingly described as 'copies' of Add. MSS 37346 and 37347 by the British Library catalogue. In fact, Add. MSS 37346 and 37347 were revised, probably by Whitelocke after the Restoration, with a number of passages praising Cromwell and the Rump, or criticising Charles II, deleted or altered, and some of the didactic matter marked for deletion. Add. MS 4991 is a fair scribal copy of Add. MSS 37346 and 37347 according to these revisions and with the earlier chapter headings removed. The fourth version of the journal, Add. MS 4902, is more drastically revised: Whitelocke removes the didactic meditations and further elaborates and polishes his memoirs and interviews. This, the most readable version of the journal, is the source for two printed editions.[11] The three later versions of the journal reproduce poems connected with the embassy by Daniel Whistler and Charles Wolseley, but not Marvell's poem, despite the esteem for it evident in Whitelocke's introductory note: 'missi etiam fuerunt ab Amico quodam Etoniensi ad Dominum Ingelo versus sequentes elegantissimi' [also the following very elegant verses were sent to Doctor Ingelo by some friend at Eton].[12]

According to a flyleaf note, Longleat MS 124a was rediscovered by John Alexander, Marquess of Bath, in one of the closets of the Old Library at Longleat House in 1859.[13] He had the volume repaired and rebound, but a number of pages are missing.[14] It is a folio volume made up of folded sheets bearing a foolscap watermark somewhat akin to Heawood No. 1954 (Schleswig, 1658). Its irregular quiring and the catchwords written at the foot of many pages suggest that the sheets were unbound when the journal was written, and that as they wrote, the scribes gathered sheets *ad-hoc*. The entries are written in several different hands: letters, documents and correspondence tend to be transcribed in a formal, compact, mixed hand; Whitelocke's memoirs of events and audiences tend to be entered in English in his cursive italic hand or in French or Latin in other distinct hands. However, there are many exceptions to these tendencies and entries sometimes switch hands or language midway. These irregularities can be partly explained by the frenetic conditions of Whitelocke's improvised chancery, which seems to have been all but overwhelmed by the volume of writing, translation and copying to be done: Whitelocke notes that he would frequently dictate letters to each of his two secretaries while writing a third himself.[15] The journal appears to have been composed through a similar division of labour, although I can find no rationale to explain why some memoirs of daily events were written in French and Latin and some in English; he needed to negotiate in French and Latin, so he might have been trying to keep himself fluent.[16] For the most part, the journal text is continuous and evenly spaced, implying that it was written chronologically. Yet gaps are occasionally left as if anticipating future insertions, and in some places it is apparent that text has been inserted later: the entry describing Whitelocke's first public audience is mostly written in one of the more formal hands, but sections are written in Whitelocke's more cursive italic hand, including a description of his attendants' dress in which his lines become increasingly crowded, suggesting a later insertion when he had been reminded of these details.[17] At some stage Whitelocke began to reorganise the journal into chapters for Add. MSS 37346 and 37347, adding chapter divisions and summaries in the margins.[18] At least one later insertion of detail dates from this stage of revision: to an entry in French describing an audience with Prince Adolphe, written in the hand usually reserved for French, Whitelocke adds in cursive English further details of their discussion and a cross-reference to a later chapter.[19] Marvell's poem is copied in a formal italic hand, which bears a number of similarities, particularly in the majuscule forms, with one of the hands used regularly in Longleat MS 124a, although that hand is elsewhere more compact and uses more secretary graphs, so I hesitate to identify them with absolute certainty.[20]

The poem is dated '7: Kal: Mart. 1653' [23 February 1653/4 by the English calendar], and it is transcribed with letters from John Thurloe dated 24 February. In the same post arrived a Latin ode addressed to Whitelocke from his friend Charles Wolseley, which is transcribed before Marvell's poem in one of the hands that appear regularly in Longleat MS 124a. The post took a month to reach Sweden: this batch of correspondence arrived on 23 March.[21] 'A Letter to Doctor Ingelo' was transcribed the same day, so Ingelo must have shown the poem to Whitelocke shortly after receiving it, making it likely that Whitelocke's copy was made directly from the presentation copy that Marvell sent to Ingelo. Whitelocke had previously shown Christina a Latin poem written by Daniel Whistler (the embassy physician), on the subject of her rumoured abdication, which she had liked.[22] On 30 March, after trying to rekindle Christina's interest in his treaty with some apparent success, Whitelocke showed her the poems by Marvell and Wolseley:

Elle est tombée sur beaucoup d'autre discours, et particulierement touchant L'Angleterre, et je lui ai donné beaucoup de contentement par la lecture de certains vers Latins, envoyés d'Angleterre (a Monsieur Ingelo) qui estoyent excellemment composes, et ausi d'une Ode qu'on m'a envoyé d'Angleterre, et que sont ici devant escrits. Les quels la Reyne m'a desire lui donner, et que je doulusse lui laisser les Articles jusques au lendemain et alors retourner vers elle.[23]

[She fell to divers other discourses, and in particular touching on England, and I gave her much contentment by reading for her certain Latin verses sent from England (to Mr Ingelo) which were excellently composed, and also an Ode that had been sent to me from England and which is written before. The queen desired that I should give these to her, and that I should leave her the articles until the following day and then return to her.]

A few years ago Hilton Kelliher discovered an incomplete text of 'A Letter to Doctor Ingelo' in Jean Arckenholtz's *Mémoires concernant Christine, Reine de Suède*.[24] This text was derived from a manuscript, now lost, in the hand of Jean Scheffer, a German antiquarian and philologist who enjoyed Christina's favour and copied documents relating to her affairs. The printed editions of Whitelocke's journal do not mention the presentation of Marvell's poem specifically, only 'other verses' given to Christina on 30 March, which Kelliher correctly supposed were Marvell's. Longleat MS 124a not only confirms that 'A Letter to Doctor Ingelo' was presented on this date to Christina, but it suggests that it was highly regarded by Whitelocke and Christina. Whitelocke's praise for the verses suggests that they were not left out of the later versions of his journal on grounds of merit; perhaps more for the relative obscurity of the poet: in Whitelocke's introductory note 'Amico quodam Etoniensi' [some friend at Eton] hints that Marvell himself does not really interest the ambassador. [25]

Kelliher argued that variants between the Arckenholtz text of 'A Letter to Doctor Ingelo' and the text as it appears in Marvell's *Miscellaneous Poems* (London, 1681 (hereafter *1681*)) show that Marvell revised the poem after he sent it to Sweden. Whitelocke's manuscript provides a complete and more accurate witness of the poem as it was presented to Christina and reveals Marvell's care for detail when he later revised the poem.[26] I cannot discuss the variants exhaustively, but I will try to draw attention to the more important differences between the texts.

Longleat MS 124a brings the Arckenholtz text into clearer focus. Most of the variants between Arckenholtz and *1681* that Kelliher suspected were errors in the transcription or printing of the Arckenholtz text do not appear in the Longleat manuscript: 'Fungitur' [for 'Jungitur', joined] (l. 8), 'agniolis' [for 'agricolis', farmers] (l. 10), 'tum' [for 'tam', as] (l. 36), 'est' [a superfluous addition] (l. 41), 'Cynthii' [for 'Cynthi', the mountain Cynthus in Delos] (l. 44), 'Paridas' [for 'pariles', equal] (l. 45), 'Qua' [for 'Quae', which] (l. 48), 'auro' [for 'auso', daring] (l. 55), 'spoliatae' [for 'spoliata', having stripped] (l. 58), 'num' [for 'nam', for] (l. 60), 'seriis' [for 'seris', late] (l. 62). 'Ac' [and] (l. 21) is the exception, which in *1681* reads 'At' [but]. Some Arckenholtz variants that Kelliher thought indicated revisions in *1681* do not appear in the Longleat manuscript. For example, 'falsos' for 'falsâ' [false] (l. 35) is probably a transcription slip in Arckenholtz and similarly 'dimisit' [sent away] for 'demisit' [cast down] (l. 33) is probably a mistake, because the sense requires the latter (Marvell's use of 'demiserit' at l. 113 and 'dimisit' in the Latin epigram inspired by a stanza of 'Eyes and Tears' implies that he knew the difference). These slips suggest that at some stage in its transmission, the Arckenholtz text was carelessly transcribed. Arckenholtz claims that he copied the poem from a manuscript in the hand of Scheffer, but Scheffer, a distinguished scholar, is unlikely to have made or copied so many slips; this leaves the possibilities that the errors originate from Arckenholtz himself, a transcriber working for him, his printer, or that Arckenholtz mistook Scheffer's hand. In two places there are variants peculiar to Arckenholtz that are possibly deliberate emendations by a Swedish scribe. Arckenholtz's text reads 'Suevam' [a Latinization of Swedish] in place of 'saevam' [savage] (l. 11) in Longleat MS 124a and *1681*. The opening lines of Marvell's poem take liberties with his subject: invoking the language of exile, he emphasises the remoteness of Ingelo's destination and questions whether people actually live in so harsh a climate.[27] The poem elegantly transforms these themes into arguments in praise of Christina and the Swedes and so it is important to the effect that Marvell's first questions are arresting. But perhaps someone thought Marvell was taking the joke too far and changed 'saevam' to 'Suevam'; this emendation breaks up Marvell's neat figure 'saevam gens mitior oram' [a milder race [inhabits] the harsh region], and Latinizes the Swedes as the Suevi (a German tribe, also called the Suebi, mentioned by Lucan and Tacitus and identified as ancestors of the Swedish people by some early modern scholars), where Marvell uses a different Latinization, 'Suecis', at line 77.[28] Both Longleat MS 124a and *1681* describe the Swedes as 'Pace vigil' [vigilant in peace] (l. 12), which the Arckenholtz text changes to the more ebullient 'Pace viget' [flourishes in peace], even though the Arckenholtz reading again disrupts Marvell's rhetorical pattern. This change might also be more than a simple misreading: vigilance in peace suggests that the Swedes are hawkishly ready to defend their strategic interests, but the Arckenholtz variant emphasises the benefits of peace. Christina's foreign policy was generally less belligerent than those of her father Gustavus Adolphus and her successor Charles X, and with the grandees of her court she sought to delay signing the treaty with the English until a peace had been agreed between the English and the Dutch; to sign beforehand would risk dragging Sweden into a war with the Dutch and Denmark that it could not afford; it would force Sweden to boycott Dutch trade and it might prolong hostilities by encouraging the English to press harder terms upon the Dutch.[29] The tension between these perspectives on the alliance is perhaps reproduced minutely in transcription, when Scheffer or another Swedish scribe found that 'viget' suited the court's mood better than 'vigil'.

Longleat MS 124a is not faultless, but its slips are comparatively few: 'Parrahsis' [for 'Parrhasis', another name for Callisto] (l. 34), 'sin' [for 'sine', without] (l. 40), and 'succerrerit' [for 'succurrerit', came to the aid of] (l. 55) are corrected in Arckenholtz's text and *1681*. The word 'straverat' [had spread out] (l. 47) is probably a misreading of the perfect subjunctive form 'straverit', which appears in Arckenholz and *1681*. The Longleat manuscript also gives correct readings in several places where *1681* makes slips, suggesting that *1681* was not carefully proof-read by a Latinist: 'perque' [through] (l. 44), 'fovet' [warms] (l. 48), 'clausi' [enclosed] (l. 54), 'Nec timuit' [nor feared] (l. 62). The Longleat manuscript also supports Kelliher's case that Marvell adjusted the metre in revising 'Quis hominum genius' [what kind of men] (l. 5) to 'Quæ Gentes Hominum' [what kinds of men] and 'Dignior haud lapsi sustulit orbis onus' [he did not bear the burden of the moved world more gracefully] (l. 50) to 'Haud ita labentis sustulit orbis onus' [he did not bear the burden of the tottering world so well], and found more apt metaphors in replacing 'obterit' [ravage] (l. 7) with 'obruit' [overwhelm] and 'substratus' [spread over] (l. 49) with 'coopertus' [covered]. Longleat MS 124a likewise confirms that a variant which Kelliher found difficult to explain is authoritative: Ingelo is consistently called Angelo. Estelle Haan has defended this reading as a pun on Ingelo and angel 'that may encapsulate, albeit good-humouredly, the religious piety and indeed the musicianship of his addressee'. [30] If this is a pun, it was widely and publicly used by Ingelo's friends: William Mewe addressed him as Angelo in September 1653, in a letter about bee-keeping, which was subsequently published in Samuel Hartlib's *The Reformed Common-wealth of Bees* (1655), and on the occasion of Ingelo's Cambridge doctorate in 1658, the vice-chancellor, Dr John Worthington (a member of Ingelo's Eton circle who wrote a reference for Marvell in 1655) called him 'Doctor Angelicus or Ingelicus'.[31] The name is used in the title 'Angelo suo Marvellius', a conventional formula of address, which heads both Whitelocke's and Arckenholtz's text. Whitelocke calls his chaplain Ingelo, so Marvell himself probably sent the poem to Ingelo with this title. For *1681* the poem acquired an explanatory title in English: 'A Letter to Doctor Ingelo, then with my Lord Whitelocke, Ambassador from the Protector to the Queen of Sweden'. This must have been written after 1658 when Ingelo became a doctor and, if not by Marvell himself, then by someone who knew who Ingelo was and what he had been doing in Sweden (Whitelocke is not named in the text).

There is no clear reason why lines 66–67 in Arckenholtz and Longleat MS 124a ('Ipsa sed et prono connivent sydera cælo / Et flores lassis procubuere stylis' [and when these stars close their eyes in the declining sky and the flowers sink down on their weary stems]) were omitted in *1681*. The first image echoes the description of night in Sannazaro's piscatory Eclogue II, in which line 14 ends 'sopito conivent sidera caelo'.[32] Sannazaro's poem was well-known and praised by Scaliger, so the allusion is hardly so obscure that Marvell would have worried about it when revising the poem.[33] Another possibility is that the lines were simply overlooked by the compositor of *1681*. However, the person who corrected and expanded Marvell's poems in Oxford, Bodleian Library, MS Eng. poet. d. 49, was apparently unaware of them or overlooked them too.

The variants in lines 73–136 of Longleat MS 124a, which are lost from Arckenholtz's text, add more colour to Kelliher's argument that Marvell revised the poem with publication in mind. *1681* grammatically corrects 'tantis' [such great ones] (l. 97) to 'Tantos' and makes some subtle stylistic adjustments which do not alter the sense: 'pergit licito solvere corda foco' [she proceeds to release her inner feelings at this lawful hearth] (l. 92) becomes 'licito pergit solvere corda foco'; 'sperare' [it might be hoped] (l. 81) becomes 'sperasse', 'petet' [will demand] (l. 116) becomes 'petit'. Marvell made another adjustment for the sake of metre in line 73, from 'In literas *Gothus* sic quod peccaverit olim' [Thus whatever sins the Goth may have committed against letters] to 'Sic quod in ingenuas *Gothus* peccaverit Artes' [Thus whatever sins the Goth may have committed against civilised education]. In the following line he replaced 'Illa' [she] with 'Una' [she alone], intensifying the compliment to Christina, who single-handedly makes up for Gothic philistinism. The revision from 'Upsalides Musæ paulo majora canemus' [Uppsalian muses, let us sing of things a little greater] (l. 85) to '*Upsalides Musæ* nunc et majora canemus' [and now Uppsalian Muses, let us sing of greater things] gives more emphasis to the transition from praise of Christina to religion and politics. Marvell alludes here to the first line of Virgil's Eclogue IV.[34] But where Longleat MS 124a echoes Virgil's line ('Sicelides Musae, paulo maiora canamus') almost word for word, *1681* makes the echo a little subtler by discarding Virgil's understating 'paulo'.

The punctuation of the Longleat manuscript differs considerably from the other texts of the poem. The punctuation of lines 7–8 is probably mistranscribed; Arckenholtz and *1681* punctuate the lines to form an unbroken series of questions, although the length of this series is different in each text. The Longleat manuscript renders lines 11–14 as questions where *1681* makes them statement. This difference gives the good report of Swedish civilisation more confidence and emphasis, where in the Longleat manuscript that emphasis falls on the praise of Christina's leadership. Shortly after Marvell wrote 'A Letter to Doctor Ingelo', Christina abdicated and converted to Catholicism, disappointing the poem's hope that she would become Cromwell's active Protestant ally. With the benefit of hindsight, questioning everything but Christina's leadership shows starkly misplaced confidence. The revised punctuation expresses more faith in the institutions of Swedish culture, even though Marvell revised line 71 to say that Christina alone expiates the Goths' sins against the arts. Longleat MS 124a renders lines 34, 51–52, 81–2, as rhetorical questions. These variants are supported by neither Arckenholtz nor *1681*, so they might have been introduced by a copyist who thought the poem needed a touch more rhetorical variety. Lines 21–24 become a statement in *1681*; as a question they are more pointed: on the topic of how Christina measures up to Elizabeth I—she did her best to invite this comparison, and her panegyrists frequently obliged[35]—Marvell reverts to questioning Ingelo directly, reminding his reader that his praise of Christina is conditional upon Ingelo's affirmation. The possibility remains that Christina will not sign the treaty as promptly as Marvell predicts: 'pia festinat mutatis fædera rebus' [she hastens honest treaties as affairs change] (l. 125). In that event Ingelo might return and report that Christina does not live up to her reputation.

Whitelocke's manuscript of 'A Letter to Doctor Ingelo' provides a more accurate witness to the presentation version of the poem than Arckenholtz's incomplete text, and it brings into sharper focus Marvell's careful revision of the piece later in his life. The insights into its transmission yielded by Longleat MS 124a are valuable not only because very little evidence survives of the manuscript circulation of Marvell's early poems, but also because it illustrates how an embassy might offer a talented, but relatively unknown poet access to the most illustrious readers.

THE TEXT

In the following transcription line numbers have been added, otherwise formatting has been preserved. The 'que' brevigraph has been silently expanded. An otiose stroke following 'tam' in line 4 has been suppressed and an ambiguous graph in 'suorum' at line 87 has been transcribed as 'o', as required by the grammar.

PLATES (see over). *The Longleat text of Andrew Marvell's* 'A Letter to Doctor Ingelo' *in the first manuscript version of Bulstrode Whitelocke's* Journal of the Swedish Embassy 1653–54: *Warminster, Longleat House, MS 124a, fols 178v–180r. (Original page size 319 × 203mm.) Reproduced by permission of the Marquess of Bath, Longleat House, Warminster, Wiltshire.*

Angelo suo
Marvellius.

Quid facis Arctoi, charissime Transfuga cæli
   Angele, proh sero cognite, rapte cito?
Num satis Hybernum defendis Pellibus Astrum
   Qui modo tam mollis nec bene firmus eras?
Quis hominum genius, quæ sit natura Locorum   [5]
   Sint homines potius, dic ibi, sintne loca?
Num gravis horrisono Polus obterit omnia lapsu?
   Jungitur et præceps Mundus utrâque nive.
An melius canis horrescit campus aristis?
   Annuus Agricolis et redit orbe labor?   [10]
Incolit, ut fertur, sævam gens mitior oram
   Pace vigil, Bello strenua, justa Foro?
Quin ibi sunt urbes, atque alta Palatia Regum
   Musarumque domus, et sua Templa Deo?
Nam regit Imperio populum *Christina* ferocem   [15]
   Et dare jura potest *Regia Virgo* viris.
Utque trahit rigidum Magnes Aquilone Metallum
   Gaudet Eam soboles ferrea sponte sequi.
Dic quantum liceat fallaci credere famæ
   Invida num taceat plura, sonetve loquax.   [20]
Ac si vera fides mundi melioris ab ortu
   Sæcula *Christinæ* nulla tulere parem,
Ipsa licet redeat nostri decus orbis *Eliza*
   Qualis Nostra tamen Quantaque *Eliza* fuit?
Vidimus effigiem, mistasque coloribus umbras,   [25]
   Sic quoque Sceptripotens, sic quoque visa Dea.
Augustam decorant, rarò Concordia, frontem
   Majestas, et Amor, Forma, Pudorque simul.
Ingens virgineo spirat *Gustavus* in ore
   Agnoscas animos, fulmineumque patrem.   [30]
Nulla suo nituit tam lucida Stella sub axe
   Non ea quæ meruit crimine Nympha polum.

March.

missæ etiam fuerunt ab Amico quodam Etoniensi
ad Dominum Ingelo versus sequentes elegantissimi

Angelo suo
Marvellius.

Quid facis Arctoi, charissime Transfuga cæli,
  Angele, proh sero cognite, rapte cito!
Num satis Hybernum defendis Pellibus Astrum,
  Qui modò tam mollis nec bene firmus eras?
Quae hominum genius, quæ sit natura locorum,
  Sint homines potius, dic ibi, sintne loca!
Num gravis horrisono Polus obruit omnia lapsu?
  Jungitur et præceps Mundus utraque nive.
An meliùs canis horrescit campus aristis?
  Amnus Agricolis et redit orbe labor?
Incolis, ut fertur, seram gens mitior oram
  Pace vigil, Bello strenua, justa Foro!
Quin ibi sunt urbes, atque alta Palatia Regum,
  Musarumque domus, et sua Templa Deo?
Nam regit Imperio populum Christina ferocem,
  Et dare jura potest Regia Virgo viris.
Utque trahit rigidum Magnes Aquilone Metallum,
  Gaudet eam soboles ferrea sponte sequi.
Dic quantum liceat fallaci credere famæ,
  Invida num taceat plura, sonetve loquax.
Ac si vera fides mundi melioris ab ortu
  Sæcula Christinæ nulla tulere parem,
Ipsa licet redeat nostri decus orbis Eliza,
  Qualis nostra tamen quantaque Eliza fuit!
Vidimus effigiem, mistasque coloribus umbras,
  Sic quoque Sceptripotens, sic quoque visa Dea.
Augustam decorant, raro Concordia, frontem
  Majestas, et Amor, Forma, Pudorque simul.
Ingens virgineo spirat Gustavus in ore;
  Agnoscas animos, fulmineumque patrem.
Nulla suo nituit tam lucida Stella sub axe;
  Non ea quæ meruit crimine Nympha polum.

Ah quoties pavidum demisit conscia lumen!
    Utque suæ timuit *Parrahsis* ora Deæ?
Et simulet falsâ ni pictor imagine vultus,   [35]
    Delia tam similis nec fuit Ipsa sibi:
Ni quod inornati *Triviæ* sint forte capilli,
    Sollicitâ sed Huic distribuantur acu.
Scilicet ut nemo est Illâ reverentior æqui
    Haud ipsas igitur fert sin Lege comas.   [40]
Gloria Sylvarum pariter communis utrique
    Est et perpetuæ Virginitatis honos.
Sic quoque Nympharum supereminet agmina collo
    Fertque choros *Cynthi* per juga, perque nives.
Haud aliter pariles ciliorum contrahit arcus   [45]
    Acribus ast oculis tela subesse putes.
Luminibus dubites, an straverat Illa sagittis
    Quæ fovet exuvijs ardua colla feram.
Alcides humeros substratus pelle *Nemæâ*
    Dignior haud lapsi sustulit orbis onus.   [50]
Heu quæ cervices subnectunt pectora tales,
    Frigidiora gelu, candidiora nive?
Cætera non licuit, sed vix ea tota, videre:
    Nam clausi rigido stant adamante sinus.
Seu chlamys Artifici nimium succerrerit auso,   [55]
    Sicque imperfectum fugerit impar opus:
Sive tribus spernat victrix certare Deabus
    Et pretium formæ nec spoliata ferat,
Junonis properans, et clara Trophæa Minervæ
    Mollia nam *Veneris* præmia nosse piget.   [60]
Hinc neque consuluit fugitivæ prodiga formæ,
    Nec timuit seris invigilasse libris.
Insomnem quoties nymphæ monuere sequaces,
    Decedet roseis heu color ille genis,
Jamque vigil leni cessit *Philomela* sopori,   [65]
    Omnibus et sylvis conticuere feræ.
Ipsa sed et prono connivent sydera cælo
    Et flores lassis procubuere stylis
Acrior illa tamen pergit, curâque fatigat.
    Tanti est doctorum volvere scripta virûm   [70]
Et liciti quæ sint moderamina discere Regni
    Quid fuerit, quid sit, noscere quicquid erit.

March

Ah quoties pavidum demisit conscia tumor!
    Utq; sua timuit Parrhasis ora Dea?
Et simulet falsa ni pictor imagine vultus,
    Delia tam similis nec fuit Ipsa sibi:
Ni quod ornati Triviae sint forte capilli,
    Sollicita sed Huic distribuantur acu.
Scilicet ut nemo est Illa reverentior aequi
    Haud ipsas igitur fert sui Legis comas.
Gloria Sylvarum pariter communis utriq;
    Est et perpetua Virginitatis honos.
Sic queq; Nympharum supereminet agmina colle
    Fert choros Cynthi per juga perg nives.
Haud aliter pariter ciliorum contrahit arcus
    Acribus ast oculis tela subesse putes.
Luminibus dubites an straverat Illa sagittis
    Quae foret exuviis ardua colla feram.
Alcides humeros substratus pelle Nemea
    Dignior haud lapsi sustulit orbis onus.
Heu quas cervices subnectunt pectora tales,
    Frigidiora gelu, candidiora nive!
Cetera non licuit, sed vix ea tota videre:
    Nam clausi rigido stant adamante sinus.
Seu chlamys Artifici nimium succurrerit auso,
    Sicq; imperfectum fugerit impar opus:
Sive tribus spernat victrix certare Deabus
    Et pretium formae nec spoliata ferat.
Junonis penetrans, et clara Trophaea Minervae
    Mollia nam Veneris praemia nosse piget.
Hinc neq; consuluit fugitiva prodiga formae,
    Nec timuit seris invigilasse libris.
Insomnem quoties nymphae monuere Napaeae,
    Decedet roseis heu color ille genis,
Jamq; vigil leni cessit Philomela sopori,
    Inimbus et sylvis conticuere ferae.
Ipsa sed et prono connivent sydera caelo
    Et florto lassos procubuere styli
Acrior illa tamen pergit, curaq; fatigat
    Tanti est doctorum volvere scripta virum.
Et licet quae sint moderamina discere Regni
    Quid ferat, quid sit, noscere quicquid erit.

7 obterit] *obruit 1681*; lapsu?] *lapsu, 1681*

8 Jungitur] *Fungitur A*; nive.] *nive? 1681, A*

9 aristis?] *Aristis, 1681, aristis A*

10 Agricolis] *agniolis A*

11 sævam] *Suevam A*

12 vigil] *viget A*; Foro?] *Foro. 1681*

13 Quin] *Cumque A*

14 Deo?] *Deo. 1681, A*

15 Nam] *Num A*

16 viris.] *viris? A*

18 sequi.] *sequi? A*

20 sonetve] *sonetque A*; loquax.] *loquax? A*

21 Ac] *At, 1681*

22 parem,] *parem. 1681, A*

23 nostri decus orbis] *(nostri decus orbis) 1681*

24 fuit?] *fuit. 1681, fuit, A*

33 quoties] *quotiens A*; demisit] *dimisit A*; lumen!] *Lumen, 1681, lumen A*

34 *Parrahsis*] Parrhasis *A, 1681*; Deæ?] *Deæ! 1681*

35 falsâ] *falsos A*

36 tam] *tum A*

38 distribuantur] *distribuentur A*

40 sin] *sine 1681, A*

41 utrique] *utrique est A*

44 *Cynthi*] Cynthii *A*; perque] *per 1681*

45 pariles] *Paridas A*

47 straverat] *straverit 1681, A*

48 Quæ] *Qua A*; fovet] *foret 1681*

49 substratus] *coopertus 1681*

50 Dignior haud lapsi] *Haud ita labentis 1681*

52 nive?] *Nive. 1681*

54 clausi] *clau si 1681*

55 succerrerit auso] *succurrerit auso 1681, succurrerit auro A*

57 Sive] *Seu A*

58 ferat,] *ferat. 1681, A*

60 nam] *num A*

62 Nec timuit] *Nectimuit 1681*; seris] *seriis A*

67–68 Ipsa sed et prono connivent sydera cælo / Et flores lassis procubuere stylis] *Omitted in 1681*; stylis] *stylis. A*

69 curâque] *curasque 1681, A*

73 In literas *Gothus* sic quod peccaverit olim] *Sic quod in ingenuas* Gothus *peccaverit Artes 1681*

74 Illa] *Una 1681*

81 sperare] *sperasse 1681*

82 sacris?] *sacris! 1681*

85 Upsalides Musæ paulo majora canemus] Upsalides Musæ *nunc &*
majora canemus 1681

92 pergit licito] *licito pergit 1681*

97 tantis] *Tantos 1681*

98 opes!] *Opes. 1681*

100 sequi;] *sequi. 1681*

103 *Olivarus*] Oliverus *1681*

108 comis] *Comis. 1681*

114 cadat.] *cadat! 1681*; *Hisperijsque*] Hesperiisque *1681*

116 petet] *petit 1681*

118 novo] *novo. 1681*

127 *Solomon*] Salomon *1681*

129 *Angele*] Ingele *1681*

136 qualiacunque] *qualiacumque 1681*

NOTES

I am greatly indebted to Hilton Kelliher, John Kerrigan, Simon McKeown, David
Money, Nigel Smith, Keston Sutherland, Neil Wright and Peter Beal for their advice
and encouragement in the production of this article. My glosses lean heavily on Nigel
Smith's translation in his edition of the *Poems* (2003). I am grateful to the Marquess of
Bath for permission to reproduce material from Longleat MS 124a, to Trinity College,
Cambridge, for assistance with funding, and to Dr Kate Harris at Longleat House for
her kind help.

1 Ruth Spalding, *The Improbable Puritan: a Life of Bulstrode Whitelocke, 1605–1675*
(London, 1975), p. 144. In addition to several published sermons, Ingelo wrote an
allegorical religious romance in prose, *Bentivolio and Urania* (London, 1660), which
reflects upon events of the Civil War and Interregnum. It was very popular after the
Restoration: a second part was published in 1664 and each part ran to four editions,
earning Ingelo a mention in Rochester's 'A Satyr against Reason and Mankind'.
This popularity has not lasted: James Sutherland finds it 'plumbs the depths of bore-
dom' (James Sutherland, *Restoration Literature 1660–1700*, The Oxford History of
English Literature, 8 (Oxford, 1969, repr. 1990), p. 207).

2 Anthony à Wood, *Fasti Oxonienses*, 3rd edn, rev. Philip Bliss, 2 vols (London,
1815–20), II, 306. According to Wood, around this period Rogers' airs were
esteemed and commissioned by 'great personages' and some were sent to the court
of Archduke Leopold, who had his musicians play them. Ingelo helped Rogers gain
a BMus. at Cambridge in 1658 and together they wrote a piece to be performed at
a banquet for the King and royal family thrown by the Lord Mayor of London soon
after the Restoration. By this point Rogers was reckoned to be the leading composer
in England.

3 See Steven C. A. Pincus, *Protestantism and Patriotism: Ideologies and the Making of English
Foreign Policy, 1650–1668* (Cambridge, 1996), pp. 15–39; Bulstrode Whitelocke, *A*

Manuscripts at Auction: January 2002 to December 2003

A. S. G. Edwards

This list is intended to provide a summary of manuscript items produced in the British Isles between 1100 and 1700 and those which were either produced abroad for a market there or which were demonstrably in the British Isles from an early stage in their history that have appeared for sale at the major auction houses in London and New York, and in other auction house or booksellers' catalogues, where these have been available to the compiler. I would be pleased to receive notice of any auction or booksellers' catalogues containing relevant items for the period from January 2001, as well as any omitted from the period covered by the present record.

The list cannot claim to be exhaustive but is offered as a guide to these materials. Where known, the names of purchasers and/or prices paid have been given, and also the present locations of the manuscripts or their subsequent appearance in booksellers' or auction catalogues. Prices and buyers for mixed collections of leaves sold as a single lot and only partly comprising English manuscripts are given after the last relevant item in each lot. The price given for items at auction is the hammer price, exclusive of buyers' premium. For those in booksellers' catalogues it is the offered price.

Items which can be dated, in whole or in part, approximately to before 1500 are indicated by an asterisk (*) before the lot or item number. Significant provenances are noted.

Generally, manuscripts chiefly of literary, rather than historical interest, have been included. Royal letters and documents are usually omitted, as are single letters written by statesmen, ecclesiastics and other public figures. Charters, grants and other items judged to be mainly of archival interest have generally been excluded, as have maps and surveys, cookery books and collections of recipes. No attempt has been made to include any manuscripts offered for sale over the internet.

Thanks are offered to the various members of the book trade and other scholars who have provided information and other assistance in the preparation of this article. I am particularly indebted to Dr Peter Beal for corrections and information.

Abbreviations
ALs(s) Autograph letter(s) signed
attrib. attributed to
Ds(s) Document(s) signed
ill. illuminated
Ls(s) Letter(s) signed

LONDON

Bloomsbury Book Auctions

5 February 2002

84 HERALDIC MS: Ill. MS on paper, copied by Henry Lilly (*c.*1589–1639), scribe and illuminator, for Richard Weston, first Earl of Portland (1577–1635), 1632.; owned by J. P. Gilson (1868–1929). Unsold.

Bonham's

13 March 2002

*902 LATIN BIBLE: single leaf on vellum, mid-thirteenth century. £380.
918. RESTORATION VERSE MISCELLANY: chiefly poem on affairs of state, by Rochester, Dryden and others; on paper; 1680s. £5,500.

Christie's

11 July 2002

*24 LATIN BIBLE: Ill. MS on vellum, produced in Paris *c.*1260, but in England by late thirteenth century; owned by C. H. St. John Hornby and William Foyle. £40,000, to David Waxman, Estates of Mind.
*35 BOOK OF HOURS: Use of Sarum, produced in Rouen for English patron, ill. MS on vellum, *c.*1470. £28,000 (post sale, to Tenschert).
*41 BOOK OF HOURS: Use of Sarum, produced in Bruges for English market; ill. MS on vellum, *c.*1430. £10,000 to Fogg.

20 November 2002

*21 OFFICE BOOK: MS on vellum, Norwich, *c.*1390–1400. £10,000.

19 November 2003

28 ANGELA OF FOLIGNO, *Liber beatae Angelae*: MS on paper; early sixteenth century, with a leaf from an English treatise of the same date on monastic obedience. £11,000 to Fogg.

30 TRIPPE, SIMON, *Christus Medicus*: MS on paper; *c.*1572; possibly the dedication copy to Robert Dudley, Earl of Leicester. £7,000 to Arthur Freeman.

3 December 2003 (Spiro Collection)

38 RALEGH, WALTER: A.L.s to unidentified recipient, 8 March 1587/8. £16,000, to Arthur Freeman.

Sotheby's

18 June 2002

*20 BOOK OF HOURS: Use of Sarum; ill. single leaf, on vellum, late fifteenth century. Previously in Quaritch, *Catalogue of Illuminated and other Manuscripts* (1931), no. 56. £12,000.
*49 BOOK OF HOURS: Use of Sarum; ill. MS on vellum, *c.*1430–50; previously Christie's 11 July, 2000, lot 54 (Foyle Sale). Unsold.

11 July 2002

10 GEORGE VILLIERS, DUKE OF BUCKINGHAM (subject): translation of Pierre Matthieu, Aelius Sejanus, histoire romaine; paper, seventeenth century. £2,600 to Maggs.

3 December 2002

*52 (b) THEOLOGICAL TEXT: fragment, on vellum; twelfth century.
*52 (c) STATUTES OF ENGLAND: single leaf, on vellum; fourteenth century.
*52 (h): GRADUAL: partial bifolium, on vellum; fifteenth century. £900 in all.

4 December 2002

*42 ENGLISH MANUSCRIPT: fifteenth/sixteenth century, bound in with printed book, Michael de Hungaria, *Sermones tredecim universalis* . . . [Louvain, 1485]. £17,500.

12 December 2002

179 GEOFFREY CHAUCER: Works, 1550 (STC 5072) with contemporary MS poem added; 6 lines (Inc: 'O venerable Chaucer principall poet and peare'). £2,000 to Baumann Rare Books.

191 JOHN DONNE: MS (11 pp) of First and Second Satires; paper, *c.*1632, together with legal precepts, once owned by John Hall; descending from the Rudston family of Hayton, East Yorkshire; on paper; *c.*1627–32. £8,500 to Quaritch. Now in the Folger Shakespeare Library, Washington, D.C.

17 June 2003

*70(a) ENGLISH SERVICE BOOK: MS fragments; on vellum; fifteenth century, with other items. £1,200.

83 BIBLE: in Latin, MS on vellum, second half of thirteenth century; from the secular college of St Michael, South Malling, East Sussex; *olim* Schøyen 11. £11,000.

*89 BOOK OF HOURS: Use of Sarum; ill. MS; on vellum; *c.*1400–20; south Netherlands, for English use; with prayers in Middle English prose. From Stonyhurst College (MS 70). £45,000.

*91 BOOK OF HOURS: ill. MS; on vellum; south Netherlands, for English market; *c.*1430–50; with prayers in Middle English prose. £14,000.

20 November 2003

16 ALCHEMY: Three volumes of notes and extracts from alchemical sources, on paper; *c.*1650. £4,000.

95 FAIRFAX, EDWARD: 'A Discoure on Witchcraft . . . in the year 1621', on paper; mid-seventeenth century. £2,200.

96 FAIRFAX, EDWARD: 'A Discoure on Witchcraft . . . in the year 1621', on paper; transcribed by Ebenezer Sibly in 1793. £600.

202 LOCKE, JOHN: A. l. s. to Cornelius Lude, 16 February, 1698/9. £7,800.

2 December 2003

*31 PSALTER and BREVIARY: single leaves from each; on vellum; possibly English. Unsold.

*83 PSALTER: in Latin, early fifteenth century; on vellum; possibly owned by John Stocksley (*c.*1475–1539), Bishop of London. £4,400.

11 December 2003

4 HERALDRY: MS on paper, *c.*1605, containing noble arms and biographical and historical notes. Unsold.

NEW YORK

Sotheby's

18 June 2002

92 ISAAC NEWTON: AMS, fragment (one leaf) from a theological work; paper, *c.*1700. Unsold.

4–5 December 2003 (H. P. Kraus Sale)

*66 BERNARD OF CLAIRVAUX, HUGH OF ST VICTOR:, MS, on vellum, from St Osyth's Essex, mid-twelfth century; *olim* Foyle, sold Christie's, 11 July, 2000, lot 5. $180,000.
310 MANER OF THE TOMBE TO BE MADE FOR THE KINGIS GRACE AT WYNDESORE: Pedigree of the Southwell family, *c.*1610; scroll on paper, in the autograph of William Dethick (1543–1612); *olim* Phillipps 18161. Unsold.

BOOKSELLERS' CATALOGUES

Julian Browning, London

Catalogue 25 (2002)

183 ROBERT HOWARD: Manuscript receipt s. 'Ro: Howard', November 1678. £65.

Maggs

Catalogue 1324: Books and Readers in Early Modern Britain (1478–1700) III (2002)

13 THOMAS BROWNE: 'Concerning Artificiall mounts and raised hills without fortificaetions attending them'. Autograph MS; bifolium, 27 October 1658. £18,500. (Previously Catalogue 1272 (1999), No. 27.)

68 JOHN JONES: Autograph dedicatory poem in his edition of *Ovid's Invective or Curse against Ibis* (1658; Wing O 678). £2,400.

Catalogue 1340 (Illuminations: 2003)

*4 PSALTER: Single leaf, possibly English, 1260–80. £2,750.
*23 BOOK OF HOURS: Single leaf from a Sarum Book of Hours probably produced in Bruges, *c.* 1460–75. £1,500.

Phillip J. Pirages

Catalogue 47 (2002)

*123 LATIN BIBLE: 2 leaves, on vellum, first half of the thirteenth century. $250 each.
*132 PSALTER: various leaves, on vellum *c.*1300. $ 275–350 each. One now in the collection of David Jupe, Reading, Berks.
*177 (8) SERVICE BOOK: on vellum, fifteenth century. $950 (for collection).

Quaritch

Early Books (October)

*55 ALEXANDER OF VILLEDIEU: *Doctrinale*, sheets of a thirteenth-century MS on vellum, used as binder's waste in a sixteenth-century, Cambridge binding by Nicholas Spierinck of Thomas More's translation of Lucian (Paris, 1514) and Erasmus's *Morae Encomium* (Basel, 1517). £4,500.

Notes on Contributors

PRISCILLA BAWCUTT is Honorary Professor of English at the University of Liverpool and Vice-President of the Scottish Text Society. She is author of *Gavin Douglas: A Critical Study* (1976) and *Dunbar the Makar* (1992). Her edition of *The Poems of William Dunbar* (2 vols, 1998) was awarded the Saltire Society/National Library of Scotland prize in 1999. Her most recent publication is a revised edition of the Shorter Poems of Gavin Douglas (2003).

MARK BLAND is Senior Lecturer in English at De Montfort University. He has published articles on both manuscripts and the book-trade. He is editor of an old-spelling manuscript-based edition of *The Poems of Ben Jonson*, his other forthcoming books including a Guide to the study of early modern manuscripts and printed books and 'The Manuscripts of Ben Jonson and his Contemporaries'.

A.S.G. EDWARDS is Professor of English at the University of Glamorgan. His *New Index of Middle English Verse* (with Julia Boffey) will be published by the British Library in 2005.

MARGARET FOREY has edited the poems of William Strode (unpublished Oxford B.Litt. thesis, 1966) and contributed articles on Strode and his contemporaries to various periodicals and works of reference, including *The Oxford Dictionary of National Biography*. Her teaching career included a part-time lectureship at the University of Durham.

EDWARD HOLBERTON is a doctoral student at Trinity College, Cambridge. He is working on the political poetry of the Protectorate.

RANDALL McLEOD is Professor of English at the University of Toronto and specialises in textual criticism. He has published papers on Harington, Shakespeare, Herbert, Keats, Shaw, and Hopkins, and recently on the continental printers Aldus (Castiglione's *Cortegiano*, 1528) and Stephanus (Hebrew bible, 1539–44). He is the inventor of the McLeod Portable Collator. Forthcoming from the Huntington Library Press is *The Peaceable and Prosperous Regiment of Blessed Queene Elisabeth: A Facsimile from Holinshed's* Chronicles 1587, in collaboration with Cyndia Clegg.

NOEL MALCOLM is a Senior Research Fellow of All Souls College, Oxford, a Fellow of the British Academy, and a General Editor of the Clarendon Edition of the works of Hobbes. He has edited Hobbes's correspondence (2 vols, Oxford, 1994) for that series, and is currently preparing an edition of *Leviathan*. His most recent publication (with Jacqueline Stedall) is *John Pell (1611–1685) and his Correspondence with Sir Charles Cavendish: The Mental World of an Early Modern Mathematician* (OUP, 2004).

TIMOTHY RAYLOR is Associate Professor of English at Carleton College, Minnesota. He is author of *Cavaliers, Clubs, and Literary Culture: Sir John Mennes, James Smith, and the Order of the Fancy* (1994) and of *The Essex House Masque of 1621: Viscount Doncaster and the Jacobean Masque* (2000). He is currently working with Stephen Clucas on an edition of Hobbes's *De Corpore*.

DAVID RUNDLE is J. P. R. Lyell Research Fellow in Palaeography and Manuscript Studies at the University of Oxford. His present project is a study of the library of Humfrey, Duke of Gloucester. He has published widely on humanism in England in the fifteenth and early sixteenth centuries and on the book-collections of Italian Renaissance clerics. He is also one of the General Editors of the Oxford Bibliographical Society.

DANIEL WAKELIN is Lecturer in English at Christ's College, Cambridge. He studies fifteenth-century English literature and manuscripts, especially in relation to humanism and reading-habits.

Index of Manuscripts

Aberdeen, University Library
28, 47, 50, 54, 67

ArundelCastle
Arundel-Harington Manuscript, 57

Cambridge, Fitzwilliam Museum
Mu 689, 52, 55, 66

Cambridge, Magdalene College
Pepys 1408, 49, 52, 55, 63, 65
2553, 47, 52, 53, 57, 59, 63, 65

Cambridge, Pembroke College
243, 28, 29, 30, 31, 36, 37, 40

Cambridge, St John's College
S. 23, 142, 145, 146, 147

Cambridge, Trinity College
O.9.8, 18
Capell W. 1, 74

Cambridge, University Library
Ee.v.5, 16
Kk.1.5, 50, 65
Ll. 5. 10, 52–3, 57, 59, 66

Cambridge, Massachusetts, Harvard
University, Houghton Library
Eng. 626, 142, 143, 144
Eng 966.3, 142, 149, 154, 160,
163

Capetown, South Africa, South African
Public Library
Grey 7.a.29, 142, 143, 144, 145, 146,
147, 154, 157, 163
Chatsworth House, Derbyshire
Hardwick MS, drawer 45, 211, 216–17
Hobbes MS A. 3, 204, 210, 211
Hobbes MS A. 4, 204, 208, 210, 217

Hobbes MS A. 5, 204, 208, 210, 215
Hobbes MS A. 7, 204
Hobbes MS B. 4, 204, 208, 210, 211, 217
Hobbes MS B. 6, 204, 210, 211, 217

Dublin, Trinity College
877, 142, 146, 148, 149-150, 152, 155,
161, 163

Edinburgh, National Archives
RH 13/35. 49, 50

Edinburgh, National Library of
Scotland
Adv. 1.1.6, 46, 53, 60–64, 65
Adv. 19.3.6, 57, 58, 66
9450, 49, 60, 67
15397, 66
16500, 49, 55, 60, 65
Dep. 314, 67

Edinburgh, University Library
Lang III.447, 47, 49, 58, 66,
Lang III.447, 54, 67

Glasgow University Library
Hunter 374, 14

London, British Library
Add. 4416, 219
Add. 4417, 211, 219, 222
Add. 4991A, 234
Add. 4991B, 234
Add. 10344, 17
Add. 12049, 75
Add. 17492, 57
Add. 29409, 66
Add. 30982, 142, 145, 152, 155, 156,
162, 163, 182, 188–91
Add. 36484, 52, 66
Add. 36529, 74

Add. 37346, 234, 235
Add. 37347, 234, 235
Arundel 23, 14
Arundel 285, 47, 50, 55, 65
Cotton Julius A. vii, 14
Cotton Otho A. vii, 15
Cotton Titus A. xxii, 28, 29–30, 31–34, 36, 37, 40
Cotton Titus A. xxiv, 74
Egerton 1910, 211, 217
Egerton 2421, 142, 145, 154, 155, 163
Harley 2471, 15
Harley 3360, 215-16
Harley 3865, 57
Harley 6796, 201–08 *passim*, 210–28 *passim*
Harley 5915, 17
RP 1845, 75
Sloane 1446, 192
Sloane 1792, 142, 150, 154, 163

London, Private Collection, 18

London, Westminster Abbey
41, 142, 150, 154, 157, 163

Los Angeles, CA, William Andrews Clark Memorial Library
T135ZB724, 48–9, 59, 67

New York, Pierpont Morgan Library
1057, 155, 156, 162

Oxford, Bodleian Library
Add. C. 262, 92, 94
Arch. Selden. B. 24, 47, 48, 57, 65
Ashmole 38, 193
Ashmole 45, 28, 31, 32, 34, 36, 37, 40
Ashmole 47, 193
Bodley 915, 15
Don. c. 50, 143
Don. d. 58, 193
Eng. poet. d. 49, 239
Eng. poet. e. 97, 142, 148, 150, 154
Eng. poet. f. 27, 193
Malone 13, 142, 149, 152, 163

Oxford, Christ Church
printed book f.3.7, 18

Oxford, Magdalen College
lat. 23, 15
lat. 39, 15
lat. 138, 15
lat. 196, 15

Oxford, Merton College
E.3.35, 18
printed book 76.a.6, 18

Oxford, New College
250, 16
256, 16
265, 18
271, 16
274, 19
277, 19
278, 19
279, 19
280, 17

Oxford, St John's College
116, 19

Paris, Bibliothèque de Sainte-Geneviève
1060, 211, 215

Philadelphia, Pennsylvania, Rosenbach Library
239/22, 83-91, 95–101, 116–18, 122
239/23, 143

San Marino, California, Henry E. Huntington Library
HM 172, 142, 143, 144, 145, 160
HM 198, 142, 143, 144, 145, 146, 147, 148, 149, 151, 152, 154, 155, 157–58, 160, 161, 162

Warminster, Wilts, Longleat House
124a, 233–51 *passim*

Washington, DC, Folger Shakespeare Library
V.a.96, 142, 144, 145, 146, 147, 155, 156, 161, 162
V.a. 170, 142, 146, 147, 151, 163
V. a. 249, 75

Washington, DC, Library of Congress
M 1490, 47–8, 52, 66

Mersenne, Marin, 201, 203, 208, 211, 214, 218, 219, 220, 222, 228
Mewe, William, 239
Middleton, Thomas, 187
Mirk, John, 57
Moleyns, Adam, 4
Monte, Pietro del, 3, 4, 6
Montgomerie, Alexander, 47, 54
Morley, George, 55, 157

Newton, Isaac, 258
Niccoli, Niccolò, 3
Nixon, Anthony, 162, 165

On husbondrie, 27, 30

Pacchi, Arrigo, 215
Palladius, *De re rustica*, 27
Payne, Robert, 215
Pell, John, 214, 218, 219, 220, 221, 222, 223, 224, 225, 226, 227
Petrarch, *Secretum*, 6
Pettie, George, 57
Petworth, Richard, 3, 4, 5, 6, 12
Piccolomini, Aeneas Sylvius, 4, 5
Pinkerton, John, 47, 55
Pynson, Richard, 40

Ralegh, Sir Walter, 167, 169, 256
Ravenscroft, Thomas, 58
Reidpeth Manuscript, *see* Cambridge University Library, Ll. 5. 10
Reidpeth, John, 52–3, 66
Rheita, Anton Maria Schyrle von, 226
Robertson, Margaret, 54, 66
Rogers, Benjamin, 233
Rolland, John, 64
Rood, Theodoric, 40
Roe, Sir John, 139
Russell, John, 41, 42

Salutati, Coluccio, 40
Scott, Sir Walter, 46
Selden, John, 140
Shakespeare, William, 167, 170, 180, 183, 187
Shirwood, John, 2

Sinclair, Henry, Lord, 49, 65
Sinclair, Oliver, 57
Sorbière, Samuel, 211, 216
Spirleng, Geoffrey, 36
Stewart, Alexander, 54
Stockesley, John, 257
Strode, William, 180–197 *passim*
Sulpizio, Giovanni, 40
Sutcliffe, Matthew, 158, 169
Swynfeld, Hugh, 5

Tait, Robert, 50, 67
Terence, 9
Thomas, Alan, 75
Thurloe, John, 235
Toly, William, 5
Tottel, Richard, 75
Trevisa, John, 28
Trippe, Simon, 256

Vegetius, *Epitoma rei militaris*, 26, 28
Viète (Vieta), Francis, 211, 214, 222, 223
Villiers, George, Duke of Buckingham, 256
Waard, Cornélis de, 219
Wallace, Adam, 57
Walton, John, 60
Warham, John, 186
Warner, Sir Edward, 78
Warwick, Earl of, 26
Wemyss, Jean, Countess of Sutherland, 54
Wemyss, Lady Margaret, 54, 67
Weston, Richard, 255
Whethamstede, John, 9
Whistler, Daniel, 234, 236
White, Thomas, 50
Whitelocke, Bulstrode, 233, 234, 235, 236, 237, 239, 241
William, Lord Knollys, 165
Wilmot, John, Earl of Rochester, 255
Wilson, John, 180, 181
Witeker (or Whiteacre or Wireker or Longchamps), Nigel, 9,10
Wolseley, Charles, 234, 235, 236
Worthington, John, 239
Wyatt, Sir Thomas, 60, 78